In Search
of More Effective
Mathematics Education

Issues in Curriculum Theory, Policy, and Research

Arthur Woodward and Ian Westbury,
Series Editors

Deliberation in Education and Society
edited by J. T. Dillon

In Search of More Effective Mathematics Education:
Examing Data from the IEA Second International
Mathematics Study
edited by Ian Westbury, Corinna A. Ethington,
Lauren A. Sosniak, and David P. Baker

The Pursuit of Curriculum:
Schooling and the Public Interest
by William A. Reid

In Search
of More Effective
Mathematics Education

Edited by

Ian Westbury
Corinna A. Ethington
Lauren A. Sosniak
David P. Baker

Ablex Publishing Corporation
Norwood, New Jersey

Printed in the United States of America

Library of Congress Cataloging-in-Publication Data

In search of more effective mathematics education : examining data
    from the IEA second international mathematics study / edited by Ian
    Westbury . . . [et al.].
        p.   cm.
    Includes bibliographical references and index.
    ISBN 1-56750-060-9. — ISBN 1-56750-061-7 (pbk.)
    1. Mathematics—Study and teaching. 2. Second International
Mathematics Study.
QA11.I439   1994
510′.71—dc20   93-46295
                                                                   CIP

Ablex Publishing Company
355 Chestnut Street
Norwood, New Jersey 07648

Contents

About the Authors

David P. Baker is an associate professor of sociology at The Catholic University of America.

Corinna A. Ethington is an associate professor of education at Memphis State University.

James Flanders is a consultant on mathematics education in Colorado Springs, Colorado.

Adam Gamoran is a professor of sociology and educational policy studies at the University of Wisconsin–Madison.

Peter L. Glidden is an assistant professor of curriculum and instruction at the University of Illinois at Urbana-Champaign.

Delwyn L. Harnisch is an associate professor of educational psychology at the University of Illinois at Urbana Champaign.

Damian P. Murchan teaches at St. Mary's National School, Ashborne Co., Dublin, Ireland.

Bengt O. Muthén is a professor in the Graduate School of Education at the University of California, Los Angeles.

Cornelius Riordan is a professor of sociology at Providence College, Providence, RI.

Finbarr C. Sloane is an assistant professor of curriculum and instruction at the University of Illinois at Urbana-Champaign.

Maryellen Schaub is a research associate in the Life Cycle Institute, The Catholic University of America.

Lauren A. Sosniak is an associate professor of education at Washington University, St. Louis.

Maria Varelas is a doctoral candidate in education at the University of Illinois at Chicago.

Ian Westbury is a professor of curriculum and instruction at the University of Illinois at Urbana-Champaign.

Introduction: The Second International Mathematics Study

Ian Westbury

Department of Curriculum and Instruction
University of Illinois at Urbana-Champaign

INTRODUCTION

Our goal in this book is to present a set of studies that: (a) explore some significant questions about mathematics teaching and learning, and (b) illustrate new methodologies for the analysis of new kinds of questions about mathematics education. The data from the Second International Mathematics Study (SIMS) are the starting point for all of the work being reported here. These data were collected in 1980–1982 from national samples from 20 educational systems and reflects the activity of approximately 3,900 schools, 6,200 teachers, and 124,000 students.[1] SIMS was the largest and most comprehensive data-collection effort on mathematics teaching

---

[1] SIMS was undertaken by the International Association for the Evaluation of Educational Achievement (IEA), an organization chartered in Belgium and now headquartered in The Hague, The Netherlands. A brief history of the some of the major IEA studies undertaken by IEA before the SIMS study is offered below. Subsequent IEA studies have focused on computer use in schools, reading, and science; a third IEA mathematics and science study is currently being planned.

and learning ever undertaken. Because of this scale, its comparative cross-cultural perspective, and its conceptualization and design, we believe that the SIMS data offers an indispensable beginning point for the exploration of many of the fundamental questions that circle around mathematics teaching and learning, not only internationally (as the name of the study might suggest) but also in the United States—and, of course, in other countries. Our hope is that this volume presents some significant, and provocative, findings about the teaching and learning and mathematics, as well as some new approaches to research, which illustrate the significance of SIMS for all inquiry on the central issue of mathematics education, the task of finding ways of more effective teaching and learning for all students.

SIMS is a well-known study—although, as I will suggest later, this familiarity may be a problem for seeing the study as a resource for further research rather than a set of all too well-known conclusions for findings. Moreover, SIMS has been extensively reported in the research literature. Three volumes discussing the cross-national findings have been published (Burstein, 1993; Robitaille & Garden, 1989; Travers & Westbury, 1989) and many more reports discussing findings from the individual participating countries have appeared in many languages. Indeed, in the last decade there have been few reports or discussions on the state of mathematics education in the United States and elsewhere that have not drawn upon the SIMS data and findings to develop and sustain their conclusions.

What remains to be done by further research that draws on the SIMS data sets? In the United States the persistent theme that has emerged from most such reports and discussions has, of course, been the low standing of American mathematics achievement seen internationally and the consequent need for "improvement" in the teaching and learning of mathematics. But, despite the attention they have been given, such widely publicized findings are of limited significance, even if the inferences that lie behind them are correct. When all is said and done, conclusions about levels of aggregate national achievement really serve only to raise questions, to create holes that we must try to understand, rather than to provide answers to the central questions that emerge from such findings. Why, to ask one obvious question, does the United States seem to be such a low achiever among the SIMS countries—*if it is*? Why, conversely, are such Asian societies as Japan and Hong Kong such high achievers—*if, indeed, they are*? The answers to such questions might seem to be clear—at least that is the impression one gets from reading much of the popular and policy-oriented discussions that claim to draw on the SIMS "findings"; however, as the chapters in this volume that pick up the theme of comparative achievement show very clearly, they are not. SIMS, I will argue in this chapter (and hope that the core chapters of this volume will make quite plain), is in fact one of the major resources for research and further studies for answering such questions. Indeed it was the study's goal to provide a data set to facilitate systematic exploration, using a cross-cultural vantage point, of the major questions that circle around more effective mathematics education within and across school systems. As I will suggest below, this goal was achieved, at least in part, by the planners of SIMS. The SIMS data sets do, as a result, provide a fundamental resource not only for the very visible task of assessing and evaluating national achievement within a cross-national perspective, but also for answering the questions that achievement patterns between and within countries seem to raise. It was our hope as we prepared this volume that the research presented might have a significance beyond the results it has se-cured and might stimulate others to consider using the resource represented by the SIMS data for yet further research. As I will suggest below, the data set is so rich a resource that its potential is almost endless.[2]

The SIMS Framework

It is not my goal in this introductory chapter to summarize the findings of the chapters that follow. They will speak for themselves. What I do need to do is describe SIMS and its background, and set a context for the balance of this book. The ambitions and the scale of SIMS created a necessarily complex study with a very complicated design and context. This background is inevitably present in all studies that use the SIMS data sets and colors very directly the ways in which any studies, including those in this volume, that use the study's data are to be understood. This larger context produced, moreover, a language and vocabulary that pervade all discussion of the SIMS data and of the ways in which findings might be inter-preted. To read all of the chapters included here, an "introduction" to this language is needed to set the stage for the substantive discus-sions of their analyses and conclusions. To do this I will describe,

---

[2] The SIMS data are available as a public-access data set from the International Mathematics Project, College of Education, University of Illinois at Urbana-Champaign.

first, the organizational background and context of SIMS and, then, the design and structure of the study and, thus, the framework that pervades all the chapters in this volume.

The IEA Studies

SIMS was undertaken within an organizational structure and a research tradition that had emerged over two decades within its sponsoring organization, the International Association for the Evaluation of Educational Achievement (IEA). An appreciation of SIMS, both of its design and of its impact in the United States and elsewhere, necessarily requires an understanding of the study's place in the IEA tradition. It is this tradition that supplies the context that provides the strengths, and creates some of the limitations, of the data that underlie all of the chapters that follow. It is a context that has also determined how SIMS has been seen by many who have read or heard discussions of the study's findings.

In 1967, with the publication of a two-volume report (Husén, 1967), the organization that was to become IEA completed its first major project, the *International Study of Achievement in Mathematics* or, as it was to be named after the second international mathematics study was launched, the *First International Mathematics Study* (FIMS). FIMS was the first large-scale cross-national investigation of school achievement that had been undertaken. As Husén (1967) wrote in the final report on FIMS, there are "many questions . . . [which] would be extremely difficult to answer from a national study simply because it is often difficult to test the value of alternative possibilities within one system" (p. 27). The hope was that FIMS could be a *study* which used differences across countries and educational systems to understand not only the forces that play on educational achievement in general, but also the effects of the specific policies and programs which can and do result in important differences in the conditions of teaching and learning; in this way the world might become a "laboratory," to use a word often invoked in the IEA tradition, within which more effective school organizational and teaching practices might be found. The goal articulated by Husén is still fundamental to all cross-cultural studies such as SIMS and lies at the heart of many of the chapters that follow.

In hindsight, however, it was perhaps the organizational achievement of IEA in successfully completing a study of mathematics across 12 countries rather than any immediate findings that was the most important and direct accomplishment of FIMS. The study showed that cross-national data could be collected, using common instruments that were built collaboratively, and that the data that resulted could yield some meaningful and interpretable findings. And, as a significant byproduct of this achievement, FIMS also created a new awareness of international differences in school achievement—with all of their seeming implications for evaluating the quality and effectiveness of national school systems and "educational cultures"; comparative achievement data of the kind that FIMS provided offered one way of answering the abstract and elusive question "How are our schools doing?"

FIMS was followed in the late 1960s by the IEA *Six Subject Survey*. In this second IEA project, both the organization and the methodologies that those who had led FIMS had developed were used to explore achievement in the broader canvasses of science, reading, literature, English and French as foreign languages, and civic education.[3] While some of the technical and organizational problems that had faced FIMS still remained unsolved in this second set of studies (see, Medrich & Griffith, 1992), the IEA *Six Subject Survey* was able to bring into very clear focus the research potential of cross-national studies. In particular, the concepts of opportunity-to-learn (OTL) and the "curriculum," the extent to which a school system, a stream or track, a course or program, and individual teachers, provided coverage of the items underlying the items on a test, emerged from the *Six Subject Survey* as a critically important factor in both the determination and explanation of school achievement. The variable of opportunity-to-learn under one name or another was to become a concept which was to find use far beyond the IEA tradition and it is the identification and recognition of the centrality of this concept which, for some, represents the key contribution (and it is a major contribution) of IEA to educational research.[4] In particular, OTL was an analytic variable which promises a way out of the theoretical problems posed by the Coleman Report, *Equality of Educational Opportunity*, with its seeming conclusion that the school did not make a difference on achievement when

---

[3] For these studies, see Carroll, 1975; Comber & Keeves, 1973; Lewis & Massad, 1975; Passow, Noah, Eckstein, & Mallea, 1976; Peaker, 1975; Purves, 1973; Thorndike, 1973; Torney, Oppenheim, & Farnen, 1975.

[4] Because the databases from the *Six Subject Survey* were more widely distributed than was the FIMS database, its data was also used in some significant and well-known secondary analyses. Heyneman's studies (see Heyneman & Loxley, 1983; Heyneman, 1986) re-examined the seeming finding of the Coleman Report that school played only a limited role in producing school achievement and his findings suggested that, under appropriate conditions, school could play a major role in educational achievement.

compared to the home. In foreshadowing the distinction between "schools" as organizational sites and the process of "schooling" (that is, curricula and teaching methods) that was to become so important theoretically during the 1980s, the *Six Subject Survey* played a major role in throwing new light on the issues which the Coleman Report had opened up.

However, despite such significant research contributions, it was, again, a simpler message that emerged into public view from the *Six Subject Survey* (and particularly from the science study) at least insofar as the United States was concerned: The United States did not score well in science at higher grade levels when compared to other countries.[5] Unfortunately, it was the image of cross-national studies that such rankings symbolized that came to determine much of both professional and popular understandings of what the IEA studies were intended to demonstrate. Indeed, when SIMS was being first proposed there was considerable resistance to the idea of U.S. participation in any new IEA study of mathematics education if all such a study was to seeking to do was demonstrate yet again the United States' low standing in the International Achievement Olympics.

Curiously however, as the initial results of SIMS emerged in the United States in the mid-1980s, this defensive reaction faded as both policy makers and mathematics educators and researchers came to revel in the national commitment to improvement that seemed to flow in the new climate of that era from the nation's (once again) low standing in mathematics achievement. However, while different from the earlier reaction, this new reading of the significance of international comparisons of achievement merely confirmed, and did not change, both professional and public perceptions of what cross-national studies were meant to do. As I have emphasized, SIMS is a much richer study than its common image would suggest. Indeed the riches that the study's data contains are extraordinary—and much greater than that found in any other large-scale cross-national (and perhaps any large-scale national) study attempted to date. These riches are an outcome of the design of the study, which in its turn was a result of the increasingly sophisticated understandings both of what large-scale national assessment studies might do and how they should be designed that had emerged in the years between FIMS and the *Six Subject Survey* and the period in which SIMS was being planned (for a brief review

---

[5] Thus, the *Six Subject Survey* found that 5 out of 18 countries significantly outperformed the U.S. at age 14 and 10 of 13 countries outperformed students in the last year of secondary school (see Medrich & Griffith, 1992).

of some of these issues see Gamoran, this volume; see also Rauden-busch & Willms, 1991; and Willms, 1992). But while, as a result of this new context for large-scale assessment research, SIMS was different in many ways from previous IEA studies, it was at the same time very much an "IEA study." To understand the character of SIMS, we must appreciate the ways in which it combined both new and older elements in its organization and design.

The SIMS Framework for Data Collection

Like FIMS and the *Six Subject Survey*, and all IEA studies, SIMS was a cooperative study undertaken by collaborating but indepen-dent national centers.[6] The need to seek consensus from the par-ticipating centers about design, instruments, and operational pro-cedures meant that all that was hoped for by the planners of the study could not come to fruition across all of the studies undertaken by national centers. But even a partial realization over the set of participating countries of what were very ambitious plans that had evolved over many years meant that the SIMS design became quite complex.[7] The variant designs and the language that I will describe below was a result of this context.

---

[6] IEA studies were and are undertaken by "national centers," research groups in universities, ministries, and other national agencies which have the organizational capability of undertaking tasks like the sampling of schools, classes and students, the management of a testing program, and the like. Such centers may be truly "national," but national centers can be also centers within provinces or states, or separate educational systems within a country. Thus, the Canadian provinces of British Columbia and Ontario, England and Wales and Scotland, and French-speaking and Flemish-speaking Belgium were separate national centers within SIMS and undertook their own studies within the overall SIMS framework. For the U.S., the national co-ordination of SIMS was undertaken at the University of Illinois at Urbana-Champaign with support from the U.S. Department of Education (through the National Center for Educational Statistics) and the National Science Foundation. The management of the overall study was undertaken by the New Zealand Department of Education under the direction of Robert A. Garden. International file building and analysis was undertaken at the New Zealand Department of Education, Wellington, the Ontario Institute for Studies in Education, Toronto, and the University of Illinois at Urbana-Champaign.

[7] Planning by IEA for a second mathematics study was begun in the mid-1970s. The data collection phase of the study was completed in 1982 after testing in one or the other of the 1980–82 academic years in the various countries. As this very brief chronology might suggest, SIMS was a massive and complex project for the 20+ national centers that undertook it—and was begun and the data collection largely completed before e-mail and fax made communication and data transfer over great distances relatively easy (for a discussion of some of the organizational and communication problems of the study, see Garden, 1990).

The designs that were advocated within the planning phase of SIMS placed a much greater emphasis than did the designs of FIMS or the *Six Subject Survey* on the notion that the second mathematics study should be a study of *mathematics* teaching and learning, from both descriptive and analytic points of view (see Travers & Westbury, 1989). Moreover, these initial visions for the study sought a design that would permit assessment not only of what a cohort of students might have learned by a single point in time (at an age or grade level), but also of the extent and nature of student learning *gains* or *growth* that were occurring in the classrooms and/or grade level of each educational system during the year of testing. The advocates of such a vision of the study also placed considerable attention on the possibility of the careful description of the patterns of teaching of the widely taught subject areas of mathematics (among them fractions, ratio, proportion and percent, algebra, geometry, and measurement at the junior secondary level; calculus, and analytic geometry at the upper secondary level), both to seek understanding of these patterns and also to permit inferences from methods of teaching to student growth between the beginning and the end of the year. And always, following the IEA credo, the ambition was to use cross-national variation as a way of capturing the differences of all kinds that might or could occur across a set of schools but could not be found within the schools of a single country.

But, within the organizational framework of the study, such a vision of what SIMS might be could only provide a set of parameters within which the collaborating national centers had to determine what kind of and how extensive a study they could support, might be interested in, and would undertake in *their* context. Inevitably, such national deliberations produced a variety of conclusions about what was desirable or feasible and, therefore, a variety of variations on the common themes that the study's planners sought.[8] Let me now turn to the task of describing both the framework of the study and the variations that emerged within the basic framework in order to set an immediate context for the chapters in this book.

---

[8] Some of these features of the SIMS design—which permitted variations across countries in the ways different national studies were undertaken—are, in turn, important in interpreting the SIMS results and what they might mean. Thus, some national centers used school-level grade cohorts (e.g., England and Wales, Scotland) or homeroom (e.g., Israel) rather than the recommended classroom-level samples. Such different frameworks for their studies make the interpretation of such countries findings uncertainly comparable to those which used the "standard" SIMS designs in some analyses.

The SIMS Model

Like other IEA studies SIMS was designed to explore and assess schooling, teaching, and learning in specific "populations" or grade levels in the school systems of the participating countries. Two such populations were selected for investigation within SIMS: all students in an early secondary grade (in the case of the United States, Grade 8) within a school system; and terminal year (in the United States, Grade 12) "specialists" in mathematics in the "secondary" stream of each school system.[9] Within the study, these target populations/grade levels were termed Population A and Population B and at each of these levels SIMS sought to collect a comprehensive set of data that would, on the basis of representative national samples:[10]

- illuminate and map both the organizational framework for the delivery of schooling and curricula within the participating countries at these levels,
- describe the curriculum or curricula in classrooms at these grade levels, and
- assess class- and group-level achievement, and student attitudes about mathematics, of classes in the target populations.

The primary overall goal was to frame a study design that could provide an understanding of the forces between and within curricula and systems of schools and between and within schools, classrooms, and teachers that might determine between- and within-country achievement profiles and patterns. Figure A outlines this

---

[9] Within the study, these target populations/grade levels were termed Population A and Population B and were formally defined internationally as:

Population A:

All students in the grade (year level) where the majority have attained the age of 13.00 to 13.11 years by the middle of the school year. [As an alternative principle of population selection, countries were permitted to select the grade at which the "curriculum" implicit in the international cognitive tests was most appropriate for students.]

Population B:

All students in the normally accepted terminal grade of the secondary education system and who are studying mathematics as a substantial part of their academic program.

[10] The details of population definitions in each participating educational system are presented in Travers and Westbury (1989). The sampling is discussed and evaluated in Garden (1987) and Travers and Westbury (1989).

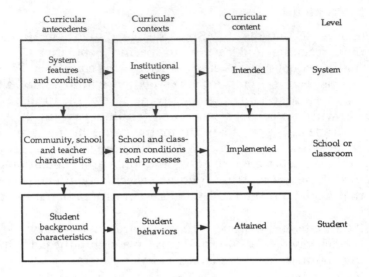

FIGURE A. The SIMS Framework

framework seen in terms of the dimensions of the key variable of "curriculum" that the studies identified and probed (see Travers & Westbury, 1989). But ultimately, of course, all of these conceptions of the curriculum converge on the classroom with its teacher, students, transactions and outcomes, and it was at this level that the instrument development and data collection of SIMS was most directly concentrated.[11]

Three related theoretical and methodological developments played key roles in determining many of the specifics of the framework within which the ambitions of SIMS were developed:

- the notion of growth as *the* criterion of school effectiveness,
- a conceptualization of the class as the primary site in which school effects were generated,

---

[11] Of course, as part of the "background" data extensive information was sought from SIMS national centers on the larger context within the educational system of each country's sample. Some of these data are reported in Travers and Westbury (1989). Moreover, as Flanders shows in Chapter 5, data collected from the SIMS questionnaires can also be used to secure data on the teaching approaches and coverage patterns of textbooks used in particular classrooms within countries—which, in turn, opens further opportunities for research.

- the emergence of (at that time) the possibility of multilevel statistical models that would permit school-, class-, and individual-level influences on achievement to be distinguished.

Together the conceptual and methodological considerations that flowed from these notions led to an intensive focus in the planning of the study on the processes by which mathematics learning was produced by teachers and teaching within classes together with a decision to use classes-within-schools as the central element for the study design to be recommended to national centers.[12]

As a result of the focus on *learning* within classes and its determinants (in contrast to the focus on the knowledge accumulated at the end of a cycle of schooling and its determinants that had been at the center both of earlier IEA studies and of most other large-scale assessment projects), the development of a framework within which "growth" in achievement within a class and grade over a year of schooling might be assessed became an overriding issue in the planning for the SIMS operational design. This in turn led to proposals for a beginning-of-year/end-of-year testing design that would permit individual- and class-level learning to be assessed as well as an intensive description of teacher "classroom processes" as a key determining context of such learning.

These discussions and proposals represented of course a new departure within the IEA tradition. As it turned out, many of the participating national centers did not wish to and/or did not have the resources to undertake a beginning-of-year/end-of-year assessment of growth patterns (or, to use the language of SIMS, a *longitudinal* study) at the Population A level and only the United States wanted to undertake such a study at the Population B level. The longitudinal study became, therefore, an option within SIMS that was selected by eight of the 20 educational systems participating in the Population A study.[13] The studies undertaken in the other systems were, in the language of SIMS, *cross-sectional studies* with

---

[12] In order to disaggregate class as distinct from school effects at the Population A level the international planning committee also strongly recommended that national committees sample two classes within each school.

[13] Even within the set of countries using the longitudinal design there were a range of more and less significant deviations from the design that was finally adopted as the "recommended design." As noted in Chapter 4, Japan was not able to use the standard longitudinal cognitive instruments because these tests had not been finally developed at the point at which the Japanese study needed to get underway.

TABLE A
Structure of the SIMS Studies
(1) Population A—Longitudinal Study
Students in grade with modal age of 13 years. Eight countries participated.

Country/System	Schools	Teachers	Students
Country/system questionnaries:	School organization questionnaire	Background, Attitudes, Practices	Core test form: 40 items
National contexts for mathematics curricula and teaching		Questionnaire	Rotated test forms: R1 (35 items)
		OTL Questionnaire	R2 (35 items) R3 (35 items)
		Each teacher indicated OTL	R4 (35 items)
Appropriateness ratings of test items in terms of the national intended curriculum		for each of the test items (5 forms)	Each student completed the core and one rotated form at the beginning and end of the school year
		Classroom Backgroumd Questionnaires Each teacher responded to questionnaires asking for information on approaches to teaching Fractions, Ratio, Proportion Percent, Algebra, Geometry, Measurement, General classroom practices	Student Background Attitudes Questionnaires Each student completed a short beginning of year questionnaire and a long end of year questionnaire.

(2) Population A—Cross-Sectional Study
Students in grade with modal age of 13 years. Twenty countries participated
(including countries in longitudinal study)

Country/System	Schools	Teacher	Students
Country/system questionnaires:	School organization questionnaire	Background, Attitudes, Teaching Practices	Core test forms: 40 items
National contexts for mathematics curricula and teaching		Questionnaire	Rotated test forms: R1 (34 items) R2 (34 items)
		OTL Questionnaire Each teacher	R3 (34 items) R4 (34 items)

TABLE A (*continued*)
Structure of the SIMS Studies
(2) Population A—Cross-Sectional Study
Students in grade with modal age of 13 years. Twenty countries participated
(including countries in longitudinal study) (*continued*)

Country/System	Schools	Teachers	Students
Appropriateness ratings of test items in terms of the national intended curriculum		indicated OTL for each of the test items (5 forms)	Each student completed the core and one rotated form at the end of the year
			Student Background, Attitudes Questionnaires
			Each student completed an end of year questionnaire.

(3) Population B
Mathematics specialists in the final year of secondary school.
Fifteen systems participated.

Country/System	Schools	Teachers	Students
Country/system questionnaires:	School organization questionnaire	Background, Attitudes Teaching Practices Questionnaire	R1 (17 items) R2 (17 items) R3 (17 items) R4 (17 items)
National contexts for mathematics curricula and teaching		OTL Questionnaire Each teacher indicated OTL for each of	R5 (17 items) R6 (17 items) R7 (17 items) R8 (17 items)
Appropriateness ratings of test items in terms of the national intended curriculum		the test items (8 forms)	Each student completed two of the eight forms or 34 items (2)
		Teacher Classroom Process Questionnaires (1) Calculus Analytic Geometry Trigonometry College Algebra General Classroom Processes	Student Background Attitudes Questionnaires Each student completed an end of year questionnaire

[1]United States, British Columbia, and Ontario only. British Columbia did not use the calculus questionnaire.
[2]United States students only completed a pretest.

TABLE B
Participation by Educational Systems in SIMS

Country/ System	Pop A		No. of classes	Pop B	
	LS	CS		LS	CS
Belgium (Flemish)	x		1		x
Belgium (French)		x	1		x
Canada (British Columbia)	x		1-2	(1)	
Canada (Ontario)	x		1-2	(1)	
England & Wales		x(2)			x
Finland		x	2+		x
France	x		2		
Hong Kong		x	1+		x
Hungary		x	1		x
Israel		x(2)			x
Japan	x		1		x
Luxembourg		x	1-6		
Netherlands		x	1		
New Zealand	x		2		x
Nigeria		x	1		
Scotland		x(2)			x
Swaziland		x	1		
Sweden		x	2		x
Thailand	x		2		x
U.S.A.	x		2	x	

[1]British Columbia used some and Ontario all the Population B *Teacher Classroom Process Questionnaires.*
[2]These systems sampled at the school or homeroom levels rather than the individual Population A mathematics classroom(s).

end-of-year testing only and without the intensive probing of class-level curricula and teaching practices that were key components of the longitudinal design. Table A outlines the elements of the longitudinal and cross-sectional designs in terms of the conceptualization of major data categories and the instruments developed for each of the studies. Table B lists the countries and educational systems which participated in one or another of the SIMS "studies," the populations which countries tested, and the design option selected.

The SIMS Sampling and Instrument Design

The comparative dimension of a study like SIMS is, of course, an outcome of a common framework for both population definition and sampling and data collection. To make meaningful comparisons across school systems the populations and samples must be the same, or at least similar, and the data that is collected common across all of the cases to be compared. Both of these issues were, of course, core problems for the design of SIMS—and the results which emerged were complex both conceptually and practically.

The process and problems of population definition and sampling are discussed in Garden (1987) and Travers and Westbury (1989). I will not repeat those discussions, which conclude that there is sufficient overall comparability of national population definitions at the Population A level to judge that the SIMS framework was able to achieve something approaching a common population at that level. At the Population B level this commonality is much more uncertain. The quality of the sampling in some countries, including the United States, was also a problem—although several critics from outside the study judged the American sample to be adequate to represent the United States school system and students and thus yield meaningful international comparisons. And, in most of the countries which participated in the longitudinal studies, the countries that are most commonly discussed in this volume, the consensus from within SIMS was that the samples that were achieved in these systems are adequate for the purposes of both international comparison and analysis.

The instruments that were designed for SIMS were the second leg of the design problem that the planners of the study had to face. The cognitive tests in particular had to carry a resolution of the problem of how the outcomes of different curricula could be meaningfully assessed and compared and offer a solution to the difficulties of the two different studies that emerged at the Population A level. What resulted was inevitably complex.

Given the differences in curricula across countries, of course it is not possible to develop a single test of mathematics achievement that either fits the situation and the curriculum of each and every country precisely. As with all cross-national research within education, what this reality means for a cross-national study of achievement was never really resolved within SIMS and, instead, of a single coherent formulation of what the tests were, various images were used at different times to describe the framework and the outcomes of the cognitive testing. Two of these images are central to the task of thinking through what the mathematics achievement data that come from SIMS are, might be, or might mean. These images can be formulated as follows:

1. The sets of cognitive tests developed for the Population A and Population B studies reflected a "core [international]

curriculum" in mathematics that represented an international consensus about the mathematics that should be sampled at the two population levels—although, of course, it was and is understood that no single country's curriculum would cover that core completely or precisely. From this vantage point, the responses to the tests of the students of each country provide a relatively firm basis for the development of national profiles of achievement that are to be, and can be, interpreted as achievement on this consensual, "core" mathematics curriculum. Thus, countries and educational systems (or subpopulations within countries) can be meaningfully evaluated in terms of their performance on either "the SIMS test" overall or on any topics and subtests reflecting those topics that are embedded within the overall international core curriculum and test.

2. The "tests" are a "menu" of items or of subtests made up of individual items and content areas. Because no country's profile of curricular emphasis is similar across all the items that made up the SIMS item pool, an operational "test" must be constructed for each and every study that might be undertaken. This task of test "reconstruction" must be undertaken in the light of both the intentions of the actual curricula of every individual educational system and/or the purposes of any particular study.

When the SIMS test data are used comparatively, it is essential to develop a point of view with regard to these interpretations of what the tests might be. This issue is, perhaps, less central when a cross-cultural test is used within a *national* context—but even then we must recognize that every national context is complex and does not necessarily have a single prescribed curriculum that can be taken as either uniformly normative or as the one curriculum against which students might be meaningfully evaluated.

In the American context, for instance, the answers to the questions "What does the SIMS test measure?" and "Does the content profile of the tests match the American curriculum?" are complex and have implications for the interpretation of the results of both international *and* national assessment and analysis. In Chapter 2, for example, Flanders suggests that the core *international* curriculum embedded within the Population A tests was inappropriate even for the "typical" curriculum of American eighth grades (that is, the SIMS Population A grade). However, while this is Flanders's conclusion about the empirical match between the content profile of the

SIMS Population A test and the American curriculum, he concludes his analysis by suggesting that it would be difficult to imagine a better implicit curriculum against which American schools might be evaluated than that embedded in the SIMS tests. In raising this caveat to his own conclusions Flanders enters a curriculum consideration into the argument about the validity of a test. The international test becomes a mirror against which American schools *should* be evaluated. In Chapter 4, I adopt a different position, one that is closer to the second of the images I sketched above: I argue that much of the SIMS item pool cannot and should not be used to assess the outcomes of American schooling. In short, there is a tension around the description and interpretation of what the SIMS tests are or might be that is omnipresent whenever the cross-national aspects of SIMS are considered. It is a tension, and ambiguity, that is found running across many of the chapters that follow.

Item Sampling.   Both the images that I describe above of what an international "test" might be encounter, of course, the issue of *how* any diverse set of curricula might and can be sampled by way of test items so as to reflect their multidimensionality, coverage, and scope. A solution to this issue involves, first, a content analysis of a set of curricula, expert judgments about what might be at the core of each country's curriculum, and then an assessment of what might be reasonably thought to be at the core of the set of national cores that emerge. Then there is the question of how this international content core might be reasonably sampled with enough items to permit meaningful measurement. The first problem is conceptual and curricular; the second is methodological.

Travers and Westbury (1989) describe the process of curriculum analysis used within the study to develop the core international curriculum that was operationalized in the item pool that emerged. I will not repeat that discussion here; it is less salient to the interpretation of the arguments of the chapters that follow than the SIMS answer to the second problem. How can that curriculum or item pool be sampled by way of a finite and manageable number of test items?

As its solution to this problem of curriculum sampling the SIMS framework for collection of the cognitive data uses *item sampling*. A large pool of items representing a sample of various content domains (mathematical topics) and levels of cognitive processes are distributed across a set of several test forms, which are then assigned differentially and randomly to subgroups of students in each classroom participating in a study. Although each subgroup in the class is tested on only some items in the item pool, the class as a whole is tested on all items—with the implication that class-level achievement over the complete item pool can be validly inferred from the performance of the subgroups, or subsamples, within classes. The actual structure for such item sampling that was used in SIMS differed in the Population A and Population B studies (see below), but in each case the use of item sampling meant that a much larger sample of items was administered to each class than to the individual students in that class.

This structure for the SIMS tests resulted in a very particular terminology for discussing the tests, one that is reflected in all of the chapters in this volume. Because of differences between the specific test structures used in the Population A and Population B studies, the framework for the cognitive tests for each of these levels needs to be discussed separately.[14]

Population A.   For the Population A study an item pool of 199 items, organized by both content domain (for example, arithmetic, measurement, and algebra) and cognitive process, was the basis for sampling the international "universe" of Population A mathematics (for the structure of the Population A item pool, see Table C). These 199 items were distributed across the five forms that made up the tests for the Population A options as follows:

- a single *core form* sampling all of the content domains; this form was administered to all students in the each system's sample of classes, and
- four *rotated forms* taken by four randomly selected subsamples of students in every class; thus one rotated form was taken by each student *in addition to the core form*.

Using this structure, achievement on the items in the core form can be used to measure individual-level achievement while class-level achievement can be measured across items on both the core and the set of four rotated forms—with the result that performance of a larger set of items can be assessed *at the class level than can be at the individual student level*. In the longitudinal study the same set of forms was used for both the pre- and posttest—with the implication that *individual-level* "growth" can be measured using data from two administrations of the core form while *classroom-*

---

[14] For a comprehensive description of the test development process, see Travers and Westbury (1989).

TABLE C
The SIMS Item Pool: Population A
(1) Cross-sectional study

Content Domain	Computation	Behavior or Cognitive Level			
		Comprehension	Application	Analysis	Total
Arithmetic	17	15	11	3	46
Algebra	18	10	8	4	40
Geometry	12	16	18	2	48
Statistics	5	8	4	1	18
Measurement	7	7	9	1	24
Totals	59	56	50	11	176

(2) Longitudinal study

Content Domain	Computation	Behavior or Cognitive Level			
		Comprehension	Application	Analysis	Total
Arithmetic	24	18	18	2	62
Algebra	14	11	6	1	32
Geometry	10	12	17	3	42
Statistics	5	10	2	1	18
Measurement	7	7	11	1	26
Totals	60	58	54	8	180

The number of items common to both versions of the Study was 156.

level "growth" can be measured using items or specially designed subtests made up from the larger set of items on both the core and rotated forms.

In the Population A study there were some differences between longitudinal and cross-sectional cognitive instruments—although the general model was the same in each option. The ambition of the longitudinal study to assess growth and its concomitants in the specific areas of the Population A curriculum that were hypothesized to be most responsive to specific teaching at the Population A level meant that more intensive sampling of some content areas was undertaken than was the case in the cross-sectional study—and this led to differences in the item pools of the two Population A studies (see Table C). The five longitudinal cognitive forms contained 180 items while the five cross-sectional forms contained 176 items. The set of items common in both studies contained 156 of the 199 items in the pool.

Population B. For the Population B study the structure of the cognitive tests was less complex. A pool of 136 items representing

TABLE D.
The SIMS Item Pool: Population B

Content Domain	Behavior or Cognitive Level				
	Computation	Comprehension	Application	Analysis	Total
Sets, Relations & Functions	2	3	1	1	7
Number Systems	5	5	6	3	19
Algebra	9	6	7	3	25
Geometry	9	8	8	3	28
Elementary Functions/Analysis	16	14	13	3	46
Statistics	4		3	—	7
Finite Math	—	2	2	—	4
Total	45	38	40	13	136

the content domains of sets, relations and functions, number systems, algebra, elementary functions and analysis (calculus), probability and statistics, and finite mathematics (see Table D) was distributed across eight forms—and each student took two of these forms. As a result, it is not possible to develop individual-level scores for Population B students. Only class-level achievement can be assessed.[15]

The Processes of Schooling in Mathematics Classes

As I suggested above, the design of SIMS was built around the assumption that the *process of schooling* (that is, the curriculum that students experience in their classrooms and the activities that are used in those classrooms) are significant determinants of school effects. This is not to say that national cultures, national patterns of school organization, teacher "quality," social class, geographic location, gender, or ethnicity are not central issues within schooling; rather, the argument is that such variables influence schooling and/or its effects by determining the ways in which the curriculum and/or opportunities to learn are distributed and interact with the larger contexts of the school *and* individual student capabilities. Thus, the SIMS planning model hypothesized that the ways in which the curriculum and opportunities to learn are *distributed* between countries and educational systems are important determinants of national achievement patterns. And, within countries it was as-

---

[15] As has already been noted, only one country, the United States, used a "full" longitudinal design for the Population B study (that is, a pretest and a posttest).

sumed that the distribution of curricula between and within schools is an important immediate determinant of patterns of achievement.[16]

Given this starting point, the development of ways to measure the elusive concept "process of schooling" became a major task in the design and development of the study. Most importantly, ways had to be developed to describe the classroom "curriculum" as a basis for:

- descriptive studies of how mathematics is treated and taught under the variety of conditions found across the participating countries and within single countries or educational systems,
- descriptive and inferential studies of the distribution of "curricula" (including teaching practices) as such patterns of distribution might be related to contextual variables, and
- inferential studies relating patterns in the distribution of "curricula" to patterns in the distribution of student achievement.

Within SIMS two approaches were used to conceptualize the "curriculum." One approach defined the "mathematics curriculum" using the SIMS item pool as its starting point and asked at national (in terms of the national "intended curriculum"), teacher, and student levels whether the content underlying the items in the pool had been "covered." Coverage and opportunity to learn were, in this view, defined in terms of the "SIMS curriculum" which, in its turn, was intended to facilitate analysis of both item specific and topic-level opportunity to learn and both item specific and topic-level achievement. The second approach asked for descriptions by teachers of their curricula and teaching practices using a framework developed out of the possibilities that can emerge from more abstract, perhaps only "theoretical," considerations of approaches to treating specific topical areas—for example, teaching practices. This second approach opened the way to going beyond content coverage narrowly conceived to an exploration of the range of ways in which given areas of content might be covered and how one or another approach to coverage might affect achievement. The first of these strategies was used in all of the options at both population levels; the second strategy was pursued intensively only in the longitudinal studies, although the teacher questionnaires used in all of the options did include a number of questions asking for information about both topical coverage and teaching methods.

---

[16] For discussions of the theoretical issues in the relationship between the processes of schooling and achievement see the chapters by Gamoran (Chapter 9) and Murchan and Sloane (Chapter 10).

Describing the Curriculum using the Item Pools as a Starting Point

Appropriateness Ratings.   All national committees were asked to evaluate all items in the item pool used in the study option they selected for its appropriateness to the national intended curriculum of their system using a three-point classification: This item is *highly appropriate, appropriate, inappropriate*.[17] The use of the appropriateness rating in particular studies provides a basis for a selection of items in cross-national studies to control for topics or areas of mathematics (and items in the pool) which were not included in one or another country's curriculum (for example, square roots or transformational geometry). The appropriateness ratio also provides data that can be used for the description of *intended* national curricula although it must always be noted that the curriculum that a school system intends or prescribes does not always match what happens in a country's classrooms.

Opportunity to Learn.   As has already been noted, what was called within SIMS the "implemented curriculum" or opportunity to learn (that is, the curriculum actually taught to students within a class as reported by each classroom teacher in the population of classes being investigated) has consistently emerged within IEA studies as one of the key variables determining achievement. Indeed, as I have also noted, the concept of opportunity to learn constitutes one of the key contributions by the IEA studies to the understanding of the determinants of educational achievement.

Within SIMS, the primary source of specific data on classroom curriculum coverage by way of the *Teacher Opportunity-to-Learn [OTL] Questionnaires*.[18] The questionnaires asked teachers to re-

---

[17] In hindsight, this approach to the description of item appropriateness proved problematic inasmuch as the questions that national committees were asked to react to did not make it clear how countries with highly differentiated curricula at either the Population A or Population B level should respond (i.e., in terms of modal or "typical" coverage, in terms of the curricula of discrete tracks or programs). In addition, the appropriateness rating posed major problems for countries like the United States which had no ministry-prescribed national curricula; in such countries the constant question was what is the "intended curriculum"; is it the curriculum embedded in the "typical" text—and, if it is, what is a "typical text?" Should the curriculum be seen as typical practice—and, if it is, who knows what typical practice is?

[18] This questionnaire was completed by teachers of the sampled classes at the time their students were completing the SIMS cognitive tests.

spond to the following questions about every item on all forms of all of the SIMS cognitive tests being used in their classes:

- Estimate the percentage of students in this class who would get the question right without guessing—the difficulty question, and
- Report whether or not your class had been taught the mathematics needed to answer the item, and if not, whether it was because the material had been taught earlier or would be taught later—the OTL question.

The task of the *OTL Questionnaires* was to capture, to the degree possible by a questionnaire, a detailed description of the actual curriculum taught in each classroom in the samples in terms of the curriculum embedded in the set of items used in each study. It should be noted that the questions, as posed on the *OTL Questionnaires*, allow several different definitions or interpretations of OTL. Two such definitions in particular represent quite different conceptions of the "curriculum": OTL can be defined as the curriculum taught to students prior to this year *and* this year[19] or it can be seen as this year's curriculum only. The use of one or the other of these definitions can obviously yield different data and embodies different conceptions of the curriculum and achievement; in the case of the first of these conceptions, the referent is clearly cumulative learning, in the case of the second "growth" although it might well be that teachers' reports of what they covered have a tighter relationship with achievement than does the more expansive conception of OTL. And it may be that the difficulty question may offer a better measure of OTL than the OTL question as such: Thus, Flanders's chapter (Chapter 2) offers an extended commentary on both the explicit coverage questions in the *OTL Questionnaire* and the implicit coverage question represented by teachers' estimates of the difficulty of items for their classes to suggest that teachers' difficulty estimates may offer a better measure of OTL than the OTL question itself.[20]

As I have noted, the strength of the OTL questions as used within SIMS is their tight linkage with the actual items in the cognitive test

---

[19] This definition of OTL is used in the published international reports on SIMS.

[20] I should also note that, in addition to OTL as defined by teachers, some countries included a question on their test booklets in which students were asked to rate whether or not they had been taught the content underlying (their perception of) the question.

forms—with all that that means for articulation between each test item and data on coverage of that item. But, while the OTL items give data analysts the power that comes from a tight coupling with items, it gives no information on topics outside the scope of the item pool and no information about the larger context of the items, the instructional methods, or the intentionalities associated with the teaching of particular items or content areas. For the longitudinal studies, this gap in the conception of the processes of schooling was addressed in part by the *Teacher Classroom Process Questionnaires* although some questions probing these areas were also included in the *Teacher Questionnaire(s)* that were part of all of the options at both population levels.

The SIMS *Teacher Classroom Practices Questionnaires* sought to capture, by way of questionnaires, a picture not only of the practices of teachers, but also of the *reasons* for these practices. The scope of these questionnaires posed burdens for the teachers of the participating countries and, as seen in the chapter by Glidden (Chapter 6), which draws on the Population B version, there is significant incomplete data. But, despite this problem for the analyst, the data from these questionnaires provides a provocative basis not only for the description of curricula and classroom practices and the reasons which lie behind those practices, but also (potentially because this has not been yet attempted yet in a sustained way—although see Burstein, 1993) for a fine-grained analysis seeking to relate specific classroom practices to growth. In this volume these data are only used in one chapter—and there it is the Population B data which are used and the focus is not growth, but, rather, the effects of system control practices on teacher decision making about curriculum. I will, however, briefly describe the overall structure of both the Population A and Population B classroom process questionnaires to complete my description of the study.

As seen in Table A, the Population A study included a set of five topic-specific classroom process questionnaires covering the areas of fractions, ratio/proportion/percent, algebra, geometry, and measurement, together with a general classroom practices questionnaire. In the Population B study there were four topic-specific questionnaires covering trigonometry, college algebra, analytic geometry, and calculus, as well as a general classroom processes questionnaire. In both sets a common framework was followed for each of the topic-specific instruments with questions in the following areas:

  sources of instructional materials and curricular
  and instructional decisions,

teaching topics/curriculum,

time allocations,

teaching methods, and

teacher opinions.

In each case general descriptions were supplemented by detailed probing in particular areas that were thought to be of general interest to mathematics educators—for example, at the Population A level, in measurement, the number formula for the area of a parallelogram ($A = bh$) or, in fractions, the concepts of common and decimal fractions; at the Population B level, in analytic geometry, the balance between two-dimensional and three-dimensional work, and vector versus nonvector approaches. In all cases the focus was on the underlying approaches to and decisions about the mathematics—which was explored in considerable detail. Thus, in some questionnaires, questions were posed to ascertain whether certain specific algorithms (used, for example, to solve proportional equations) were taught using only numerical exercises or by means of a symbolic presentation first followed by numerical examples, or vice versa. In the Population B versions the use of aids and models, approaches to the presentation of formulas, and teachers' use of and attitudes towards applications were also addressed. Peter Glidden's discussion in Chapter 6 illustrates both the kind of data that is available from the Population B questionnaires and the kinds of issues which can be explored using the data that these questionnaires provide.

Schools, Teachers and Students

I suggested earlier that the SIMS framework was built on the assumption of the centrality of the processes of schooling in the determination of school effects. As a starting point for the design of the study's data collection and instrument development, this assumption led, as I have suggested, to considerable attention being given to the need for a comprehensive description of both the curriculum and teacher enactment of the curricula. However, the study's plans also called for extensive data collection on the participating schools, teachers and students. Thus, as seen in Table A, each of the SIMS options included a:

School questionnaire covering issues such as school size, location, length of school year, teacher/student ratios, number of teachers qualified in mathematics, etc.;

Student questionnaire covering student backgrounds, students' educational expectations, parental support, and importantly, attitudes towards mathematics and mathematics teaching[21]; and a

Teacher questionnaire covering background data from teachers of the participating classes, teacher attitudes about mathematics and mathematics teaching (which can be linked to the responses of their students to the same questions), classroom characteristics, teaching practices, time devoted to a set of standard Population A or Population B teaching topics, homework patterns, sources of the classroom curriculum, textbooks used, etc.[22]

Analyzing the SIMS Data

The design of the SIMS database provides opportunities for many different kinds of analysis of curricula and teaching, both cross-nationally, in subsets of the participating countries, in single countries, and within and between strata in individual countries. The focus of analysis in such studies can be the test item (as seen in the chapters by Harnisch (Chapter 8) and Muthén (Chapter 11)), or the student, class, teacher, national subsystem, or country. In all cases such analysis can exploit the linkages of the nested, hierarchical design in which student outcomes can be linked with specific classroom curricula and contexts *and* with student and teacher background characteristics, school contexts, and, ultimately, national contexts.

We can identify two broad approaches to analyses of the SIMS data. First, there are comparative and national *descriptive studies* answering the question "What is the state of affairs regarding . . .?" Such studies have and can address: (a) the formal cognitive and attitudinal outcomes of mathematics teaching at the student, class, school, subsystem, and system level or aspects of the curriculum, teaching processes, and/or "mathematics"; (b) the outcomes of the processes within school systems (and their contexts) which are associated with, for example, patterns in the distribution of curricu-

---

[21] In the longitudinal studies, questionnaires probing student attitudes towards mathematics and mathematics instruction were administered at both the beginning and the end of the year.

[22] The data on teaching practices that were available from the *Teacher Questionnaires* is the only data available from the cross-sectional studies on teaching practices. The *Teacher Questionnaire* data are illustrated in the chapter by Schaub and Baker (Chapter 5) comparing U.S. and Japanese teaching practices and, as is made clear in that chapter, the data do yield important insights into the differences between these two countries.

la and opportunity to learn, of teaching practices, of teacher quality, enrollment patterns, etc.; and (c) what may be thought of as the contexts and frameworks for mathematics teaching, as seen, for example, in Sosniak, Ethington, and Varelas's (Chapter 3) intriguing exploration of the ideologies of American teachers and Flanders's (Chapter 2) exploration of the curriculum of U.S. Grade 8 textbooks. The focus of such studies can be on discrete variables or on clusters of variables of different kinds and at different levels. And, of course, the unique power of the data set is its capacity to ask the question "What is the state of affairs . . ." in a comparative context.

Second, the SIMS data also support inferential studies undertaken at student, teacher, subsystem, national and cross-national levels using the variety of indicators of inputs, processes, and outcomes that are available within the SIMS data set. The most obvious cluster of such studies centers on the general problems of school and curriculum effects—and such work is illustrated here in the chapters by Gamoran (Chapter 9) and Murchan and Sloane (Chapter 10)—but as seen in Baker, Riordan, and Schaub's chapter (Chapter 7), the study supports an analysis that ranges far from the problem of school effects as traditionally conceived. And for all such analysis, the significance of the SIMS data derives from the interaction that I described above between the conceptions of both "theory" and methodology that were merely glimpses in the eyes of some when the study was being undertaken and the framework for data collection. The study is built upon a complex organizational model of schooling and the production of student achievement rather than a simplistic educational production function model and it incorporates a focus on the classroom and classroom processes as crucial determinants of learning, with a specific focus on the role of the mathematics curriculum and the mathematics teacher as a "manager" of learning.

My goal in this introductory chapter has been to set the Second International Mathematics Study in its context, and provide a framework and a vocabulary for interpreting the work that is reported in the chapters that follow. I have not attempted to discuss in any sustained way the substantive significance of the work that has emerged from the analysis of the SIMS data that is represented here. However, I can foreshadow some of this significance by mentioning briefly the themes that will be developed in the following pages.

We have organized the chapters which make up this volume into three broad sections: Part I, which we have called "Teaching and Learning of Mathematics in Classrooms"; Part II, "School Structures, Social Structures, Gender and Mathematics Education"; and

Part III, "New Methodologies for Research in Mathematics Education." Part I includes four chapters, each of which focuses on the successes or problems of American classroom teaching or on the problem of assessing that success. Part II includes three chapters exploring "larger" issues that surround classroom teaching—the organization and control of curricula and teaching, and gender. Whereas the chapters in Part I draw (with one exception) on the SIMS U.S. data only, the chapters in Part II are explicitly comparative and show, we believe, how the comparative perspective that is so central to SIMS can illuminate the problem of effective mathematics instruction in the United States. Part III contains three chapters which use the SIMS data to illustrate some powerful new methods for investigating teaching and learning, multilevel methods and instructionally sensitive psychometrics; many of these possibilities derive from the characteristics of SIMS design which, because it anticipated many of the methodological developments which emerged in the years since the data was collected, is a data set in which the substantive and methodological possibilities that these new approaches offer can be realized.

The theme of all that was done in SIMS and of this volume is more effective mathematics teaching and learning. What I hope that this chapter and what follows does is show what a rich resource SIMS offers for exploring this fundamental issue. SIMS, as I suggested earlier, does much more than define what may be a problem. It, more importantly, offers a *resource* that is being used, and can be used further, to both define and seek answers to what is clearly a multifaceted and complex set of issues. If this volume encourages others to consider the host of possibilities around the host of issues being raised here it will have done what we hoped it might do.

REFERENCES

Burstein, L. (Ed.). (1993). *The IEA study of mathematics III: Student growth and classroom processes.* Oxford: Pergamon.

Carroll, J. B. (1975). *The teaching of French as a foreign language in eight countries* (International Studies in Evaluation V). New York and Stockholm: Wiley and Almqvist & Wiksell.

Comber, L. C., & Keeves, J. P. (1973). *Science education in nineteen countries* (International Studies in Evaluation I). New York and Stockholm: Wiley and Almqvist & Wiksell.

Garden, R. A. (1987). *Second international mathematics study: Sampling report.* Washington, DC: National Center for Educational Statistics, U.S. Department of Education.

Garden, R. A. (1990). An overview of the SIMS study (ERIC ED 325 360). In K. J. Travers & I. Westbury (Eds.), *Second international mathematics study: Studies.* College of Education. Champaign; University of Illinois at Urbana-Champaign.

Heyneman, S. P. (1986). *The search for school effects in developing countries: 1966–1986* (EDI Seminar Paper No. 33). Washington, DC: World Bank.

Heyneman, S. P., & Loxley, W. A. (1983). The effect of primary school quality on academic achievement across twenty nine high and low-income countries. *American Journal of Sociology, 88,* 1162–1194.

Husén, T. (1967). *International Study of Achievement in Mathematics* (2 volumes). Stockholm and New York: Almqvist & Wiksell and Wiley.

Lewis, E. G., & Massad, C. E. (1975). *The teaching of English as a foreign language in ten countries* (International Studies in Evaluation IV). New York and Stockholm: Wiley and Almqvist & Wiksell.

Medrich, E. A., & Griffith, J. E. (1992). *International mathematics and science assessments: What have we learned?* (NCES 92-011; National Center for Educational Statistics, Research and Development Report). Washington, DC: Office of Research and Improvement, U.S. Department of Education.

Passow, A. H., Noah, H. J., Eckstein, M. A., & Mallea, J. R. (1976). *The national case study: An empirical comparative study of twenty-one educational systems* (International Studies in Evaluation VII). New York and Stockholm: Wiley and Almqvist & Wiksell.

Peaker, G. (1975). *An empirical study of education in twenty-one countries: A technical report* (International Studies in Evaluation VIII). New York and Stockholm: Wiley and Almqvist & Wiksell.

Purves, A. C. (1973). *Literature education in ten countries* (International Studies in Evaluation II). New York and Stockholm: Wiley and Almqvist & Wiksell.

Raudenbusch, S. W., & Willms, J. D. (1991). The organization of schooling and its methodological implications. In S. W. Raudenbusch & J. D. Willms (Eds.), *School, classrooms, and pupils: International studies of schooling from a multilevel perspective.* San Diego CA: Academic Press.

Robitaille, D. F., & Garden, R. A. (1989). *The IEA study of mathematics 2: Contexts and outcomes of school mathematics.* Oxford: Pergamon.

Thorndike, R. L. (1973). *Reading comprehension in fifteen countries.* International Studies in Evaluation III. New York and Stockholm: Wiley and Almqvist & Wiksell.

Torney, J. V., Oppenheim, A. N., & Farnen, R. F. (1975). *Civic education in ten countries* (International Studies in Evaluation VI). New York and Stockholm: Wiley and Almqvist & Wiksell.

Travers, K. J., & Westbury, I. (1989). *The IEA study of mathematics I: International analysis of mathematics curricula.* Oxford: Pergamon.

Walker, D. A. (1976). *The IEA six subject survey: An empirical study of education in twenty-one countries* (International Studies in Evaluation IX). New York and Stockholm: Wiley and Almqvist & Wiksell.

Willms, J. D. (1992). *Monitoring school performance: A guide for educators.* Washington, DC and London: The Falmer Press.

I

TEACHING
AND LEARNING
MATHEMATICS
IN CLASSROOMS

1

When Teaching Problem Solving Proceeds Successfully in U.S. Eighth-Grade Classrooms

Lauren A. Sosniak

Department of Education
Washington University
St. Louis, MO

Corinna A. Ethington

College of Education
Memphis State University
Memphis, TN

Recent calls for change in mathematics education—and there have been many (for example, Mathematical Sciences Education Board, 1990, 1991; National Council of Teachers of Mathematics, 1980,

1989; National Research Council, 1989; Porter, 1989a; Romberg, 1990; Sowder, 1989; Stevenson, Lee, & Stigler, 1986; Stigler & Stevenson, 1991)—typically put problem solving at their center. Teachers and textbooks alike are said to give problem solving short shrift (see also Barr, 1988; Brown, Cooney, & Jones, 1990; Porter, Floden, Freeman, Schmidt, & Schwille, 1988; Romberg & Carpenter, 1986), and U.S. students are much less successful with problem solving than with computation (see also McKnight, Crosswhite, Dossey, Kifer, Swafford, Travers, & Cooney, 1987; Mullis, Dossey, Owen, & Phillips, 1991). These findings are particularly troublesome because problem solving is said to be the heart of mathematics education, both for its relation to the subject of mathematics itself and for its contributions to individuals and society alike (National Council of Teachers of Mathematics, 1989; Putnam, Lampert, & Peterson, 1990; Romberg, 1990; Sowder, 1989).

The calls for change in mathematics education, change in support of student attention to and success with mathematical problem solving, focus simultaneously on change in the ways teachers and students think about mathematics, and change in the ways students are helped to come to know the subject. First, "the notion that mathematics is a set of rules and formalisms invented by experts, which everyone else is to memorize and use to obtain unique, correct answers, must be changed" (Romberg, 1990, p. 472). Mathematics must be understood *not* as a set of procedures for finding single right answers, but rather as a language with signs and symbols and terms that help us investigate, reason, and communicate. Second, the process of teaching and learning also must shift from drill-and-practice, from rote learning of algorithms, to regular and sustained work with interesting problems.

Mathematical problem solving must become central if mathematics education is to respect the nature of the discipline. It must become central, also, if business and industry are to be well served by our schools. And mathematical problem solving must become central if we are interested in developing the capacity for lifelong learning, "so that students can explore, create, accommodate to changed conditions, and actively create new knowledge over the course of their lives" (National Council of Teachers of Mathematics, 1989, p. 4).

The research reported in this chapter examines the problem of teaching mathematical problem solving. It does so by focusing closely on a group of teachers who evidence considerable success teaching eighth-grade students to be mathematical problem solvers. We examine the thought and action of these teachers, as a group; and we examine the group of successful teachers in comparison with a group of teachers not as effective in teaching problem solving.

Our focus on within-group similarities and between-group differences is guided by two considerations. First, it is guided by a move taking place in research on teaching most generally, from a technical to a thoughtful view of the nature of the work, from a search for a set of practices for teachers to follow to a search for a set of principles that might guide teachers in their individual efforts with students around mathematical content (Porter, 1991). Second, our efforts are guided by a concern for a set of principles that maintains respect for the ecological character of classroom instruction. We attend, in turn, to teacher thinking and action, students and their work in the classroom, the nature of the content with which teachers and students work and the manner in which that content is represented, and, finally, the context within which teachers and students work with mathematics content. Our intent is not only to examine each of these dimensions of mathematics education in school, but also to consider consistency or inconsistency of principles across dimensions, and to consider the power of a group of principles for explaining successful work with problem solving.

A POINT OF DEPARTURE: PROVOCATIVE CASES

The particular SIMS data we are interested in are those associated with an anomaly we identified in the sample of "typical"[1] eighth grade U.S. mathematics classes. Examining teacher reports of opportunity to learn (OTL) for all problem-solving/applications items on the SIMS core test (13 items coded level 3, and the single item coded level 4),[2] we were able to identify seven items for which a fair

---

[1] On the U.S. SIMS eighth-grade survey, classes were classified as *algebra*, *enriched*, *typical*, and *remedial*. No definitions are offered for these terms, but the achievement patterns for students in the different groups suggests that these classifications are substantively meaningful. Because there does seem to be a substantive difference in the four types of classes, and because the bulk of classes are labeled *typical*, we decided to include in our sample only *typical* classes to avoid possible confounding of our analyses.

[2] SIMS items were developed and coded using Wilson's (1971) modified version of the taxonomy of educational objectives (Bloom, Engelhart, Furst, Hill, & Krathwohl, 1956). Items were coded as *computation* (Level 1), *comprehension* (Level 2), *application* (Level 3), and *analysis* (Level 4). The core test, given to all students, included 40 items distributed to categories as follows: *computation* = 16, *comprehension* = 10, *application* = 13, *analysis* − 1.

The air temperature at the foot of a mountain is 31 degrees. On top of the mountain the temperature is −7 degrees. How much warmer is the air at the foot of the mountain?

A. −38 degrees
B. −24 degrees
C.   7   degrees
D.   24 degrees
E.   38 degrees

Cloth is sold by the square meter. If 6 square meters of cloth cost $4.80, the cost of 16 square meters will be:

A. $12.80
B. $14.40
C. $28.80
D. $52.80
E. $128.00

In the discus-throwing competition, the winning throw was 61.60 meters. The second-place throw was 59.72 meters. How much longer was the winning throw than the second-place throw?

A.   1.12   meters
B.   1.88   meters
C.   1.92   meters
D.   2.12   meters
E. 121.32 meters

A model boat is built to scale so that it is ⅒ as long as the original boat. If the width of the original boat is 4 meters, the width of the model should be:

A. 0.1   meter
B. 0.4   meter
C.   1   meter
D.   4   meters
E. 40 meters

A painter is to mix green and yellow paint in the ratio of 4 to 7 to obtain the color he wants. If he has 28 liters of green paint, how many liters of yellow paint should be added?

A.   11
B.   16
C.   28
D.   49
E. 196

Four 1-liter bowls of ice cream were set out at a party. After the party, 1 bowl was empty, 2 were half full, and 1 was three quarters full. How many liters of ice cream had been EATEN?

A. 3¾
B. 2¾
C. 2½
D. 1¾
E. None of these

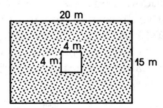

A square is removed from the rectangle as shown. What is the area of the remaining part?
A. 316 m²
B. 300 m²
C. 284 m²
D.   80 m²
E.   16 m²

FIGURE 1.1   Problem-Solving Items Differentiating Successful from Ineffective Instruction

number of teachers (63 of 142) agreed that their students had the opportunity to learn the material necessary to solve each of the items. These items sampled nicely higher order work with mathematics across a range of specific content (see Figure 1.1). Calculating growth scores (posttest minus pretest) for each of the 63 classes on each of the seven items, and running a cluster analysis[3] on those growth scores, revealed two distinct clusters: 27 classes had significantly higher growth scores than the other 36. Examining the average growth scores for the set of seven items for each of the 63 classes revealed 14 classes with overlapping growth scores and 49 classes with growth scores that did not overlap at all.[4]

In other words, we were able to identify two nonoverlapping groups of teachers whose students differed significantly in the progress they made learning problem solving and application items even though all the teachers reported covering the material necessary for their students to solve the problems. The two groups were not only statistically different in their outcome with respect to student growth of knowledge and skill in problem solving, they were dramatically so. The successful teachers were slightly more than two standard deviations more effective than the less-successful teachers. Average growth on the seven problem-solving items was .1948 for the successful group of students and .0043 for the students in the unsuccessful classes; the standard deviation of all the growth scores was .092. (Using the pooled within-group standard deviation of .043, this difference is even more dramatic.)

---

[3] The seven growth scores were entered into a cluster analysis routine using the SPSS[x] CLUSTER program. This clustering routine, in brief, initially considers all cases as members of a single cluster and then forms subsequent clusters based on a pattern similarity measure (in this case, the squared Euclidean distance). Three alternative solutions were considered: two group, three group, and four group. The two-group solution was found to be the most interpretable solution, identifying teachers whose students on average exhibited considerable growth and teachers whose students exhibited little or no growth. A discriminant classification analysis indicated that 95.2 percent of the teachers were correctly classified using this two-group solution.

[4] As we worked with data associated with these two groups of cases, we discovered a small number of instances when complete data for variables associated with teachers' work with curriculum and students was not available. To ensure that our analyses of these variables involved the same group of teachers and classes, we subsequently eliminated cases for which complete data was not available. In the end, our two nonoverlapping groups included 21 classes in which students learned to solve the more difficult problem-solving items, and 23 classes where, despite opportunity to learn, students apparently were much less successful learning to solve advanced problem-solving items.

We investigated further to explore the reasonable possibility that the initial ability of the students with whom the teachers were working would account for the eventual outcome. Instead, we found that the students of these two groups of teachers began the school year with equivalent average achievement on the 40-item core pretest. The groups of students were significantly different in their problem-solving performance at the end of the academic year *despite* equivalent initial mathematics achievement at the start. (See Table 1.1 for means and standard deviations.)

Thus, holding constant the variables traditionally considered among the most important influences on student achievement (e.g., Carroll, 1963; Porter, 1989a)—opportunity to learn and student aptitude (here, initial achievement)—two groups of teachers were dramatically different in their effectiveness in problem-solving instruction. The unusually successful teachers formed a group large enough to examine carefully using the variety of data available, and the two groups of teachers and their students allowed us a means of comparison and contrast as we explored some principles of teaching problem solving successfully.

Before we proceeded with comparisons of the two groups, we tested one further consideration: Was it possible that the group of teachers ineffective at teaching mathematical problem solving were simply poor teachers—ineffective at teaching of any sort—thus blurring questions about mathematical problem-solving instruction and

TABLE 1.1
Means and Standard Deviations for Explanatory Variables

	Effective Group (N = 21)	Ineffective Group (N = 23)
Growth on seven items	.195 (.044)	.004*** (.043)
Pretest performance	36.160 (.078)	32.280 (.086)
Pre-post growth on the 26 lower level items	.1703*** (.062)	.0597*** (.068)
Difficulty of items taught by respective groups (lower mean indicates higher difficulty)	2.666 (.594)	2.930*** (.581)
Importance of problem solving (scale)	1.224 (2.568)	−1.064** (2.797)
Importance of problem solving (item)	4.762 (.436)	4.348** (.487)
Importance of use of mathematics (scale)	7.250 (1.293)	7.087 (1.379)
Mathematics as a discipline (scale)	6.286 (1.821)	5.087* (1.443)
Teacher work with curricular content (scale)	7.269 (7.005)	2.964* (5.432)
Importance of nurturing student engagement (scale)	21.905 (3.419)	21.913 (3.541)
Importance of calling on nonvolunteers	2.857 (.727)	2.435* (.590)

$*p < .05$; $**p < .01$; $***p < .001$

bringing to the fore questions about teaching more generally? Analysis of pre- to posttest growth on the 26 lower-level (Level 1 and Level 2) core-test items revealed that the "ineffective" group of teachers could not be dismissed so easily. This group of teachers was successful at helping students acquire knowledge and develop skill around lower-level eighth-grade mathematics content (see Table 1.1). Thus, we felt confident that comparing the two groups in search of principles of effective problem-solving instruction was a meaningful endeavor.

WORKING WITH SIMS DATA

As we noted earlier, our search for principles of effective teaching of problem solving was guided by a concern for respecting the commonplaces of teaching. We began with the very basic assumption that teachers teach something (content), to someone, in some manner, within some context. Thus, it was important to us to examine the teachers and their teaching (actions they took and thoughts they had about their work as teachers and as teachers of mathematics; education and teaching experience which might bear on thought and action), the subject matter (what was emphasized and what was part of the null curriculum—the curriculum not taught), the students (demands on them from their teachers; their background—most generally and more specifically vis-à-vis mathematics), and the context of teaching and learning (characteristics of a school such as size, number of students in a class, amount of mathematics instruction provided each week, and grouping patterns for students to classrooms).

We were interested primarily in principles of effective problem-solving instruction that would relate to the work of teachers with students and subject matter in classrooms. Classroom-level work is the most direct influence on student achievement, while issues of student and teacher background and school organization can only support or detract from what takes place in the classroom. Thus, we focused our preliminary search on variables that would bear most directly on teacher and student work in the classroom; we considered questions of teacher and student background and school organization to be sources of alternative explanations for successful teaching. We relied heavily, but not exclusively, on the SIMS teacher questionnaire for our data.

When possible, we tried to examine within-group similarities and between-group differences by using sets of items in the database to construct scales against which the two groups could be compared. Scales, composed of sets of items addressing different representations of a construct are, obviously, better measures of a principle than single items; when we have groups of items with common consistency and we see the commonality of the construct underlying those items we have a more accurate and meaningful measure. As will become obvious later, due to the nature of the database and the problem at hand it became necessary to examine single items in some instances.

SEARCHING FOR PRINCIPLES OF EFFECTIVE PROBLEM-SOLVING INSTRUCTION

Teacher Decisions about Eighth-Grade Mathematics Content

As we noted at the outset, all of the teachers represented in this study reported as one of their content decisions providing an opportunity to learn the material necessary to solve seven of the higher level items on the core SIMS test. Our subsequent examinations of content decisions attempted to put that finding in context: what did teachers include, along with the opportunity to learn, that was necessary to solve the seven problem-solving items, and what did they choose to leave out? What was emphasized and de-emphasized in the curriculum as a whole that surrounded the problem-solving content?

We were interested, first, in whether the two groups of teachers crated different curricula for their students, and, if they did, how those curricula were different. We compared the profiles of the two groups of teachers with respect to teachers' reports of opportunity to learn the material necessary to solve each of the remaining 33 items on the SIMS core test. We did this both by comparing the percentage of teachers in each of the two groups reporting teaching each of the 33 items, and by comparing the average OTL scores for each item for each group of teachers.

We found that the two groups of teachers did indeed create different curricula for their students. The effective group of teachers were more likely to report both opportunity to learn the material necessary to solve higher level (as defined within SIMS) items, and more likely to report omitting teaching to lower level items. In turn, the comparison group was more likely to provide OTL for the lowest level items on the core test, and less likely to provide OTL for higher level items. Thus, opportunity to learn the material necessary to solve the seven problem-solving items was surrounded in one instance by attention focused on more difficult mathematics on the whole; it was surrounded in the other instance by attention to the easier mathematics from the set of choices.

Teaching Thinking about Eighth-Grade Mathematics Content and Objectives

Difficulty of SIMS Test Items.   In an effort to understand the curricular differences for the two groups of teachers, we turned to an examination of teacher beliefs about item difficulty. We wondered, for example, whether it was possible that the groups of teachers had different perceptions about what was easy and hard—different from the SIMS developers and different from each other. We were interested more specifically in whether the teachers' beliefs about the eighth-grade mathematics content defined by the SIMS test developers were different in such a way as to explain why the successful group of teachers were more likely to emphasize the content that SIMS developers considered more difficult.

We examined the question of whether the two groups of teachers held different beliefs about what was easy and hard about eighth-grade mathematics content by focusing on teacher reports of the percentage of students who they estimated would get the item correct without guessing. Doing so revealed that the groups of teachers agreed with each other about which items would be more or less difficult for their students, and, further, the perceptions of easy and difficult items matched the SIMS developers' coding of the items. (See Table 1.1 for means and standard deviations for variables discussed in this section.) In sum, the groups of teachers differed in what they reportedly included and excluded from their curricula, but agreed with each other and with experts on what was easy or hard for eighth-grade students to learn. Teacher content choices thus can be understood as clear choices about what is of most worth for students to spend their time on in relation to common understanding about the easiness or difficulty of the content.

The Importance of Mathematics Problem-Solving Content to the Eighth-Grade Curriculum.   The next questions we examined were whether different content choices were related to teachers thinking more broadly about the eighth-grade mathematics curriculum. Teachers were asked their opinion about how important it was to emphasize different types of mathematical content. In our effort to create a scale around the importance of problem solving and mathematical application we identified five items that we believed should fit together and would represent a reasonable range of types of problem solving and application. We included in our scale-building effort the following items:

- emphasis should be placed on teaching applications involving common fractions and decimals,
- problem-solving activities should be emphasized more than computations with fractions and decimals,
- applications with proportions should be emphasized more than solving proportional equations,
- applications involving consumer arithmetic (discount, interest, etc.) should be emphasized when students study percent,
- solving word problems is . . . important.

Teachers responded to the first four items using a five-point scale for agreement (1 = strongly agree, 5 = strongly disagree); they responded to the last item using a five-point scale for importance (1 = very important, 5 = not important at all). We recoded all items so that higher values always reflected more importance.

The five items did not group together particularly well ($\alpha = .518$), although the scale did distinguish significantly between the two groups of teachers, with the successful group emphasizing a problem-solving/application orientation. Omitting any one or two items from the scale still would not have significantly improved the internal reliability of the scale. Thus, we opted to examine more carefully the single item we believed best represented the category of teacher belief about the importance of problem solving and application: the item asking specifically about the importance to the teacher of solving word problems. This single item also revealed a significant difference between the two groups, with the successful teachers holding the stronger belief about the importance of emphasizing problem solving.

General Objectives for Eighth-Grade Mathematics. The SIMS data also allowed us to examine the teachers' general objectives for eighth-grade mathematics, independent of specific mathematics content. Another way, then, of testing teachers' beliefs about the importance of emphasizing problem solving and application was to examine responses to questions about the emphasis that should be placed on objectives that might tap at an orientation toward the use of mathematics rather than learning the procedures associated with mathematics. We reasoned that the following items would hold together well as a scale round the question of the importance of mathematics use, and then that teachers' responses to the scale would be significantly different:

- become interested in mathematics,
- develop an attitude of inquiry,
- develop an awareness of the importance of mathematics in everyday life.

The three items do hold together as a scale (α = .665). However, this general measure of objectives for eighth-grade mathematics does not distinguish between the two groups of teachers. At this most general level, independent of specific mathematics content, both groups of teachers believe it is more important than not to emphasize these objectives.

Teacher Thinking about Mathematics as a Discipline

In our further effort to understand the differences in curricular decisions and thinking for the two groups of teachers, we turned to an examination of teacher thinking about the subject of mathematics itself. We were interested in whether the teachers' beliefs about mathematics as a subject most generally were related to their content decisions and/or beliefs about eighth-grade curricular emphases.

To examine the teachers' beliefs about the nature of mathematics as a subject matter, we created a scale of items which represents an approach to distinguishing between mathematics as conceptual (idea-based, higher order) or procedural (rule-based, lower level) knowledge. We included in our scale the following two items which represent alternative perspectives on the place of rules and mathematics—on one hand there is an emphasis on rules, on the other there is an emphasis on the ideas rather than the rules of mathematics:

- There is always a rule to follow in solving math problems.
- In mathematics, problems can be solved without using rules.

Again, teachers responded to these items on a five-point scale, this time from strongly disagree (1) to strongly agree (5). The second item thus was recoded so that higher values always represent a more conceptual view of mathematics.

The internal consistency reliability of the two items was reasonably strong ($\alpha = .6184$). Comparing the two groups on this scale, we also found a statistically significant difference between the groups. The successful teachers were more likely than the ineffective teachers to perceive mathematics as conceptual rather than rule governed.

Teacher Work with Curriculum Content

The SIMS database allowed us also to examine teachers' thinking about their work as teachers of mathematics. In particular, it allowed us to examine the influences on their decisions about how best to represent mathematics in class. To do so, we created a scale including responses to the question: How difficult would it be for you to teach the target class satisfactory under each of the following circumstances . . .? The "circumstances" we included in our scale were those having to do without:

- problem sets you have written yourself;
- tests you have written yourself;
- examples to talk about that you have made up yourself;
- advice you have received in the past year from administrators (e.g., principal, curriculum supervisor, department head);
- advice you have received in the past year from other teachers;
- the official syllabus;
- published tests;
- published workbooks or published problem sets;
- published textbooks;
- knowledge of what is on external exams (not selected by you) taken by your students.

We recoded the last seven of the ten items so that the scale would represent values around a reliance on self versus a reliance on external sources for work representing curriculum to students.

The internal reliability coefficient for the scale was high ($\alpha = .755$), and the scale did distinguish significantly between the two groups of teachers. The successful teachers were significantly more likely than the ineffective teachers to find it difficult to teach without their own problem sets, tests, and examples; the ineffective teachers were significantly more likely to find it difficult to teach without external guidance.

Thinking about Work with Students:
The Conditions for Learning

Our examination of teacher beliefs about work with students turned in two directions. First, we were interested in the attention teachers give to nurture student engagement with mathematics and mathematics classes—being positive generally in class and personal in their work with individual students. Second, we were interested in the attention teachers believed it would be important to give to promoting student involvement in class irrespective of attending to needs and feelings of specific students.

Teachers were asked a series of questions about what teachers might do to make their teaching more effective, and were asked to rate each item with regard to what they thought personally was of more or less importance. The items were rated on a scale such that 1 = little or no importance, 2 = some importance, 3 = major importance, and 4 = highest importance. Included in the list of suggestions were eight we thought would distinguish teachers who were nurturing of students most generally and individuals more specifically from those who were less so. The items we used to create this scale asked teachers to rate, with respect to importance, the following pedagogical strategies:

- have something good to say about the answers students give in class whether the answers are correct or not;
- allow discussions to continue longer than planned when students show particular interest;
- try to develop warm, personal relationships with students;
- give abler students assignments which are truly difficult for them to solve;
- give less able students assignments that are simple enough that they can progress without making many mistakes;
- ask questions to determine the specific weaknesses of less able students and assign tasks accordingly;
- give assignments which are tailored to the particular instructional needs of individual students;
- change the sequence and duration of activities for the sake of variety.

This set of items did result in a high internal consistency reliability ($\alpha = .6923$). However, it did not distinguish between the two groups of teachers. In fact, the two groups responded almost identically, being more positive than not to a personal and nurturing approach to teaching.

In our effort to examine beliefs teachers held about the importance of working actively to engage students in classwork and in
learning mathematics irrespective of attending to needs and feelings
of specific students we tried various approaches to creating a scale,
all unsuccessful. What we found, however, in our efforts to group
various issues of pedagogy around this idea of demanding student
participation and serious attention to mathematics, was one item
which consistently asked to be considered on its own: the emphasis
teachers placed on the value of calling on students who do not
volunteer to answer questions. Examining this variable alone, we
found that the two groups of teachers were significantly different in
their responses. The successful teachers believed this was much
more important for improving the effectiveness of teaching than did
the ineffective teachers.

TEACHING AND LEARNING IN CLASSROOMS: COLLECTING OUR FINDINGS

Using data from SIMS to examine a variety of dimensions of teaching and learning mathematical problem solving—curriculum content emphasized, teacher objectives for the eighth-grade mathematics, teacher views of the discipline of mathematics, the nature of
teacher work with the curriculum, and the nature of teacher work
with students—we find an interesting pattern of within-group similarity and between-group differences. The successful approach to
helping students acquire problem-solving knowledge and skill
seems notable for its demands—on both teacher and students and
with regard to subject matter.

Teaching problem solving successfully, rather than ineffectively,
was associated with an emphasis on the most difficult mathematical
concepts and skills in the curriculum (opportunity to learn more
difficult mathematical ideas and skills; emphasis on problem solving and word problems). It was associated with teachers asking
much of themselves when considering how to represent the eighth-
grade curriculum to and with their students, relying primarily on
teacher-created problem sets rather than district mandates or
school-selected materials (personalized teaching). It was associated
with teachers pressing their students to get involved in the process
of learning (calling on nonvolunteers). And it was associated with
teacher beliefs that mathematics itself is principally an intellectual
rather than a procedural matter (rule orientation).

Interestingly, successful teaching of problem solving was not distinguished from ineffective teaching by two variables we had anticipated might be important: topic-independent objectives for eighth-grade mathematics emphasizing usefulness of mathematics, and a nurturing attitude toward student engagement. In both instances, both groups of teachers were more positive than the average and were not significantly different from each other.

In sum, teaching problem solving successfully involved teachers working assertively and with intelligence, and calling on their students to do the same, with the most demanding aspects of the curriculum. It was "active mathematics teaching" (Good, Grouws, & Ebmeier, 1983) of a different sort: calling on cognitive activity from teachers and students alike around difficult mathematical content and mathematical objectives. The less successful approach was more notable for being less demanding, for smoothing the way for teachers and students alike—working with easier content, relying on external influences for teacher work with that content, and merely inviting, rather than pressing for, student engagement with curricular content.

The model of demanding teaching we were developing for helping to understand effective problem-solving instruction needed to be put to the test. How important, as a set, were variables associated with demanding teaching—variables of curricular content emphasized (difficult problems emphasized), teacher views of the discipline of mathematics (conceptual rather than rule governed), teacher objectives for the eighth-grade mathematics (word problems important), the nature of teacher work with the curriculum (personalized teaching), and the nature of teacher work with students (calling on nonvolunteers)? We examined the power of this set of variables for explaining the difference in the success of the two groups using a regression model which would allow us to determine the difference between the two groups that would have been expected if they had been the same on the variables we examined. That is, we were interested in identifying what part of the observed difference in the average growth scores of these two groups of students would be explained by the differences in the "demanding" characteristics of teacher thought and action.

After controlling for the differences in the previously described variables, the coefficient for the variables representing the two groups of teachers was .143. The original difference between the groups was .191. This reduction of .048 represents approximately one-half a standard deviation. Together, the five variables account

TABLE 1.2
Regression Results With Average Growth on Seven
Items as Dependent Variable

Independent Variables	β	β
Group	−.191*	−.143*
PROBDIF		.007
RULEORIENT		−.002
WPIMP		.007
PRSNTCH		.002
CALLNONVOL		.016

*$p < .001$

for approximately one-fourth of the difference in student achievement between the successful and unsuccessful teachers. (See Table 1.2.)

Our findings seemed impressive, but we recognized that they needed to be considered in relation to more traditional explanations for successful teaching. Would background knowledge and experience of the teacher, and various aspects of school organization, be as powerful, or perhaps even more powerful, in explaining eventual student success with problem solving as were the set of variables associated with demanding teaching? That was the question we turned to next.

SEARCHING FOR ALTERNATIVE EXPLANATIONS

Explanations for successful teaching and learning frequently look less closely than we have at teachers' work with curricular content and a group of students, and more closely at background and contextual variables such as characteristics of teachers, students and schools themselves. We recognized the possibility that characteristics of the teachers and students, and of the schools within which teaching and learning took place, might well influence successful learning of mathematics, perhaps even more strongly than the variables embedded in classroom work which we reported on earlier. Thus, in order to make sense of our earlier findings, we went in search of alternative explanations for successful and ineffective work with mathematical problem solving by examining more traditional variables associated with the context for teaching and learning.

The Teachers and Students

Is there something about the backgrounds of teachers or students themselves which might account for the differences we found in the teaching and learning? Were the teachers differently educated, for example? Or did the teachers have different amounts of experience? Were the students differently prepared for their class-work?

In the search for differences related to teacher education (different preparation of the teachers for their work), we considered the following variables from the SIMS teacher questionnaire: semesters of postsecondary mathematics; semesters of postsecondary mathematics pedagogy, and semesters of postsecondary general pedagogy. A MANOVA revealed no statistically significant difference between the groups. (See Table 1.3 for means and standard deviations for both teacher and student alternative explanation variables.)

TABLE 1.3
Means and Standard Deviations for Teacher and Student Alternative Explanation Variables

	Successful Group	Ineffective Group
Teacher Variables		
Educational Background:[a]		
Semesters postsecondary mathematics	10.222 (5.642)	9.500 (4.747)
Semesters postsecondary mathematics pedagogy	2.444 (1.617)	2.187 (1.328)
Semesters postsecondary general pedagogy	5.278 (3.461)	5.312 (4.882)
Teaching Experience:[b]		
Years of teaching	17.524 (12.250)	11.727 (7.032)
Years teaching 8th grade	9.143 (5.703)	6.682 (4.654)
Student Variables		
Student Pretest Attitudes:[c]		
Importance of problem solving	3.729 (.203)	3.604 (.190)
Ease of problem solving	3.319 (.239)	3.366 (.291)
Like of problem solving	2.956 (.306)	2.889 (.284)
Teachers' Perception of Students:[d]		
Range of abilities	2.143 (.793)	2.130 (.757)
Mastery of previous material	68.333 (17.701)	59.957 (21.845)
Student SES[e]	.608 (.949)	−.655 (1.220)

[a] Wilks lambda = .989; $df = 3,30$; $p = .954$
[b] Wilks lambda = .911; $df = 2,40$; $p = .154$
[c] Wilks lambda = .877; $df = 3,40$; $p = .149$
[d] Wilks lambda = .956; $df = 2,41$; $p = .397$
[e] $t = 3.81$; $df = 42$; $p < .001$

In search of differences related to different amounts of experience teaching, we considered both reported years of teaching and reported years of teaching eighth-grade mathematics. A MANOVA revealed no statistically significant differences between the groups of teachers. It seems important in this instance to note tendencies that might prove to be significant if we were working with a larger sample: The successful teachers had more years of experience teaching (mean of 17.5 vs. mean of 11.7; $p = .063$), and the successful teachers also reported more years teaching eighth-grade mathematics (mean of 9.1 vs. 6.7; $p = .128$).

In our search for differences related to student background, in addition to the earlier reported variable of initial ability as measured by pretest scores on a test of general mathematics ability, we also examined initial attitudes toward problem solving (using student-reported data from the beginning-of-year student questionnaire), the range of abilities of the students in the class and class mastery of the previous curriculum (using teacher perceptions of these latter two variables), and student SES (using student-reported data from the end-of-year student questionnaire).

We examined student responses on the pretest to questions about the importance of problem solving, the ease of work with problem solving, and students' liking of work with problem solving. The responses of the two groups of students were essentially the same on all three variables. A MANOVA including teacher-reported range of abilities of the students in the class (mean $= 2.1$ for both groups), and class mastery of the previous curriculum (68.3 percent entered with sufficient degree of mastery of previous curriculum for the successful teachers; 60 percent for the unsuccessful teachers; $p = 1.72$), also revealed no significant difference between the groups.

Our measure of student SES was a composite measure created by summing, after standardizing, mother's and father's education and occupation. On this measure we did find a statistically significant difference between the two groups of students (see Table 1.3). It seemed important, then, to examine how much of the problem-solving achievement difference between the two groups would be explained by student SES alone. Rerunning our earlier regression analysis, using SES rather than teaching variables, the difference between the groups, if they had been the same on SES, is .172. The proportion of the difference between the two groups explained by SES alone is 10 percent; this is certainly meaningful, but also considerably smaller than the approximately 25 percent accounted for by the variables of demanding teaching on their own.[5]

---

[5] A common approach to the study of student achievement is to examine characteristics of a school organization or the institution of schooling. Because

SUMMARIZING THE EMPIRICAL INVESTIGATIONS

We began our search for principles of successful problem-solving instruction with a naturally occurring and theoretically interesting sample. Two groups of eighth-grade mathematics teachers agreed that they were providing opportunity for their students to learn a range of mathematical problem-solving items and the groups of students working with these teachers began the school year with equivalent mathematical achievement; at the end of the year one group of students demonstrated considerable progress learning problem solving, while the other group had made virtually no progress at all. The groups of teachers and their students allowed us to take seriously Carroll's (1985) assertion that allocation of time in relation to student ability is necessary, but not sufficient, to promote successful learning. The groups provided us with an opportunity to examine more carefully the conditions which, in addition to opportunity to learn and student aptitude, support success with problem solving.

Our particular interest in this search for principles for teaching effective problem solving centered on the role of schooling, and, more specifically, the role of teachers and their work with curriculum content and groups of students. We were mindful also of the need to consider influences of teacher and student background and school organization. Our analyses thus were conducted in two waves: first, examining teachers' thoughts and action in relation to work with curriculum and groups of students; next, examining more traditional variables of teacher and student background and school organization which might reasonably be expected to influence student achievement in school.

Our analyses compellingly demonstrated the power of classroom-level influences over and above allocation of time to specific content. We found that classroom teachers' beliefs and actions around work with students and curriculum content accounted for a considerable amount of the difference in student achievement between the two groups. The successful approach to helping students acquire problem-solving knowledge and skill involved what we now think of as *cognitively demanding instruction*: teachers thinking about mathematics as more conceptual than rule governed, emphasizing work

---

school size, number of students in a class, minutes of mathematics instruction per week (number of periods × length of periods) might be expected to account for differences in student achievement, we included these variables in a MANOVA which revealed no statistical significance. We used chi-square procedures to examine grouping patterns (homogeneous or heterogeneous) patterns for the schools, and again found no statistically significant difference.

with word problems and, more generally, difficult rather than the lower level eighth grade mathematics content; working personally with the eighth grade content to find ways of representing it to students; and, demanding that students, too, get personally involved with the difficult subject matter whether or not the students are inclined to do so on their own.

In our analyses, the successful and ineffective groups were not distinguished by a variety of variables frequently associated with the study of effective instruction. There were no statistically significant differences between the groups with respect to topic-independent objectives emphasizing the usefulness of mathematics, nor with respect to nurturing attitudes toward student engagement. There were no statistically significant differences between the groups with respect to amount of teacher experience and education; there were no statistically significant differences around school and district decisions regarding grouping for instruction, class size, and the like. Of the traditional explanatory variables we studied, only student SES distinguished the two groups and provided an alternative source of explanation for the differences in achievement.

Student SES, a proxy measure for various unexamined educational actions and opportunities typically taking place outside the school, did account for some of the difference in the problem-solving achievement of the two groups. It was considerably less powerful than the set of variables we associate with demanding teaching, but still it was important. Because variables of demanding teaching are alterable and SES as it is currently conceptualized is not, and because variables of demanding teaching reflect most directly on our work as educators and SES does not, we believe it is reasonable to focus attention principally on the idea of demanding teaching. Still, we would probably be well advised to pause for a moment and reflect on the continued power of SES in models of school learning. Clearly, if we could untangle the educational meaning of SES with some clarity, then models of school learning could be enriched by entering into those equations the alterable variables associated with learning outside of school which support the efforts and intentions of the school. The intimate relations between education in and out of school continue to be an obvious source of influence and potential that neither we nor the educational community at large have studied sufficiently.

Important Limitations of this Study

This study is limited not only by our attention almost exclusively to school influences on learning mathematical problem solving, but also by several conceptual and technical problems well known to researchers studying effective practice or working with survey data. For example, our findings regarding demanding teaching suffer, as all studies of this sort do, from a form of the naturalistic fallacy. Because this study relies on existing practice for its understandings, the results we find can, at most, only point to the best of currently available practice. Whether best practice as it currently exists is a proper stepping stone to best practice as it ought to be is a question worthy of debate. Still, we would argue that if we were able to bring instruction up to the best of currently available practice around principles of demanding teaching, we would in fact be making instruction radically different from what is currently found in U.S. classrooms. It would be different in its content and its method as well as in the dispositions teachers and students bring to mathematics and their work with mathematics in the classroom.

Our findings are limited also by the nature of survey data. Survey data provide only a crude sense of teacher thought and action and the interaction of teachers with students and content. Thus, the data we have worked with are important for provisional understanding, but limited in serious ways. We cannot know with any certainty what teachers and students are doing and thinking during daily classroom activity. We cannot know whether common accounts of thought and action might turn out to be quite different in meaning if the survey respondents were probed in greater detail, or whether different reports that appear here to be statistically significant might dissolve if the matters at hand were investigated more closely. Further, careful classroom observation and in-depth interviews with the same groups of teachers might reveal variables far more potent for comparing the groups than were available in the survey data.

These are inevitable limitations of working with survey data, and, particularly, conducting secondary analyses. They are serious limitations that demand we present our findings as provisional, and that we be explicit about the need for multiple tests of our conclusions using alternative samples and research methodologies. These limitations notwithstanding, we believe the results of this investigation are worthy of careful attention and serious follow-up.

We point to the small numbers of teachers and students included in this study, a feature typically thought of as a limitation, and note instead the very fact of the statistical significance we were able to achieve with these small numbers. More importantly, we believe, the statistical significance is noteworthy because of the potential theoretical power of the findings. Our findings fit nicely with and provide extensions for contemporary understanding of both effective teaching and effective instruction in mathematics. The fit of "demanding teaching" into the long-term search for effective mathematics instruction is the subject to which we will turn in the next and final section of this chapter.

RETHINKING EFFECTIVE INSTRUCTION
FOR MATHEMATICAL PROBLEM SOLVING

In many respects, our findings support years of work on effective teaching and effective instruction in mathematics (see Romberg & Carpenter, 1986). Our work supports the argument made by many before us that the content covered in a classroom does make a difference to student achievement. It also supports arguments that teacher thinking and teacher beliefs are related to student achievement. More specifically, like Peterson, Fennama, Carpenter, and Loef (1989), we find that teachers who hold a conceptual rather than rule-governed orientation toward mathematics and an orientation toward emphasizing mathematics applications and problem solving secure higher levels of student achievement around problem solving than do teachers who hold alternate perspectives. Finally, our work supports the idea that teacher investment in thinking about "representations" (Wilson, Shulman, & Richert, 1987)—teachers' taking pedagogical content knowledge seriously—makes a difference in student achievement.

Support for these developing lines of work is important. But more important still is an element of our work that we think sets it in a somewhat different arena. The demanding approach to teaching and learning that we have identified here is particularly interesting not primarily for the individual ideas about mathematics education we have been able to support, but rather for the support this study provides for what Doyle (1988) calls *curriculum enactment research*.

Curriculum enactment, "an umbrella term for the processes by which schooling is accomplished in classroom settings" (Doyle, 1988, p. 18), includes an integrated focus on content, pedagogical processes, and the management of classroom action systems. Curriculum enactment research is an advance in research on effective teaching and effective mathematics instruction, Doyle claims, in that it works to take into account the various dimensions of teaching and learning in school, balancing and examining each dimension in relation to the others. The various dimensions include the two most common in research on effective teaching—pedagogical processes and management of classroom action systems—and one relatively neglected in the educational research literature—*curriculum content*.

The search, in curriculum enactment research, is for the development of structural explanations in which "objects and activities do not have meaning as autonomous entities apart from the system of relations in which they are embedded" (Doyle, 1988, p. 19). And, from our perspective, the variables we have examined are signs within a system of demanding teaching. Our findings should not generate a fragmented and algorithmic image of teaching practice. Rather, the whole of our findings, a whole which attends seriously to intentions and activities and their relationships, seems greater than the sum of parts.

The whole of our findings around demanding teaching points to the limits of what Jackson (1986) calls "painless pedagogy." Jackson contends that over historical time the practice of teaching clearly has moved in the direction of reducing discomfort for students and teachers alike. This is not merely happenstance, he argues, nor an unintended consequence of other priorities, but rather "the search for painless pedagogy has inspired educational reformers throughout modern history" (p. 102). While Jackson clearly acknowledges the movement as progress most generally, he notes also that the endless quest for painless pedagogy is not without problems.

> No one except a sadist would advocate the introduction of discomfort and suffering into the educational process for its own sake. . . . But the crucial question, which quickly emerges when all cartoons are laid aside, is how much discomfort can be eliminated from the educational process without risking the loss of something even more important than relative comfort: education itself? (p. 111)

It is not only the goal of reducing discomfort for students that Jackson believes needs to be examined; the goal of reducing discomfort for teachers also may be problematic. "Teachers may wish to reduce the discomfort associated with their work. . . . The question is whether the reduction of discomfort can be and sometimes is purchased at the sacrifice of other goals more central to the teacher's task" (Jackson, 1986, p. 112).

We believe that our search for principles for successful problem-solving instruction touches on the limits of painless pedagogy, and points to the end of the line for this form of progress in teaching policy and practice. If teachers avoid emphasizing difficult curriculum content in class, and if they allow students to avoid public work with difficult content, are they not sacrificing education itself? If teachers themselves rely principally on external sources for guidance around content representation, if they themselves are not invested in thinking seriously about the nature and the meaning of the content they are intending to teach, can they still be teaching reasoning and investigation and communication via mathematical signs and symbols and terms?

The whole of our set of findings also points to the policy dilemma of commitment versus control (e.g., Rowan, 1990), or, as Porter (1989b) has phrased it, "the pros and cons of telling teachers what to do" (p. 343). It would be easy to suggest, following from our analyses, that curriculum be defined around more difficult rather than easier mathematical content, that teachers be directed to learn to value and emphasize in class mathematical applications and problem solving, and that teachers be directed to prod students into work with this content even if students would not choose to do so on their own. However, respecting the idea of curriculum enactment as a search for structural explanations which are not algorithmic in their implications, respecting the thoughtfulness that mathematical problem solving itself and problem-solving instruction demand, and respecting the intelligence demonstrated by the group of teachers in this study who were successful teaching problem solving, we find ourselves unwilling to suggest such prescriptions. More important, we believe, may be standard setting around the very practice of thinking about curriculum enactment in the service of teaching problem solving.

The point is not automaticity around principles of demanding teaching; rather, it is that teachers and researchers and others concerned with the education of children in schools engage seriously in asking questions about the content emphasized in classroom settings, the manner in which teachers and students work individually and together with that content, and the aims toward which content and manner are directed. The successful teachers in our study seem to have done just that, represented best, perhaps, by the fact that they more than their counterparts took seriously the need for thoughtful rather than procedural work representing content to students. Demanding teaching requires that teachers ask questions about content and method, examine their intentions and their means for realizing them, and strive for fit between aims and activities. Demanding teaching is, itself, higher order thinking, problem solving, nonalgorithmic, interpretive, constructivist.

We are not arguing here for teacher autonomy as it is typically understood. As Nickson (1988) notes, "It is clear that the notion of teacher autonomy within the context of the mathematics classroom can be taken too far and that many teachers would welcome intervention and guidance of an appropriate sort" (p. 248). We are arguing for autonomy embedded within *obligation*: obligation to a subject matter, to the idea of education within school settings, and to the society served by schools and their teachers. Obligation to subject matter, the idea of education, and the society served by our schools thus provides its own guidance. Such an approach is our answer, for the moment, to Shulman's (1983) question: "If the responsible and effective teacher must be both free and obligated, how shall we define the proper mix of those typically incompatible virtues?" (p. 486) Autonomy and obligation are not necessarily incompatible virtues, they may indeed be mutually supportive.

Of course for teachers to exercise autonomy within obligation the teachers must be supported for both. Stigler and Stevenson's (1991, p. 45) analysis of a U.S. system of schooling which "prepares [teachers] inadequately and then exhausts them physically, emotionally and intellectually while denying them the collegial interaction that every profession relies upon for the growth and refinement of its knowledge base" suggests there are necessary prescriptions for change if successful teaching is to become the rule rather than the exception. As we read it, these prescriptions are principally for change of our system of schooling, rather than prescriptions for change directed toward matters of curriculum enactment in classrooms.

We must continue to examine classroom tasks (e.g., Doyle, 1986, 1990), the nature of tasks that support successful rather than ineffective work with curriculum that we hold in highest regard, and the nature of embedding principles of successful teaching appropriately in educational policy and practice. We believe that this study represents a reasonable early effort toward creating a model for successful curriculum enactment. This model integrates teacher autonomy and obligation, and educational organizations with their missions. More specifically, demanding teaching calls on teachers to work actively with complex material, and to ask students to do the same. It calls on teachers to work with intelligence, informed by supportive communities. Demanding teaching takes seriously, simultaneously, subject matter, the reflective and interactive demands of teaching groups of students in settings called classrooms, the reflective and interactive demands of learning, and the relationships between organizations and their intentions. Demanding teaching is unlikely ever to be thought of as a move in the further direction of painless pedagogy. But demanding teaching aims for a different sort of progress for students and society alike.

REFERENCES

Barr, R. (1988). Conditions influencing content taught in nine fourth-grade mathematics classrooms. *Elementary School Journal*, *88*, 387–411.

Bloom, B. S., Engelhart, M., Furst, E., Hill, W., & Krathwohl, D. (1956). *Taxonomy of educational objectives: Cognitive domain*. New York: Longman.

Brown, S. I., Cooney, T. J., & Jones, D. (1990). Mathematics teacher education. In R. W. Houston (Ed.), *Handbook of research on teacher education*. New York: Macmillan.

Carroll, J. B. (1963). A model of school learning. *Teachers College Record*, *64*, 723–733.

Carroll, J. B. (1985). A model of school learning: Progress of an idea. In C. W. Fisher & D. C. Berliner (Eds.), *Perspectives on instructional time*. New York: Longman.

Doyle, W. (1986). Content representation in teachers' definitions of academic work. *Journal of Curriculum Studies*, *18*, 365–379.

Doyle, W. (1988, June). *Curriculum in teacher education*. Division K Vice Presidential Address, AERA, New Orleans, April 1988.

Doyle, W. (1990). Classroom knowledge as a foundation for teaching. *Teachers College Record*, *91*, 347–360.

Good, T. L., Grouws, D. A., & Ebmeier, H. (1983). *Active mathematics teaching*. New York: Longman.

Jackson, P. W. (1986). *The practice of teaching*. New York: Teachers College Press.

Mathematical Sciences Education Board. (1990). *Reshaping school mathematics: A philosophy and framework for curriculum*. Washington, DC: National Academy Press.

Mathematical Sciences Education Board. (1991). *Counting on you: Actions supporting mathematics teaching standards*. Washington, DC: National Academy Press.

McKnight, C. C., Crosswhite, F. J., Dossey, J. A., Kifer, E., Swafford, J. O., Travers, K. J., & Cooney, T. J. (1987). *The underachieving curriculum: Assessing U.S. school mathematics from an international perspective*. Champaign, IL: Stipes.

Mullis, I. V. S., Dossey, J. A., Owen, E. H., & Phillips, G. W. (1991). *The state of mathematics achievement: Executive summary*. Washington, DC: National Center for Education Statistics, U.S. Department of Education.

National Council of Teachers of Mathematics. (1980). *An agenda for action: Recommendations for school mathematics of the 1980s*. Reston, VA: Author.

National Council of Teachers of Mathematics. (1989). *Curriculum and evaluation standards for school mathematics*. Reston, VA: Author.

National Research Council. (1989). *Everybody counts: A report to the nation on the future of mathematics education*. Washington, DC: National Academy Press.

Nickson, M. (1988). Pervasive themes and some departure points for research into effective mathematics teaching. In D. A. Grouws, T. J. Cooney, & D. Jones (Eds.), *Perspectives on research on effective mathematics teaching* (Vol. 1). Reston, VA: National Council of Teachers of Mathematics.

Peterson, P. L., Fennama, E., Carpenter, T. P., & Loef, M. (1989). Teachers' pedagogical content beliefs in mathematics. *Cognition and Instruction, 6,* 1–40.

Porter, A. (1989a). A curriculum out of balance: The case of elementary school mathematics. *Educational Researcher, 18,* 9–15.

Porter, A. (1989b). External standards and good teaching: The pros and cons of telling teachers what to do. *Educational Evaluation and Policy Analysis, 11,* 343–356.

Porter, A. (1991). Good teaching of worthwhile mathematics to disadvantaged students. In M. S. Knapp & P. M. Shields (Eds.), *Better schooling for the children of poverty.* Berkeley, CA: McCutchan.

Porter, A., Floden, R., Freeman, D., Schmidt, W., & Schwille, J. (1988). Content determinants in elementary school mathematics. In D. A. Grouws, T. J. Cooney, & D. Jones. (Eds.), *Perspectives on research on effective mathematics teaching* (Vol. 1). Reston, VA: National Council of Teachers of Mathematics.

Putnam, R. T., Lampert, M., & Peterson, P. L. (1990). Alternative perspectives on knowing mathematics in elementary schools. In C. B. Cazden (Ed.), *Review of research in education* (Vol. 16). Washington, DC: American Educational Research Association.

Romberg, T. A. (1990). Evidence which supports NCTM's Curriculum and Evaluation Standards for School Mathematics. *School Science and Mathematics, 90,* 466–479.

Romberg, T. A., & Carpenter, T. P. (1986). Research on teaching and learning mathematics: Two disciplines of scientific inquiry. In M. C. Wittrock (Ed.), *Handbook of research on teaching* (3rd ed.). New York: Macmillan.

Rowan, B. (1990). Commitment and control: Alternative strategies for the organizational design of schools. In C. B. Cazden (Ed.), *Review of research in education* (Vol. 16). Washington, DC: American Educational Research Association.

Shulman, L. S. (1983). Autonomy and obligation: The remote control of teaching. In L. S. Schulman & G. Sykes (Eds.), *Handbook of teaching and policy.* New York: Longman.

Sowder, J. T. (Ed.). (1989). *Setting a research agenda* (Vol. 5). Reston, VA: National Council of Teachers of Mathematics.

Stevenson, H. W., Lee, S. Y., & Stigler, J. W. (1986). Mathematics achievement of Chinese, Japanese, and American Children. *Science, 231,* 693–699.

Stigler, J. W., & Stevenson, H. W. (1991). How Asian teachers polish each lesson to perfection. *American Educator,* pp. 13–20, 43–47.

Wilson, J. W. (1971). Evaluation of learning in secondary school mathematics. In B. S. Bloom, J. T. Hastings, & G. F. Madaus (Eds.), *Handbook on formative and summative evaluation of student learning*. New York: McGraw-Hill.

Wilson, S. M., Shulman, L. S., & Richert, A. E. (1987). '150 different ways of knowing': Representations of knowledge in teaching. In J. Calderhead (Ed.), *Exploring teachers' thinking*. London: Cassell.

2

Student Opportunities in Grade 8 Mathematics: Textbook Coverage of the SIMS Test

James Flanders

Colorado Springs, CO

What do the textbooks used in eighth-grade classrooms say about the mathematics curriculum? Recent summaries of research and debate about the role of textbooks in education are easy to find, and the conclusions paint a disconcerting picture. Textbooks are widely used in classes, with about 90 percent of mathematics and science teachers claiming they use a single text (Weiss, 1987). Textbooks tend to define limits to the content of the curriculum, and content not found in texts is rarely reported taught (McKnight, Crosswhite, Dossey, Kifer, Swafford, Travers, & Cooney, 1987; Brown, 1973).

Other researchers have focused on text content as representative of the knowledge students might be expected to encounter in schools, and the findings generally indicate a focus on low-level comprehension. In mathematics, Nicely (1985, 1986) found that a majority of problems on complex numbers and decimals in texts were of the lowest cognitive levels. In an analysis of a 30-year sample of elementary mathematics texts, Nibbelink, Stockdale, Hoover, and Mangru (1987) express concern that recent textbooks attempt to dictate rigid algorithms for problem solving.

A few researchers have dealt with the challenge posed to students using textbooks, the most comprehensive being Chall and Conard's (1991) summary of over three decades of study into reading, science, and social studies texts. They conclude that more challenging books lead to more student development, that challenge varies by grade level, and that challenge has been decreasing over the years. Generally, the challenge in mathematics texts is scattered and shallow. Kuhs, Schmidt, Porter, Floden, Freeman, and Schwille (1979) found that of all the topics found in at least one of four fourth-grade mathematics textbooks, only 28 percent were in all four books. In a related study, Porter, Floden, Freeman, Schmidt, and Schwille (1986) found that over 70 percent of topics covered in classrooms received less than half an hour of instruction in a year. Many of these topics received less than ten minutes of coverage per year, and textbook coverage was similar to that observed in the classrooms. In their study, Graybeal and Stodolsky (1986) analyzed fifth-grade mathematics teacher-guides and documented over 500 suggested activities for a two-week period.

While topics in a single year are many and scattered, topics across the K–8 mathematics textbook curriculum are repeated over and over, presenting mathematics as a tedious repetition of arithmetic skills (Flanders, 1987). This methodical trivialization of mathematics in K–8 texts is followed by a tremendous increase in new material in ninth-grade algebra texts, leading to the hypothesis that student difficulties in algebra are less a function of the subject matter and more a function of the inconsistent challenge represented by the textbook curriculum.

The scattered coverage of many topics in a given year combined with repetition of a similar scattering year after year almost seems designed to keep a student from becoming self-motivating. Instead, the textbook curriculum seems to encourage either student anxiety (because they didn't get the skills the first time and don't see them again for a year) or student boredom (because they got the skills the first time and have nothing new to challenge them). Teachers could intervene to mediate the inconsistent challenges in texts, but there is evidence that teachers, especially beginning ones, do not do well defining curriculum independently of textbooks (Ball & Feiman-Nemser, 1988).

There is even evidence that texts help teachers to make the situation worse. In studying teachers' management of review in instruction, Good, Grouws, and Ebmeier (1983) found that textbooks that continually reteach topics tend to encourage teachers to slow their pace and procrastinate about covering new material, further decreasing the challenge presented to students. Kuhs et al. (1979) document the lack of consistency of topic sequencing in fourth-grade mathematics texts. Phillips and Kane (1972) found that textbook ordering of topics was no better a predictor of student success than random ordering. Independent studies have shown that geometry and algebra teachers depend heavily on texts for content and sequence of presentation (Brown, 1973; Klingler, 1988). Perkins (1983) found that the items in the last quarter of elementary mathematics books were not covered in class. Rowley (1988) found that 57 percent of teachers in his study reported that they decided what to teach based on what was next in the text as compared to 43 percent basing decisions on student needs.

Garnier (1988) defined curriculum according to text content and used the SIMS data to compare eighth-grade classes over a wide range of attitudinal and achievement data. Editions of the four texts she identified are among those in the current study,[1] and she presents a breakdown of problems in the texts by SIMS problem type. Her results establish arithmetic to be the topic receiving the most emphasis in the three eighth-grade books belonging to K–8 text series. Garnier also supported the other findings about inconsistent sequencing. While arithmetic and algebra precede chapters on measurement, geometry, or probability in all four books, the sequencing within these two major groupings differed between books.

---

[1] Garnier studied *Mathematics Around Us* (Bolster, Cox, Gibb, Hansen, Kirkpatrick, McNerney, Robitaille, Trimble, Vance, Walch, & Wisner, 1974), *Holt School Mathematics* (Nichols, Anderson, Dwight, Flournoy, Kalin, Schluep, & Simon, 1974), *Modern School Mathematics: Structure and Method* (Dolciani, Wooten, Beckenbach, & Markert, 1970), and *Heath Mathematics* (Rucker & Dilley, 1979). Unfortunately, the first two texts are not the editions used by the SIMS classes, and some classes Garnier (1988) thought used *Modern School Mathematics* used a different edition. However, her analysis of text content is independent of class use and is useful.

THE STUDY

Identification of Textbook Use by SIMS Classes

This current study began with 215 copies of teacher responses to the SIMS teacher questionnaire. The teachers report the use of 40 different texts including some distinct editions of texts with the same name.[2] The 215 responses were pushed through three filters. The first filter separated responses by completeness. Only those classes for which the precise text and edition information were given or can be deduced are included in this study. A second filter identified only those editions of textbooks used by enough classes to warrant looking at some descriptive statistics. Seven groups of classes were so identified, each using one of seven different texts. This study is concerned only with *typical* Grade 8 mathematics and the final filter eliminated the one of this group of classes which used an algebra text.

There are 84 classes using six different textbooks examined in this study; their texts and frequencies are summarized in Table 2.1. The two editions of *Modern School Mathematics: Structure and Method* are significantly different in coverage and placement of items and item types and had enough users to consider as two separate texts. *Holt Mathematics*, on the other hand, had two significantly different editions represented, but only five classes used one of them, and the less-used edition is not studied.

Compared to the national sample of eighth-grade classes, this sample of 84 classes is over-representative of private schools and under-representative of East-central urban areas. Ninety-three percent of the study teachers report frequent use of the text, about the same proportion found for the nation as a whole.

SIMS Test Item Coding

A copy of each of the six eighth-grade textbooks was examined for the appearance of each item on the SIMS test. If the item did appear, it was categorized as either *new material* (if it did not appear in the same publisher's seventh grade text), or *old material* (if it did appear there). A few SIMS items appear in the textbooks exactly as written on the test, but it became clear from a pilot coding of one of the texts that slight differences in problems should not lead to categorizing an item as not in the text. All items were coded as *in* or

---

[2] This information proved difficult to obtain and is available from the author.

TABLE 2.1
The Six Most Commonly Used Textbooks in Eighth-Grade SIMS Classes

Title	Publisher	Ed.	Count
Mathematics Around Us	Scott, Foresman	1978	36
Holt School Mathematics	Holt, Rinehart, and Winston	1974	13
Heath Mathematics	D.C. Heath	1979	9
Houghton-Mifflin Mathematics	Houghton-Mifflin	1978	7
Modern School Mathematics: Structure and Method (1st edition)	Houghton-Mifflin	1975	10
Modern School Mathematics: Structure and Method (2nd edition)	Houghton-Mifflin	1982	9
Total			84

not in each text. Items coded as in a text were then coded as new or old according to the following guidelines:

- In if it appears: in the text exactly; with slightly different instructions to the student; with a different operation, type of number, or a specific expression varies slightly; as an application of the same mathematics, but the context differs; or the item is less difficult than a similar one in the text.
- New (n) if it is in the eighth-grade text and is not in the seventh grade text of the same series.
- Old (o) if it is in the eighth-grade text and is also in the seventh-grade text.
- Not in (x) if it is not in the eighth-grade text.

If an item teetered on the edge of being coded in or out, it was coded in, the intent being to remain conservative in favor of text coverage in a manner consistent with previous text evaluation studies (Flanders, 1987). A page number was recorded for each item coded as being in a text. If an item appeared more than once, the page of the first appearance was noted.

Teacher Expectation and Opportunity to Learn Responses

For each item on the core and rotated forms of the SIMS test, the Population A teachers responded to the following questions on the SIMS opportunity to learn questionnaire.

1. What percentage of the students from the target class do
    you estimate will get the item correct without guessing?
    1) Virtually none
    2) 6–40%
    3) 41–60%
    4) 61–94%
    5) Virtually all
2. During this school year, did you teach or review the mathe-
    matics needed to answer the item correctly?
    1) No
    2) Yes

Responses to the teacher expectation question (Question 1) are
referred here to as *EXP* responses. Responses to the second question
are referred to as *OTL* responses. Responses to both questions are
available from all but one of the 84 teachers of the most used
textbooks.

For each textbook, an EXP mean for each item was calculated by
averaging responses of the teachers using the book, giving a real
number from one through five, inclusively. Similarly, a textbook
OTL mean for each item was calculated, yielding a real number from
one through two. Grand EXP means and OTL means across texts
were obtained by averaging in 83 responses for each item, respectively.

RESULTS

Textbook Coverage of SIMS Test Items

To obtain an overview of the textbook coverage of the SIMS test,
each test item was inspected for coverage in a majority of texts
(modal coverage). The results are summarized in Table 2.2.[3] As
described above, the categories *new*, *old*, and *x* represent items that
were coded as new, old, and not in a majority of texts. The category
no refers to items coded as new in three texts and old in the other
three. The category *nox* refers to items new in two texts, old in
another two, and not in the remaining two. The *mix* category includes items that were in three of the texts and not in the other
three. The numbers in parentheses in the *Total* row of Table 2.2 are
percents of the 180 items.

---

[3] For analyses of coverage by individual textbook, see Flanders (1992).

TABLE 2.2
Coverage of SIMS Items by Content Domain

Type	N	new	old	no	nox	x	mix
Arith	62 (34)	2 (3)	30 (48)	0 (0)	0 (0)	24 (39)	6 (10)
Alg	32 (18)	5 (16)	3 (9)	0 (0)	1 (3)	20 (63)	3 (9)
Geo	42 (23)	4 (10)	2 (5)	1 (2)	0 (0)	34 (81)	1 (2)
Stat	18 (10)	1 (6)	8 (44)	0 (0)	0 (0)	7 (39)	2 (11)
Meas	26 (14)	0 (0)	4 (15)	0 (0)	1 (4)	20 (77)	1 (4)
Total	180 (100)	12 (7)	47 (26)	1 (1)	2 (1)	105 (58)	13 (7)

Key: *new* = new in at least four texts
    old = old in at least four texts
    no = new in three, old in three texts
    nox = new in two, old in two, and not in two texts
    x = not in at least four texts
    mix = in three texts, not in three texts.
Note: cell entries are count (percent of type).

The most striking observation from Table 2.2 is that over half the SIMS items are not covered in the majority of these textbooks. As expected, most of the items covered are review of content appearing in the corresponding seventh-grade texts. The number of items in the irksome *mix* category is quite small, only 7 percent of all SIMS items, indicating a strong agreement in text content.

Table 2.2 also gives the counts of items cross-classified by text coverage and the five content domains identified in the SIMS design: arithmetic, algebra, geometry, statistics, and measurement. Cells in the body of Table 2.2 include a count and, in parentheses, a percent of item type. For example, 2 of 62 (3%) of SIMS arithmetic items are new in a majority of texts. Note that statistics items are covered almost as much as arithmetic items. This is interesting because middle school mathematics is considered to be primarily a review of arithmetic. Further, the statistics content is not significantly more new to the text than is the arithmetic content.

To the degree that eighth-grade mathematics is typically pre-algebra, by chronology if not by name, the relatively higher coverage of algebra items than geometry items is predictable. The common wisdom that geometry and measurement topics are almost exclusively saved for the year after an algebra course is also supported by this data. Geometry and measurement items are the least covered content domains. Well over half of SIMS algebra (63%), geometry (81%), and measurement (77%) items are not covered in the majority of these textbooks. All measurement items covered are review in a majority of texts, indicating the low priority given to this topic. The majority of the algebra and geometry items covered by eighth grade texts are new.

Placement of Items in a Majority of Texts.   To determine an overall picture of where items are located in textbooks, all pages were counted in each text from the opening of the first chapter through the last chapter test. (Supplementary exercises at the end of texts, glossaries, appendices, answer pages, and indices were not included in this count.) These counts were averaged to find that a typical text for these SIMS classes is 394 pages long. Then, for each item in a majority of texts, an average page position was calculated by standardizing the position of the item in each text as a percent of the way through the text, and averaging the results.

An overview of page position of items throughout an average text is given in Table 2.3. Seventy-seven percent of items are found in the first 60 percent of the average text, and the mean page position is close to 50 percent, primarily because of the large number of items in the 50–60 percent range. The placements of new and old items within an average text are significantly better. New items are centered around 62 percent of the way through the text, while old items are centered at the 44 percent mark.

TABLE 2.3
Average Placement of SIMS Items
in a Majority of Texts

Decile	Coverage				Total
	n	*o*	*no*	*nox*	
1	0	1	0	0	1
2	1	6	0	0	7
3	0	4	0	0	4
4	1	7	0	0	8
5	1	7	1	0	9
6	3	14	0	2	19
7	1	3	0	0	4
8	1	4	0	0	5
9	4	1	0	0	5
10	0	0	0	0	0
Total	12	47	1	2	62

Key: *n*   = new in at least four texts
 o   = old in at least four texts
 no = new in three, old in three texts
 nox = new in two, old in two, and not in two texts

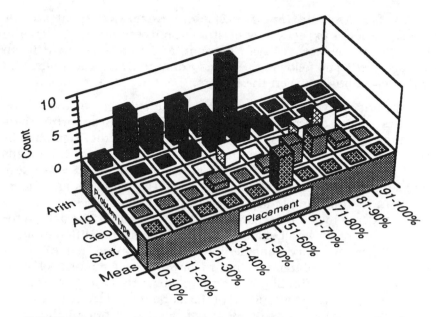

FIGURE 2.1   Average Placement in Textbooks of SIMS Items by Content Domain
Note: Placement is percent of the way through an average textbook

Placement of Items by Content Domains.   A cursory analysis of most texts shows that chapters covering geometry, probability, and statistics tend to be in the latter half of the books. Figure 2.1 shows that arithmetic items are covered in the first 60 percent of the average text, with no other SIMS problem type appearing in the first 30 percent of the books. Algebra items are covered in midtext. On average, measurement items are all in one decile, reflecting the appearance of a measurement chapter in about the same place in every text. Statistics items show a clustering similar to measurement items, indicating similar statistics chapter placements across texts. The placement of geometry is more variable.

Teacher Expectation and Opportunity to Learn Responses

Eighty-three of the 84 teachers of the six texts identified in this study responded to the questions about expectation for student success (EXP) and student opportunity to learn (OTL) SIMS items. This section presents these responses examined according to textbook coverage and item placement in texts.[4]

---

[4] For analyses of EXP and OTL by individual textbook, see Flanders (1992).

Teacher Expectations for Student Success. What are the average teacher expectations of student success on SIMS items in the light of coverage, content domain, and item placement in an average text? The following sections examine these questions, and the interactions between the factors.

Expectations and Item Coverage. The averages of teacher responses to the expectation question of the SIMS opportunity-to-learn questionnaire are summarized in Table 2.4, distinguished by coverage. Counts in Column 1 are of items with grand EXP means (M) in the range $1 \leq M < 1.5$; in Column 2 of items in $1.5 \leq M < 2.5$; and so forth. The totals of columns show that, on average, the 83 teachers in this sample are pessimistic—expecting less than half their students to get items correct without guessing. The data in the table show that, overall, expectations on items with different levels of text coverage vary considerably, whether examined from the broad perspective of items in, not in, or mixed in a majority of texts, or the detailed distinction of items in the texts being new or old. Teacher expectation for student performance on SIMS items covered in a majority of texts is greater than for items not in the texts. Understandably, expectation is also higher for old items than for new ones.

Expectations and Content Domain. Counts of grand EXP means by content domain determined in the same way as for Table 2.4 are illustrated in Figure 2.2. (The circles at the top of the plot for geometry in Figure 2.2 represent two EXP values beyond the 80 percent range shown by the connected part of the diagram.) The overall pessimistically skewed distribution of grand EXP means is

TABLE 2.4
Categorized Grand EXP Means by Coverage

Coverage	EXP					Total
	1	2	3	4	5	
new	0	6	6	0	0	12
old	0	3	24	19	1	47
no	0	0	0	1	0	1
nox	0	0	2	0	0	2
x	5	55	41	4	0	105
mix	0	5	8	0	0	13
Total	5	69	81	24	1	180

Note: EXP categories range from 1 = virtually none, to 5 = virtually all, students will succeed.

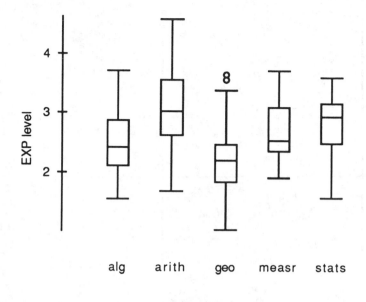

Content Domain

FIGURE 2.2   Boxplots of Grand EXP Means by Content Domain

apparent for algebra, geometry, and measurement items. It is particularly evident for the algebra and geometry items each of which has median expectation level of two, at which only 6–40 percent of students are expected to succeed. The algebra and geometry expectations are consistent with the common notion that algebra and geometry are not appropriate topics for study until arithmetic has been mastered to some arbitrary (and perhaps excessively high) degree.

Expectations and Item Placement.   Figure 2.3 shows teacher expectations for student success on items covered in the majority of texts according to average item placement standardized to a percent of the way through a text. The most striking pattern in the figure is the general downward trend of the data points, showing that teacher expectation for success is significantly higher for items found in the front half of an average text than for items in the back half. Note that three of 12 new items (marked with an *x*) are found in the last half of an average text, and five of those are over three-quarters of the way through the book. Teacher expectation on half the 12 new items is well below average. On the other hand, old item placement is about evenly split between halves of the book, with teacher expectations at or above average.

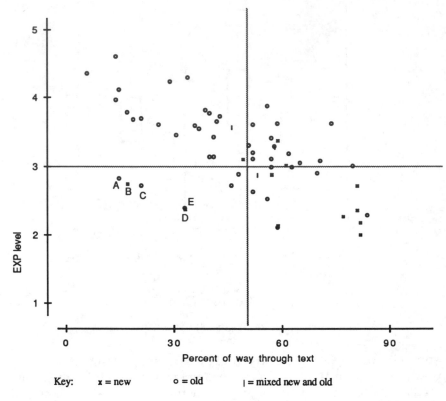

Key: x = new   o = old | = mixed new and old

FIGURE 2.3   Grand EXP Means by Average Placement by Item Coverage

Figure 2.4 highlights the same data points according to content domain. The points identified in the figure as representing old items are primarily old arithmetic items. Three of the four algebra items in the first half of an average text are old algebra problems, and of the two geometry problems in the first half of the average book, one is review in a majority of texts, the other in half the texts. With one exception, all the new items are algebra and geometry and are mostly in the back of the book. To the extent that teachers follow their text, the scene is set for students not to study new topics and/or non-arithmetic topics.

The items plotted in the third quadrant of Figures 2.3 and 2.4 are interesting in that they are separate from the main cluster of points. What are these items found early in an average text, yet for which teachers hold little expectation of student success? Referring to the labels on Figures 2.3 and 2.4, A represents an item which tests ability to rewrite an expression using the distributive property.

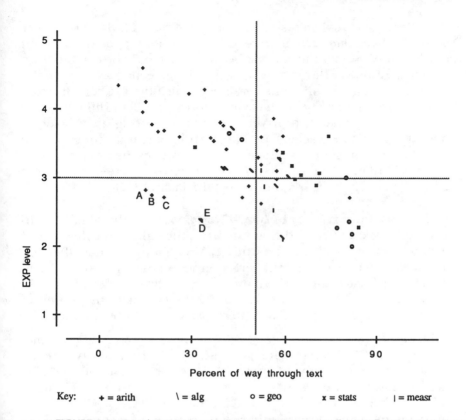

Key: + = arith   \ = alg   o = geo   x = stats | = measr

FIGURE 2.4   Grand EXP Means by Average Placement by Content Domain

Points B and D are new items, both testing use of exponents. B asks for n in $10^2 \times 10^3 = 10^n$ (and is classified, curiously, as an arithmetic item) and D asks for scientific notation for 0.00046 (and is called an algebra item). Point C represents an item which asks for a rewrite of 3.23×10^5 in decimal form. Point E represents an estimation application using decimals.

It is not difficult to guess why teachers rank these five items with below-average EXP levels even though they appear in the first third of texts. The two new items may be ranked low because they are new material, and in none of the texts are the necessary skills for success on the items used beyond the one-day lesson in which they are presented. The same reasoning applies to the second scientific notation problem, which is old to the texts because positive powers of ten are introduced in the seventh-grade book, but is seen only once there, and once again in the eighth-grade book.

The decimal problem reads: *The speed of sound is 340 meters per second. How long will it take before the sound of a car horn reaches your ears if the car is 714 meters away?* The combination of metric units, a rate, and reading may be perceived as making the problem difficult for students not likely to be fluent in solving problems involving only one of these attributes. (Student difficulty may also have more to do with fewer teachers presenting the problem— only two-thirds of teachers provided an opportunity to learn this item.) Interestingly, the average pretest score on the item is a comparatively high 43 percent. Unfortunately, the posttest average is only 47 percent, perhaps indicating the lack of OTL.

Teacher Opportunity to Learn Reports.   On the whole, teachers of the six books in this study are much more positive about giving students a chance to study SIMS-type items than they are about expectations of student performance on the SIMS items themselves. They also claim to teach an average of two-thirds of the SIMS items not in the text. We now examine the OTL data in relation to coverage, content domain, and item placement in texts overall.

Opportunity to Learn and Item Coverage.   Table 2.5 summarizes grand OTL means for items in and not in the majority of texts. As with the presentation of grand EXP means, the data in the table are categorized into discrete responses. In this case an OTL mean (M) is coded as *no* if $1 \leq M < 1.5$, and *yes* if $1.5 \leq M \leq 2$. The overwhelming message from these data is that, on average, teachers of the six texts claim to provide an opportunity to learn 142 of 180 SIMS items (79%). Mean OTL is 1.7 so, basically, these teachers claim to teach most of the items. Patterns of OTL for different types of text coverage are different from both coverage perspectives: for

TABLE 2.5
Categorized Grand OTL Means by Coverage

	OTL		
Coverage	no	yes	Total
new	1	11	12
old	2	45	47
no	0	1	1
nox	0	2	2
x	34	71	105
mixed	1	12	13
Total	38	142	180

broad "in, not in, or mixed" coverage, and for detailed "new, old, or mixed" coverage. Even though most items are taught, the opportunity to learn items in texts is still greater than the opportunity to learn items not in the text. Also, OTL for new items is less than that for old items, though more new items are reported taught than not taught.

Opportunity to Learn and Content Domain.   Distinguished by content domain, average OTL responses are illustrated in Figure 2.5. OTL responses differ significantly by content domain, and for all but one domain, significantly more items are taught than not. The exception is geometry, where 20 of 42 items are reported by a majority of teachers as not being covered in class.

Opportunity to Learn and Item Placement.   Page placements of SIMS items as a percent of the way through an average text are plotted against grand OTL means in Figures 2.6 and 2.7, with the former highlighting distinctions between new and old items, and the latter demonstrating content domain. Points representing all but four items are plotted in the top half of the graph, dramatically indicating the fact that teachers report teaching virtually all the items found in the majority of texts. There is a downward-sloping

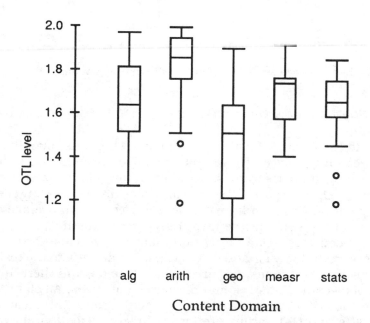

FIGURE 2.5   Boxplots of Grand OTL Means by Content Domain

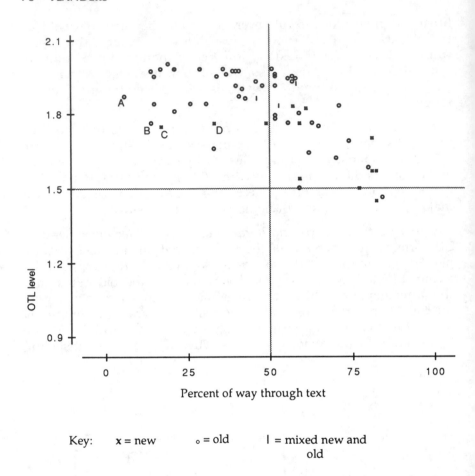

Key: x = new   o = old | = mixed new and
                                            old

FIGURE 2.6 Grand OTL Means Versus Average Placement by Item Coverage

trend to the cluster of placement versus OTL points much like the one seen for the placement versus grand EXP mean data, a decrease that further supports the observation that items found later in a text are less likely to be part of the implemented curriculum. Any effect of placement on OTL is minimal, however, because an average of 95 percent of the items in the text are reported taught.

New items receive later attention than review items. Of the eight items with the lowest grand OTL means, five are new to the texts. Of those same eight items, five are geometry items, and there are one each of algebra, statistics, and measurement items. All eight items are in the last 41 percent of pages. As with grand EXP means, the highest grand OTL means are for arithmetic items found early in most of the texts. It should be noted that the two items which test

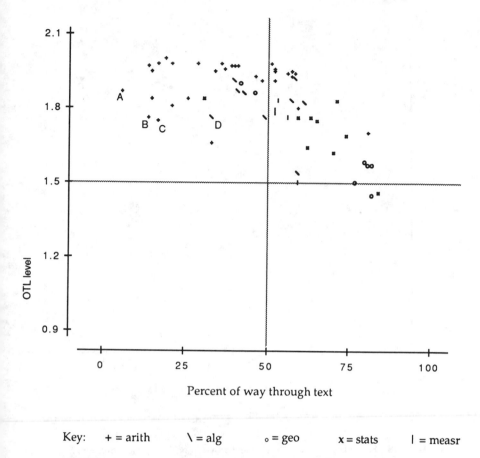

Key: + = arith   \ = alg   o = geo   x = stats   I = measr

FIGURE 2.7   Grand OTL Means Versus Average Placement by Content Domain

simple multiplication (Point *A* on Figures 2.6 and 2.7) and subtraction (Point *B*) of whole numbers do not have the highest grand OTL means, suggesting that teachers do have some sensitivity to the issue of reteaching. Still, the items are taught by about 80 percent of the 83 teachers. The two new items in the first third of the books are two items mentioned in a previous section, one being an arithmetic item asking for the exponent of a product of powers of ten (Point *C*), and the other an algebra item asking for a scientific notation form of 0.00046 (Point *D*).

Expectations and Opportunity to Learn Compared.   Figures 2.8 through 2.11 illustrate a comparison of grand OTL and grand EXP responses in light of coverage of items *in*, *not in*, or *mixed* in a

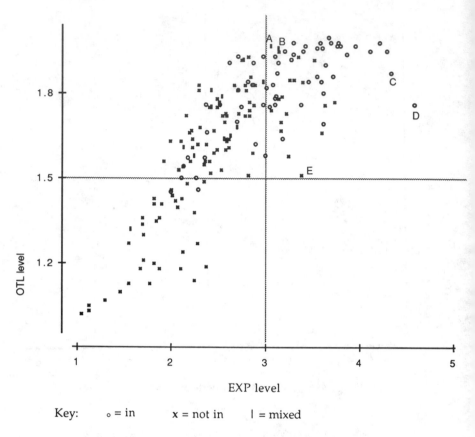

Key: o = in   x = not in | = mixed

FIGURE 2.8   Scatterplot of Grand OTL Means by Grand EXP Means by Modal Coverage

majority of the six texts, and by content domain. In Figures 2.10 and 2.11 coverage and problem type are shown simultaneously to (hopefully) generate a better view of the four-dimensional nature of the relationships.

Figure 2.8 shows grand OTL means plotted against grand EXP means with coverage highlighted. Points marked with an o represent items found in a majority of the texts, those marked x are not found in most texts, and those marked | are in three texts and not in the other three. Figure 2.9 is a graph of the same points with content domain highlighted. Points marked with a + are arithmetic items, \ are algebra, o are geometry, x are statistics, and | are measurement items. The same two keys are used for Figures 2.10 and 2.11, respectively, in which the same set of points is broken into subsets.

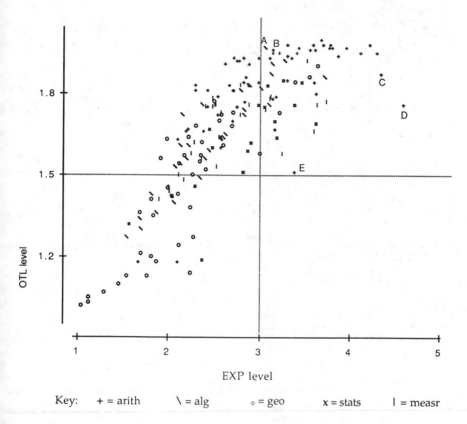

FIGURE 2.9 Scatterplot of Grand OTL Means by Grand EXP Means by Content Domain

Points in Quadrant *1* of the graphs represent SIMS items which shared high hopes of student success and high reports of teaching. Most of the items graphed highest in Quadrant 1 are problems found in the texts, and Figure 2.9 confirms the fact that they are arithmetic items (symbol +). Figure 2.10a isolates problems according to whether or not they are in a majority of texts, and shows how arithmetic items in Quadrant *1* make up a large part of the items in the texts. Further, Figure 2.10d identifies them as old arithmetic items. With only one exception, they are also items testing old arithmetic skills, as opposed to applications, estimation problems, or other types requiring more depth of analysis than pure calculation. The problems furthest to the right at the top of Quadrant 1, showing greater expectation for success, are multiplication, addition, and subtraction problems using decimals and fractions. Those near the

(a). Items in or mixed in most texts. (N = 75).

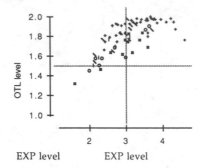

(d). Items not in most texts (N = 105).

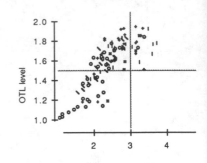

(c). Items new or mixed new in most texts (N = 15).

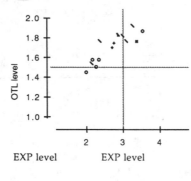

(d). Items old in most texts (N = 47).

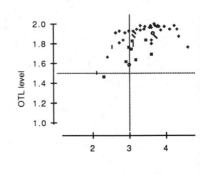

Key: + = arith   \ = alg   o = geo   x = stats | = measr

FIGURE 2.10   Grand OTL Mean by Grand EXP Mean by Coverage and Content Domain

vertical line at EXP Level 3 involve percents, mixed numbers, and ratios.

The two items with mixed status in Quadrant 1 of Figure 2.8 are applications. The one marked A has the distinction of being the highest ranked algebra item on the EXP and OTL scales (an application of integer subtraction). The other is an application of ratios (Point B). Two other points of interest in Quadrant 1 are marked C and D, the former asking for 162 × 47, the latter for 1054 − 865. They represent evidence that not all teachers reteach every type of arithmetic problem at the eighth-grade level. At least these two items are distinguished as the ones most likely for students to answer correctly. Point E in Quadrant 1 represents the least taught item with the greatest expectation for student success: it asks stu-

(a). Arithmetic item coverage (N = 62).

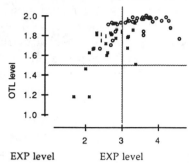

(b). Algebra item coverage (N = 32).

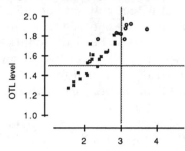

(c). Geometry item coverage (N = 42).

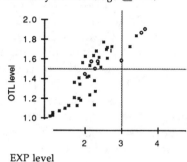

(d). Statistics item coverage (N = 18).

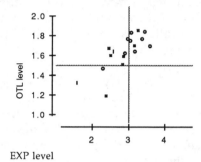

(e). Measurement item coverage (N = 26).

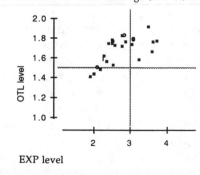

Key:

o   = in

x   = not in

| = mixed

FIGURE 2.11   Grand OTL Mean by Grand EXP Mean by Content Domain and Coverage

dents to add 3 weeks and 5 days to 9 weeks and 6 days. It is valuable to ponder why this type of problem is not worth teaching to eighth-grade students, nor including in their texts, but 1054 − 865 is.

Three items high in Quadrant 1 are not found in a majority of these texts, though there is no reason why they could not fit into the scope of the books as written. One asks for the product of 2^3 and 3^2, another for a fractional representation of a digit in a decimal, and the third an estimate of the area of a rectangle given two sides. All might be considered to be multistep problems, which are notably absent from the texts identified in this study. In several of those texts, in fact, one or two lessons are entitled "two-step problems" or the equivalent, giving a distinct impression to the reader that such problems are an exception to the rule and much more difficult than other problems.

Quadrant 3 represents items at the other extreme of teacher attention—ones that students are not expected to solve successfully and are not taught. The high degree to which teachers report teaching items covered in texts is starkly evident in the fact that only two such items have grand OTL means qualifying them as not taught. One of these two is an item on probability, the other an application of similar triangles. Twenty of the 36 items in Quadrant 3 are about geometry, and none of those are found in a majority of texts. This amounts to almost half of the 42 geometry items found on the SIMS tests. Geometry item distribution is isolated in Figure 2.11c. Of the two old geometry items found in texts, one asks students to identify which angle is acute, the other asks for the third angle given two angles in a triangle. The other two geometry items in Quadrant 1 ask for identification of a parallelogram and of a figure congruent to a given figure. The highest expectation and most OTL is for the lowest level skills.

The majority of the bottom 13 geometry items on the OTL scale are projective geometry and transformation geometry items of a kind seldom found in U.S. eighth-grade textbook curricula of the early 1980s. Two of those 13 are nontraditional problems, one asking whether a pattern can be folded into a cube, and the other asking for identification of an elevation of a cube with a corner cut off. The two arithmetic items found in Quadrant 3 are also nontraditional. One asks for the number of matchsticks that would occur in a given iteration of a pattern. The other asks for the sum of an unseen row of a triangular pattern of numbers. These kinds of nontraditional problems might appear in puzzle sections of texts or as suggestions in teachers notes, but are virtually never part of the tested curriculum.

Measurement and statistics items are generally reported as taught (see Figures 2.11d and 2.11e). The two statistics items lowest in Quadrant 3 include one which asks for a decision about the best way to pick a sample of a population (Item 65), and is not in a majority of texts even though at least half a chapter is devoted to statistics in every text. The other item is arguably one of the most difficult on the SIMS test, having an international achievement score of 20 percent, the score expected from guessing. It is a word problem describing a proportion and asking for the measure of the central angle of a sector of a pie chart that would represent that proportion. Interestingly, a version of this item is found in three of the texts.

Algebra items are sprinkled throughout the distribution of EXP by OTL points (see Figure 2.11b) with applications of two-variable algebra and representations of functions represented in Quadrant 3, none of which are found in a majority of texts. Most of the algebra items in Quadrant 1 test skills using integers, while one requires substituting a number into an equation, and one requires identifying a missing coordinate in a table of values given an equation.

SUMMARY

The six texts most used by SIMS Population A classes were analyzed for item coverage and item placement. *Well over half the SIMS items are not covered in a majority of these texts, and over a quarter of them were not covered in any text.* Greater percentages of arithmetic and statistics items are covered in most texts than algebra, geometry, or measurement items. Most of the algebra and geometry items in texts are new, while most of the other problem types are review of items covered in seventh-grade texts. On average, items are normally distributed throughout the texts, with reviewed items appearing more in the first half of the books. Arithmetic items are found in the first half of an average text. Algebra and geometry items are normally distributed, though the mean geometry placement is almost two-thirds of the way through an average text. Statistics and measurement items are found in the second half of an average book.

On average, the teachers of these texts are generally pessimistic regarding student success on items not in or new to the text, and on algebra or geometry items. They are generally optimistic about student performance on items reviewed in the text and on arithmetic items. Overall, they expect better than average results on items found in the front half of a text, and average results on items in the back half. In general, teacher reports about which items they teach are positive for all coverage levels, item types, and item placement in the text. Teacher confidence and motivation as judged by correlations between expected student success and decisions to teach are generally high.

DISCUSSION

The SIMS Test and the U.S. Eighth-Grade Curriculum

How representative is the SIMS test of the curriculum represented by the six textbooks in the current study? Consider the following results:

Result 1:   Over 50 percent of the SIMS items are not found in a majority of the six textbooks most used by SIMS classes, and roughly 25 percent of SIMS items are found in none of the six books.

Result 2:   Only 61 percent of the items in a majority of the six texts in this study are common to all six (i.e., 38 of 62 items). Thus, only 21 percent of all SIMS items are in all six books.

Result 3:   Greater percentages of SIMS arithmetic and statistics items than algebra, geometry, and measurement items are found in the texts.

Taken as a whole, the texts most commonly used in SIMS classes indicate that the SIMS test is not representative of U.S. eighth-grade mathematics. Yet it is difficult to imagine exactly how the SIMS test might be methodically improved with respect to the U.S. curriculum. Part of the difficulty for U.S. participation in the design of the test was the lack of a clear national mathematics curriculum (Crosswhite, Dossey, Swafford, McKnight, Cooney, Downs, Grouws, & Weinzweig, 1986). The low coverage of SIMS items reported here might seem to support this lack, but the fact that only 7 percent of the SIMS items are *mixed* (that is, they are not clearly in or out of a majority of the texts) indicates high agreement across texts on which mathematics to put in or leave out.

Result 3 points to textbook agreement on the mathematics topics felt to be important to eighth-grade students. Arithmetic is important to textbook authors—84 percent of the arithmetic items are in at least one text. Geometry and measurement are not so important—48 percent of geometry items and 46 percent of measurement items are in none of the texts. Eighty-one percent of geometry items are not covered in a majority of texts, nor are 77 percent of measurement items.

What message to test creators might be taken from the texts in this study? If we take the 62 items found in a majority of the six texts as typical of eighth-grade priorities in mathematics in typical classes, the relative weights given the five problem types are as shown in Table 2.6 (calculated from the data in Table 2.2). Also included in Table 2.6 are the relative weights of the content domains on the SIMS test. Comparing the 62-item U.S. typical curriculum and SIMS "curriculum" leads to the conclusion that a test reflective of the mathematics in U.S. texts should have about half again as many arithmetic and statistics items, about half as many geometry and measurement items, and about the same number of algebra items. It seems obvious that such emphases would not be appropriate for a program which prepares students for algebra and geometry, nor one that challenges them with new material. That is, *the mismatch of the SIMS test and U.S. texts may reflect a weakness of the U.S. curriculum or the texts rather than a problem with the test.*

The common coverage found in texts indicates a virtual obsession for holding students accountable to an arbitrarily high degree of mastery on a few algorithmic arithmetic procedures to be done with paper and pencil. This conclusion is supported by the following two results.

Result 4:   The ratio of new items to old items in the texts is 1 to 4 for items in a majority of the texts, and 1 to 6 for items common to all six texts.

Result 5:   Most new items are in the second half of texts, and are algebra or geometry items. Old items are predominantly in the first half of texts. On average, only arithmetic items, predominantly review, are in the first 30 percent of these books.

In Dewey's (1916) words, these textbooks are guardians of the past rather than windows to the future. The algebra and geometry items, which were probably newest to the students, were covered least and latest in their textbooks. The SIMS items students encoun-

TABLE 2.6
Content Domain Emphasis—62 Items In a Majority
of Texts Compared to the SIMS Test

Type	62 items %	SIMS %
Arith	52	34
Alg	15	18
Geo	11	23
Stat	15	10
Meas	8	14

tered most often in their texts were arithmetic and statistics problems they may very well have seen in their seventh-grade books. It should also be noted that the order of topics in seventh grade texts is almost identical to the order in the eighth-grade books, so if a problem late in a text was not covered, it was probably even more likely that it was not covered in seventh grade either. Statistics items are late in all the texts except one, so student encounters with statistics items are especially questionable—at least if topics are studied in the order the books are written.

It is frustrating that measurement items are so poorly covered in texts given the easy connection of arithmetic to measurement applications. Lack of connection between any topics in these texts seems to be more by rule than by oversight, but oversight does account for some coverage errors. In most of the texts, for example, an understanding of the concept of average is assumed in problems throughout the textbooks, but lessons introducing average as if students had never seen it before appear in statistics chapters toward the ends of the books. Similarly, problems assuming an ability to understand distance measures are used as applications in arithmetic chapters, but lessons on distance do not appear until measurement or geometry chapters found later in texts.

While the results of the current study suggest less coverage of arithmetic, more geometry and measurement, and earlier treatment of statistics, they do not necessarily suggest development of a more common textbook curriculum toward those ends. Judging by the 118 SIMS items not found in at least four of these texts, there is a shared avoidance of a great deal of mathematics which is deemed appropriate for eighth-grade students by the SIMS test designers. An appropriate recommendation to authors and publishers is that textbooks be developed that at least allow teachers and students access to the wide range of topics of the SIMS test. It would be nice to choose from among texts with different emphases in content, rather than five or six texts covering similar ranges of topics at similar shallow levels of coverage, differing primarily in topic sequencing. This approach has precedent in the materials developed by the *Middle Grades Mathematics Project*, in which modular books each cover a different topic (see, for example, Lappan, Fitzgerald, Winter, & Phillips, 1986).

Teaching and Textbooks

One of the most instructive aspects of this study is its look at the teacher–textbook relationship as compared to classroom observations or teacher surveys. Observations of the text in use help researchers get at the nuances of text coverage, evaluate teacher understanding of material, and a host of other variables. Surveys of teacher use of texts, such as those conducted by market researchers for publishing companies, get at general patterns of teacher expectations and attitudes about textbooks. The current study examines the text in use via the indirect connection of teacher responses to whether they taught SIMS items, how well they expected their students to perform on the items, and textbook coverage of the items, and so sheds a different kind of light on whether teachers depend on their books, or not. Consider the following results.

Result 6:   Teachers of the six texts in the current study report a high incidence of teaching virtually all of the SIMS items, with slightly less emphasis on geometry items than items of other problem types.

Result 7:   Teachers of the six texts in the current study have high expectations for student success on old arithmetic items in texts, and lower expectations for items not in texts, and for algebra and geometry items found in the texts.

Result 8:   Teachers report less teaching of, and less expectation of student success on, items later in the textbooks.

Teachers expect student to succeed on SIMS items found in the text, not to succeed on items missing from texts, and claim that items not in the text are taught anyway. Only 51 percent of the teachers in this study report using materials other than the text, so many of these teachers seem to be sources of the nontext mathematics, but not confident ones. In other words, even though teacher motivation to teach items is strong, teacher confidence is very much tied to the book.

Perhaps the most interesting perspective into the teacher–textbook relationship is represented in Figures 2.3 and 2.4, which show the drop in teacher expectations for student success relative to item position in texts, and Figures 2.6 and 2.7, which show similar, but less dramatic, drops for OTL by placement. Lower EXP and OTL coincides with geometry, measurement, statistics, and new items in general in texts, as opposed to arithmetic or review items. Algebra coverage is the most balanced in distribution throughout texts. These distributions may explain the slightly higher teacher motivation to teach algebra over geometry and measurement that was found in the current study.

What implications do these results have for teachers? It is sad that overall expectation for student success by teachers is low for the presumably more challenging material, but perhaps this result is simply an indicator of the mismatch of the SIMS test items and the eighth-grade textbook curriculum. For the texts in this study, coverage of new material, especially geometry and measurement, is often disjointed and in arbitrary sequence (mathematics found later in a text often did not depend on mathematics earlier in the book). So teachers could be encouraged to use such texts selectively, using arithmetic chapters only when necessary for review.

Instead of challenging students with new mathematics, however, teachers seem to substitute the challenge of achieving 90 percent mastery on meaningless drills. (A definition of mastery is probably attributable to Wilson (1926), who claimed that 100 percent accuracy is the only acceptable objective in mathematics.) Requiring all students to be able to perform any arithmetic algorithm with any numbers imaginable before letting them encounter algebra or geometry is like requiring all students to learn all nursery rhymes by heart before being allowed to read a story, or master every conceivable musical scale on an instrument before playing a tune.

What are implications of the results of this study for authors and publishers? One approach to balancing content and increasing challenge is to integrate topics throughout a text and limit the practice of giving students many similar exercises in many scattered topic areas. This practice is encouraged in the National Council of Teachers of Mathematics (NCTM) *Curriculum and Evaluation Standards* (1989), and is beginning to be evident in some of the newest editions of middle school texts. In *Transition Mathematics*, Usiskin, Flanders, Hynes, Polonsky, Porter, and Viktora (1992) have tackled the problem of helping seventh- and eighth-grade students begin secondary mathematics rather than merely review K–6 mathematics, and have done it in a highly integrated manner. The fact that the text is probably the current best selling text at this level is a strong sign to publishers and authors about what teachers want.

Further Research

The focus of the current study has been on the curriculum *available* to eighth-grade students so a next step is to investigate whether the curriculum was understood by students. How did student achievement vary with respect to SIMS items in or not in the textbooks? With respect to new or old items in the texts? With respect to teacher EXP and OTL for items in, out, new, or old? Garnier (1988) reports that textbook differences do not explain variance in achievement so answers to these questions might be expected to yield little new information about student performance.

But with or without analysis of student achievement data, there are interesting directions for further research using the data from SIMS. Coverage and teacher EXP and OTL data can be analyzed with respect to comprehension levels of SIMS items. It would be enlightening to discuss text coverage of specific items, or groups of items, in greater depth. The treatments of the order of operations, for example, were greatly different in these texts, with most books avoiding combination of operations as if it were anathema. In light of the treatments, did student achievement, teacher coverage, or expectations, vary by text on the SIMS item that asks students to evaluate $(22 \times 18) - (47 + 59)$?

RESOLUTION

Publishers cannot be content to claim that teacher opinions or recommendations of text evaluation committees serve as research. What motivates teachers or politicians is not necessarily what helps students achieve. Authors must write responsibly for teachers who sequence instruction according to mathematics, and should integrate the mathematics in texts to avoid giving preferential treatment to arithmetic, or review exercises in general. Authors should show more systematic thinking in the presentation of mathematics in context, rather than as a set of rules. Publishers and authors should consider their seventh-grade texts as unsuccessful if their eighth-grade books contain virtually the same mathematics scope and sequence.

Getting active scholars to write textbooks is a problem because of the restrictions publishers put upon them to obey teacher opinion research. Research needs to be conducted to determine if teacher opinions regarding textbooks translate into better student understanding of mathematics. A "mentioning" approach to textbook writing is bound to fail to help students (see Apple Christian-Smith, 1991; Tyson-Bernstein, 1988), even if it sells books, and authors and their publishers must take responsibility for this decision. This approach also masks an unwillingness of publishers to take risks— to accept the challenge of continually presenting appropriate new mathematics to book users, not just new packages of old content. It is to be hoped that the success of the *UCSMP* materials in particular will embolden other publishers to take risks. It is also to be hoped that these materials are treated as the first draft of a technologically aware 7–12 mathematics curriculum that they are. Serious re-search into their effectiveness, and into alternative approaches, needs to be encouraged.

To take risks also requires getting expert advice from researchers trained in textbook analysis and who are given time and encouragement from universities. The university community must re-evaluate what research means in order to help fill this need in the textbook publishing world. Mathematics educators must also take more notice of the importance of texts to teachers. In the Netherlands, for instance, the situation is such that the teachers who participated in SIMS underreported covering items in texts—exactly the opposite of the results of this study (Warries, 1986). There is very little evidence that proper training of teachers in the learning or instruction of mathematics is content-independent, and, like it or not, content is very much guided by textbooks.

Teachers cannot let texts lead them to assumptions of appropriate content, especially when that content is not based on research. Teachers should know that books can be different, in fact should be different, especially at the eighth-grade level, given the great expanse of untouched mathematics in front of their students. Other teachers can take heart from the higher EXP and better coverage of the SIMS items by teachers of the two editions of *Modern School Mathematics: Structure and Method*, especially given the fact that only one-third of the classes using these texts were in SIMS *enriched* classes (Flanders, 1992). If the decision to teach is a function of expectation, then teachers should use a text with more new content and embrace that content with confidence.

If teacher expectations increase due to having taught an item, teachers should teach more new items and not be bound by vague definitions of "basic" mathematics. The differences of EXP for items placement in the texts of this study should encourage teachers to analyze texts for logical sequencing of new and old topics—they should be encouraged to teach plotless books out of order. While teachers in this study are relatively well motivated to teach algebra items, they are not for geometry and measurement. Teachers need to think about the fact that students need pregeometry as much as prealgebra, and an understanding of measurement regardless of subsequent courses, so they should not settle for books with trivial treatments of these subjects. Motivation of students is a function of the motivation of teachers, and eighth-grade teachers need to follow the recommendations in the NCTM *Standards* for beginning secondary school mathematics, not repeating elementary school arithmetic.

Overall, the curriculum balance represented by the SIMS test is a reality I would rather have students encounter than the one found in most of the books in this study, especially the basal ones. If these texts represent our society's best authority on mathematics, the authority is fragmented, has as priorities the indoctrination of students into outdated arithmetic skills and algorithmic understanding of any other mathematics, all presented in arbitrary sequence. Encouraging improvements in content have been noted in recent editions of texts, but fragmentation seems to remain the mode. We cannot waste our students' time reteaching arithmetic in eighth-grade. We cannot claim that arithmetic is the key to mathematical understanding, at least the pencil-and-paper doing of it. We cannot expect students to be independent thinkers if the mathematical story is not told independent from teachers. We cannot help students grow by repressing new mathematics.

REFERENCES

Apple, M. W., & Christian-Smith, L. K. (Eds.), (1991). *The politics of the textbook*. New York, Routledge.

Ball, D. L., & Feiman-Nemser, S. (1988). Using textbooks and teachers' guides: A dilemma for beginning teachers and teacher educators. *Curriculum Inquiry, 18*, 401–423.

Bolster, L. C., Cox, G. F., Gibb, E. G., Hansen, V. P., Kirkpatrick, J. E., McNerney, C. R., Robitaille, D. F., Trimble, H. C., Vance, I. E., Walch, R., & Wisner, R. J. (1978). *Mathematics around us*. Glenview, IL: Scott, Foresman.

Brown, J. K. Jr. (1973). *Textbook use by teachers and students of geometry and second-year algebra*. Doctoral dissertation. University of Illinois at Urbana-Champaign.

Chall, J., & Conard, S. S. with Harris-Sharples, S. (1991). *Should textbooks challenge students? The case for easier or harder books*. New York: Teachers College Press.

Crosswhite, F. J., Dossey, J. A., Swafford, J. O., McKnight, C. C., Cooney, T. J., Downs, F. L., Grouws, D. A., & Weinzweig, A. I. (1986). *Second international mathematics study: Detailed report for the United States*. Champaign, IL: Stipes.

Dewey, J. (1916). *Democracy and education*. New York: The Free Press.

Dolciani, M. P., Beckenbach, E. F., Brown, R. G., Kane, R. B., & Wooten, W. (1982). *Mathematics: Structure and method. Course 2*. Boston: Houghton-Mifflin.

Dolciani, M. P., Wooten, W., Beckenbach, E. F., & Markert, W. (1975). *Modern school mathematics: Structure and method. Course 2*. Boston: Houghton-Mifflin.

Duncan, E. R., Quast, W. G., Cole, W. L., Haubner, M. A. H., & Sparks, T. M. (1981). *Mathematics*. Boston: Houghton-Mifflin.

Flanders, J. (1992). *Textbooks and the SIMS test: Comparisons of intended and implemented eighth-grade mathematics*. Doctoral dissertation. University of Chicago.

Flanders, J. (1987). How much of the content in mathematics textbooks is new? *Arithmetic Teacher, 35*, 18–23.

Garnier, H. E. (1988). *Curricula comparisons: Examination of eighth-grade mathematics instruction data from the Second International Mathematics Study in the United States*. Doctoral dissertation. University of California, Los Angeles.

Good, T. L., Grouws, D. A., & Ebmeier, H. (1983). *Active mathematics teaching*. New York: Longman.

Graybeal, S. S., & Stodolsky, S. S. (1986). *Instructional practice in fifth-grade math and social studies: An analysis of teacher's guides* (ERIC ED 276 614). Paper presented at the Annual Meeting of the American Educational Research Association, San Francisco, CA.

Klingler, G. M. (1988). *A naturalistic study of algebra I verbal problem instruction and learning*. Doctoral dissertation. Michigan State University.

Kuhs, T., Schmidt, W., Porter, A., Floden, R., Freeman, D., & Schwille, J. (1979). *A taxonomy for classifying elementary school mathematics content* (Research Series No. 4). East Lansing, MI: Michigan State University, Institute for Research on Teaching.

Lappan, G., Fitzgerald, W., Winter, M. J., & Phillips, E. (1986). *Similarity and equivalent fractions*. Menlo Park, CA: Addison-Wesley.

McKnight, C. C., Crosswhite, F. J., Dossey, J. A., Kifer, E., Swafford, J. O., Travers, K. J., & Cooney, J. (1987). *The underachieving curriculum: Assessing U.S. school mathematics from an international perspective*. Champaign, IL: Stipes.

National Council of Teachers of Mathematics. (1989). *Curriculum and evaluation standards for school mathematics*. Reston, VA: National Council of Teachers of Mathematics.

Nibbelink, W. H., Stockdale, S. R., Hoover, H. D., & Mangru, M. (1987). Problem-solving in the elementary grades: Textbook practices and achievement trends over the past thirty years. *Arithmetic Teacher, 35*, 34–37.

Nicely, R. F., Jr. (1985). Higher order thinking skills in mathematics textbooks. *Educational Leadership, 42*, 26–30.

Nicely, R. F., Jr., Fiber, H. R., & Bobango, J. C. (1986). The cognitive content of elementary school mathematics textbooks. *Arithmetic Teacher, 34*, 60-inside back cover.

Nichols, E. D., Anderson, P. A., Dwight, L. A., Flournoy, F., Kalin, R., Schluep, J., & Simon, L. (1978). *Holt school mathematics*. New York: Holt, Rinehart, & Winston.

Perkins, J. (1983). *Pivotal skills in elementary mathematics instruction* (ERIC ED 250 159). Los Alamitos, CA: Southwest Regional Laboratory.

Phillips, E. R., & Kane, R. B. (1972). *Validating learning hierarchies for sequencing mathematical tasks* (ERIC ED 064 405). Washington, DC: Department of Health, Education, and Welfare; Office of Education.

Porter, A. C., Floden, R. E., Freeman, D. J., Schmidt, W. H., & Schwille, J. R. (1986). *Content determinants* (Research Series No. 179). East Lansing, MI: Michigan State University, Institute for Research on Teaching.

Rowley, J. T. (1988). *A study of how teachers plan their lessons: Students needs vs. maintaining activity flow*. Doctoral dissertation. University of San Francisco.

Rucker, W. E., & Dilley, C. A. (1979). *Heath mathematics*. Lexington, MA: D. C. Heath.

Tyson-Bernstein, H. (1988). *A conspiracy of good intentions: America's textbook fiasco*. Washington, DC: Council for Basic Education.

Usiskin, Z., Flanders, J., Hynes, C., Polonsky, L., Porter, S., & Viktora, S. (1992). *Transition mathematics*. Glenview, IL: Scott, Foresman.

Warries, E. (1986). *Implications of three recently completed IEA studies for teaching and teacher education in the Netherlands* (ERIC ED 273 668). Paper presented at the Annual Meeting of the American Educational Research Association, San Francisco, CA.

Weiss, I. R. (1987). *Report of the 1985–86 national survey of science and mathematics education*. Research Triangle Park, NC: National Science Foundation.

Wilson, G. M. (1926). *What mathematics shall we teach?* Boston: Houghton-Mifflin.

3

The Myth of Progressive and Traditional Orientations: Teaching Mathematics Without a Coherent Point of View*

Lauren A. Sosniak

Department of Education
Washington University
St. Louis, MO

Corinna A. Ethington

College of Education
Memphis State University
Memphis, TN

Maria Varelas

College of Education
University of Illinois at Chicago
Chicago, IL

* An earlier version of this chapter was published in 1991 under the title Teaching mathematics without a coherent point of view: Findings from the IEA Second International Mathematics Study, *Journal of Curriculum Studies, 23,* 119–131.

Curricula of different sorts lead to different patterns of outcomes. That generalization, obvious as it might seem, was a finding of no small importance when outlined in Walker and Schaffarzick's (1974) review of experiments that compared subject matter achievement of students using the "new" curricula developed in the United States during the late 1950s and the 1960s with the achievement of students using more traditional curricula. Neither the "new" nor the "traditional" curricula could be said to be "superior"; rather, each type resulted in patterns of achievement that reflected patterns within the curricula themselves. Identifying patterns of outcomes resulting from different curricula became a problem in its own right.

Walker and Schaffarzick's analysis was based on, and thus limited by, a definition of curriculum as "materials in use." Working from this definition, the researchers concluded not only that content inclusion and emphasis were powerful determinants of achievement, but also that these variables might logically be expected to be more powerful than variables such as the nature of teaching and learning or the context within which instruction takes place. Walker and Schaffarzick made only passing reference to the possibility that interrelationships between content covered and the manner in which it is covered may alter substantially the curricular effects.

Ironically, subsequent reviews of the curricular innovations of the 1950s and 1960s suggest that the success of these programs (whether measured by effects on students or by continued use of the programs in schools) was limited in no small measure by inconsistencies or incompatibilities between the content emphasized in the packaged materials and the demands of working with that content in classrooms. The "new" curricula frequently presented views of the subject matter that did not match well with the views held by classroom teachers; the curricula assumed teaching strategies that were not familiar to or comfortable for classroom teachers; the curricula assumed roles and responsibilities for students that were inconsistent with the ways teachers typically expected students to behave in classrooms (cf. Jackson, 1983; Lazerson, McLaughlin, & McPherson, 1984). The mismatch between the curricular intentions of the packaged materials and the manner in which teachers (and school cultures) structured work with those materials in classrooms apparently contributed substantially to the general ineffectiveness of the programs.

The research reported in this chapter was an attempt to build from, and hopefully integrate, the two lines of curricular work reported above. We were interested in testing with the SIMS data the extent to which different patterns of outcomes would be evident in mathematics curricula of different sorts. Our definition of "curricula of different sorts" was to be more broadly conceived than the definition used by Walker and Schaffarzick (1974); it would take into account both aims and means and especially the relationships between the two. We were interested in the effects of curricula that were theoretically consistent in their points of view across a variety of dimensions. We reasoned that the greater the coherence expressed in a curriculum (defined with reference to both "matter" worth attending to and some "manner" of unpacking that substance in a classroom), the more obvious and powerful should be the effects of the curriculum. That is, curricula with coherently different orientations should result in patterns of outcomes that are not only different in nature but also dramatic in their differences.

Most generally, our framework for thinking about curricular orientations and curricular coherence was informed by Tyler's (1949) classic work on the elements and relationships involved in curriculum planning. Tyler argues throughout his small book for consistency. He calls, for example, for objectives consistent with one another and mutually consistent with the activities in which students are asked to engage in the service of realizing those objectives. Consistency of these sorts is important, Tyler (1949) argues, to "permit some degree of integration and coherent unification in the mind and action of the student so that the maximum psychological benefit of learning can thus be derived" (p. 41). Inconsistency, on the other hand, will result in a less efficient and less effective educational experience.

> In some respects educational experiences produce their effects in the way water dripping upon a stone wears it away. In a day or a week or a month there is no appreciable change in the stone, but over a period of years definite erosion is noted. Correspondingly, by the cumulation of educational experiences profound changes are brought about in the learner. . . . In order for educational experiences to produce a cumulative effect, they must be so organized as to reinforce each other. (p. 83)

Somewhat more specifically, our framework for thinking about curriculum, and our guide for the analyses we would conduct of curricular points of view more broadly conceived, was influenced also by the work of Schwab (1970, 1973). Schwab (1970) reminds us that curriculum work is concerned with choice and action. He argues that in the course of choice and action we must treat equally the ends and means of education, and understand both as "mutually determining one another" (Schwab, 1970, p. 36). He argues further that the choices we make and actions we take require defensible decisions balancing simultaneously "four commonplaces of equal rank: the learner, the teacher, the milieu, and the subject matter" (Schwab, 1973, pp. 508–509).[1] This outline for thinking about curriculum helped us organize conceptually questions that were asked of teachers as part of the SIMS data, study teachers' responses to those questions, and define ways of testing the consequences of different curricular orientations.

Finally, our plan was more specific still. We were interested most particularly in testing the effects of two specific curricular orientations reflecting what Jackson (1986) calls traditions within the domain of educational thought and practice. Jackson labels these orientations "the mimetic and the transformative," terms which he says encompass the differences expressed in long-standing debates between "traditional" and "progressive" educators, over "subject-centered" and "child-centered" practices, and the like.[2] In brief, and without trying to do justice to Jackson's discussion, one of the traditions is concerned primarily with the transmission of factual and procedural knowledge while the other emphasizes qualitative transformations in the character and outlook of the learner.

Our problem at the start, then, was to identify groups of teachers whose curricular orientations best represented one or the other of two enduring traditions in educational thought and practice, and then to study the effects on students of working within one or the other of the traditions. The problem was much larger than we imagined. In this chapter we report on our attempts (largely unsuccessful) to identify teachers of mathematics who hold a clear and consistent curricular point of view which emphasizes either a "progressive" or "traditional" orientation, and we discuss the ways we have come to understand the results of our analyses.

---

[1] The importance of attending to teachers' views of learning, teaching, and the subject matter itself as variables of considerable significance in studies of curricula and their consequences also has been highlighted recently by researchers concerned primarily with studies of mathematics (see, for example, Leder & Gunstone, 1990; and Romberg & Carpenter, 1986).

[2] Cohen (1988) writes at length about similar traditions, which he calls "a great collision between inherited and revolutionary ideas about the nature of knowledge, learning and teaching" or "traditional and innovative instructional doctrines" (p. 44).

METHODS OF INVESTIGATION

Sample and Data

The SIMS data we were interested in were those collected on U.S. students in the eighth-grade. Further, since we had reason to believe that different eighth-grade class types logically could be expected to emphasize different curricular concerns that might confound the analyses planned, we decided to limit our sample and study to only *typical* classes.

The SIMS data were particularly amenable to a study of curricular orientations and their consequences for several reasons. First, the data included both teachers' responses to a set of questions about their choices and actions, and students' responses to a variety of questions that could be used to define in various ways the outcomes of curricular orientations. Second, the survey administered to teachers addressed a wide range of themes. These included questions about curricular objectives considered more or less important (aims), teaching strategies believed to be more or less effective (means, emphasizing the role of the teacher), ways of organizing students in classrooms and asking students to work in support of learning (means, emphasizing the role of the students), and, most generally, teachers' broad conceptions about the subject matter of mathematics. These particular question sets allowed us to study curricular orientations in light of Schwab's framework loosely defined. Third, the response categories provided with each of the sets of questions included options that could be identified as falling more closely within either the "progressive" or the "traditional" orientation. The data thus would allow us, theoretically, to identify teachers emphasizing either a "progressive" or a "traditional" curricular orientation across a variety of dimensions, and then to study the effects on students of working for a year within one or the other coherent curricular point of view.

Procedures

Our aim was to develop scales representing each of the curricular orientations (progressive and traditional) within each of the four dimensions of a curricular point of view. These scales would be constructed by summing across groups of items within each area that conceptually represented a particular orientation. Using these scales we could then identify those teachers with a coherent point of view, be it progressive or traditional, for they would consistently score high on one scale and low on the other within each of the four areas. Our plan then was to develop scales representing various curriculum outcomes regarding achievement and engagement, and then to study the relationships between teachers' curricular points of view and student outcomes. The results of our investigations led us to eliminate the latter portion of our intended analyses. The following section describes the results of our work on teachers' curricular orientations, organized by the dimensions we were concerned with in the study. The results for each analysis reported below are based on only those teachers who had complete data on all items involved in the analysis.

RESULTS

Curricular Objectives for Eighth-Grade Mathematics

The SIMS teacher questionnaire asked teachers to identify how much emphasis they give to a set of broadly conceived curricular objectives in their work during the year with a target eighth-grade class. Each objective was rated on a scale such that: 1 = relatively more emphasis, 2 = about equal emphasis, and 3 = relatively less emphasis. Included in the list of nine curricular objectives teachers were asked to rate, were five we believed should conceptually divide teachers more oriented toward either the progressive or the traditional orientation. We reasoned that teachers with a progressive curriculum orientation would emphasize the following objectives:

- develop an attitude of inquiry;
- become interested in mathematics;
- develop an awareness of the importance of mathematics in everyday life.

On the other hand, teachers oriented toward the traditional point of view should place less emphasis on the above objectives and more emphasis instead on facts and skills, as reflected in the following objectives:

- know mathematical facts, principles, and algorithms;
- perform computations with speed and accuracy.

We combined these groups of items into two scales that conceptually represented opposing points of view relative to curricular objectives. The resulting internal consistency reliabilities of the scales (α = .57 for the progressive point of view; α = .47 for the traditional point of view; N = 143) proved to be too low for us to be able to use them and reliably distinguish between groups of teachers.

On the chance that the reliabilities for the scales were biased by awkward wording or multiple interpretations for some of the response categories, we decided to focus on a single objective from each group that we believed conceptually best reflected the particular point of view. *Develop an attitude of inquiry* was chosen to reflect the progressive approach, while *perform computations with speed and accuracy* was chosen to reflect the traditional approach. We then proceeded to test the hypothesis that teachers who held a progressive point of view would place more emphasis on developing an attitude of inquiry and less emphasis on performing computations with speed and accuracy, while teachers with a traditional point of view would do the opposite.

The results of a chi-square test of independence (χ^2 = 3.716, p = .446) indicated that the hypothesized inverse relationship between responses to these items was not present. In fact, responses to one item were independent of responses to the other. In other words, teachers emphasizing one approach were as likely as not also to emphasize the other. Of the 143 teachers in this sample who responded to both items, only ten exhibited a consistent point of view in their responses to the two items: six with a traditional orientation and four with a progressive orientation.

Effective Teaching

The SIMS teacher questionnaire provided a list of "suggestions of what teachers might do to make their teaching more effective," and asked teachers to rate each item with regard to what they thought personally was of more or less importance. The items were rated on a scale such that: 1 = little or no importance, 2 = some importance, 3 = major importance, and 4 = highest importance. Included in the list of 41 suggestions were seven we thought conceptually should distinguish the more student-centered, progressively oriented teachers from teachers with a traditional curricular orientation. The former, we thought, would rate as more important the following three suggestions:

- provide an opportunity for students to discover concepts for themselves;
- allow discussions to continue longer than planned when students show particular interest;

- take student preferences into account when planning lessons.

On the other hand, we believed that the more traditional, subject-centered teachers would place less emphasis on the above strategies and be more likely to rate as more important the following suggestions:

- present the content in a highly structured fashion;
- before an activity begins, give students detailed step-by-step directions on what they are to do;
- make sure the students know exactly what they should be doing at any given time;
- immediately correct false statements made by students.

As before, we developed scales using each group of items and tested the scales for their internal consistency reliability. Again, the resulting reliabilities were too low ($\alpha = .48$ for the progressive and $\alpha = .42$ for the traditional; $N = 144$) to use confidently in subsequent analyses. Once again we selected the single teaching practice that would best reflect the opposing points of view. *Provide an opportunity for students to discover concepts for themselves* was considered to best reflect the progressive approach to teaching, while *give students detailed step-by-step directions on what they are to do* was selected to represent the traditional approach.

Arguing as before, that teachers with consistent points of view would consider one teaching practice highly effective and the other much less so, we again tested our hypothesis with a chi-square test of independence. In order to look for general tendencies rather than extreme positions, Categories 1 and 2 were combined as were Categories 3 and 4 on each item. The results here were as before: teachers' ratings of the important of the two teaching practices were independent of each other ($\chi^2 = 1.286, p = .257$). That is, a teacher valuing a discovery approach was as likely to value giving detailed, step-by-step instructions to students as not. Of the 144 teachers who responded to these questions, only 34 responded in a manner indicating a consistent point of view: 17 responded consistent with a progressive point of view, and 17 were consistent with a traditional curriculum orientation. It is important to note also that 104 of the 144 teachers rated both of these seemingly contradictory items as of major or highest importance.

Student Activity in the Service of Learning

The SIMS teacher questionnaire asked teachers to estimate the amount of time students spent in four different sorts of activity settings for a typical week and for the last week of instruction. The activity settings were identified as:

- doing seat work or blackboard work (students preparing individual written answers to assigned exercises or problems, but not counting tests and quizzes);
- listening as a whole class to you give lectures or explanation;
- working in small groups;
- taking tests and quizzes.

We reasoned that a teacher with a more progressive or transformative curricular orientation would report more time with students working in small groups, and less time with students listening to teacher lectures or explanation, than a teacher with a traditional or mimetic curricular orientation. The latter sort of teacher should report the reverse with regard to distribution of student time. (Seatwork and testing situations were excluded from our analysis of progressive or traditional student activity, because the nature of the problems students might be asked to work on in either of these activity settings could, conceivably, support either progressive or traditional concerns.)

The SIMS data reveal that, as a group, teachers ask students to engage in seatwork activity more frequently than any other activity, and test situations more frequently than group work (105.8 minutes of seatwork; 84.2 minutes spent listening to lectures and explanations in a typical week; 36.5 minutes spent in small group work; 41.8 minutes taking tests and quizzes). Still, we believed that the time spent listening to lectures and explanations and working in small groups was sufficiently large to warrant further investigation. Of the 178 teachers, 154 (87%) reported spending more time on teacher lectures or explanations than on group work, 24 teachers (13%) reported spending more time with students engaged in small group work than they did lecturing or explaining.

Teacher Views of the Subject Matter of Mathematics

The SIMS teacher questionnaire asked teachers to "express on a five point scale the extent of agreement between the feeling expressed in each statement and your personal feelings." The scale ranged from 1 = strongly disagree to 5 = strongly agree, with 3 = undecided. Included among the statements were those that emphasized a "dynamic" or "process" nature of mathematics, and those that emphasized a "static" nature of mathematics. We reasoned that the progressive teacher should be more likely to be in strong agreement with statements such as:

- a mathematics problem can always be solved in different ways;
- trial and error can often be used to solve a mathematics problem;
- there are many different ways to solve most mathematics problems.

The traditional teacher, on the other hand, should be more likely to agree with statements suggesting a more static concept of mathematics, statements such as:

- there is always a rule to follow in solving a mathematics problems;
- there is little place for originality in solving mathematics problems;
- learning mathematics involves mostly memorizing.

Here we used the same approach taken with the curricular objectives and perceptions of effective teaching. We created scales representing the opposing points of view by summing across the above groups of items. As before, the internal consistency reliabilities were too low to feel confident of the ability of the scales to differentiate among teachers with respect to point of view (α = .41 for the traditional orientation, and α = .58 for the progressive orientation). Next we selected the single item we considered most representative of each of the two curricular orientations: *there are many different ways to solve most mathematics problems* for a progressive, "process" view of mathematics, and *learning mathematics involves mostly memorizing* for a traditional point of view. We reasoned that teachers holding one point of view would be in agreement with one statement and disagreement with the other. Again collapsing Categories 1 with 2 and 4 with 5 to examine the direction of teacher thinking rather than the strength of teacher positions, this was tested with a chi-square test of independence. The results (χ^2 = 14.94; p = .005) indicated that with regard to questions about the nature of mathematics as a subject matter this group of teachers did show consistency in their points of view. An extreme proportion of these teachers (110 of 174) espoused a progressive point of view; only nine held a consistent traditional orientation.

Identifying Teachers With Consistent Points of View Across Curricular Dimensions

The results of the analyses of particular dimensions of the mathematics curriculum left us uneasy about the extent to which the sample of teachers of typical eighth grade mathematics classes in the United States are teaching with a coherent curricular orientation, either progressive or traditional. Although the majority of the teachers expressed a progressive orientation to the subject matter itself (110 holding a progressive point of view; nine holding a traditional point of view), the numbers were skewed dramatically in the reverse for the activity settings they structured for students. And the number of teachers who were consistently progressive or traditional either with regard to their curricular objectives or their beliefs about effective teaching was extremely small.

Still, because we were able to identify a number of teachers who were "progressive" and "traditional" within each of the variables of this study, we believed it might be possible to identify also a number who were consistent across the curricular commonplaces. Even relatively small-sized groups of teachers expressing coherent progressive and traditional orientations across the curricular variables would allow us to study the effects on student outcomes of these different points of view, because the number of students influenced by these teachers would create reasonably sized groups for further study.

Our analyses in search of teachers with a coherent point of view across the four curricular variables, either progressive or traditional, revealed not a single instance of such consistency. On the chance that one of the four variables we used was solely responsible for this finding, we repeated our search for a coherent point of view across any three of the variables. Omitting beliefs about effective teaching from the analysis did not change the results at all: none of the 178 teachers held a consistent point of view, either progressive or traditional, across the remaining three variables. Omitting curricular objectives from the analysis revealed one teacher of the 178 holding a coherent traditional point of view and two others consistently progressive in their orientation. Omitting student activity from the analysis revealed two teachers with a progressive orientation and none with a traditional orientation across the remaining three variables. Omitting the nature of the subject matter itself from the analysis left us with two teachers consistently traditional in their orientations and none consistently progressive.

Thus, while our aim was to study the effects on students of alternative curricular orientations, we were unable to do so because of the inability to identify teachers who held a theoretically coherent point of view, either traditional or progressive, for their work as eighth-grade mathematics teachers. In our effort to make sense of this finding we conducted one further analysis consistent with curriculum work: a search for teachers coherent with regard to either the aims or the means of eighth-grade mathematics. We reasoned that if such teachers were found in reasonable numbers, we would be better able not only to make sense of the teachers' point of view but also to draw clear implications for work with preservice and inservice teachers.

Looking only for teachers with a coherent point of view regarding aims, using the variables of curricular objectives and the nature of the subject matter itself, we identified four teachers of the 178 with a consistent progressive orientation and none with a consistent traditional orientation. Looking only for teachers with a coherent point of view regarding the means, using the variables of effective teaching and student activity, we identified 15 teachers with a consistent traditional orientation and three who were consistently progressive. Clearly, from a curricular point of view, the teachers responding to the SIMS teacher questionnaire provide no compelling evidence for a theoretically coherent orientation toward their work.

DISCUSSION

We began with an investigation into what seemed like a simple but nontrivial question: What are the consequences for student engagement and student achievement of different curricular orientations in the teaching of mathematics? We had in mind a test of two particular curricular orientations with long histories of discussion in our educational literature; data from SIMS seemed, on the face of it, to be well suited for this investigation. The plan was to identify two groups of eighth-grade mathematics teachers, each clearly and strongly representing either a "progressive" or a "traditional" curricular orientation, and then to study the effects of the distinct orientations on the students studying with those teachers.

What we learned in the course of turning plan into action was something different from, but no less important than, the knowledge we were seeking at the start. In short, we learned that eighth-grade mathematics teachers in the U.S. apparently teach their subject matter without a theoretically coherent point of view. They hold positions about the aims of instruction in mathematics, the role of the teacher, the nature of learning, and the nature of the subject matter itself which would seem to be logically incompatible. Even within each of these dimensions of curricular orientation, the teachers have little trouble agreeing with two or more statements which would seem to reflect entirely different conceptions of eighth-grade mathematics, conceptions which would seem to be incompatible in action and outcome. This is especially so with regard to teachers' reports of their objectives and their beliefs about effective teaching strategies.

We began this study with a belief that consistency in curricular orientation is important. Our belief was supported by curriculum theory most generally (Tyler, 1949; Schwab, 1970, 1973), research on teaching mathematics more specifically (Romberg & Carpenter, 1986; Leder & Gunstone, 1990; Thompson, 1984), and critiques of the less-than-successful curriculum reform movement of the 1950s and 1960s (Jackson, 1983; Lazerson, McLaughlin, & McPherson, 1984). We were careful in our analyses to respect the varying degrees of strength with which teachers might hold particular positions and to search only for consistency in the direction of orientation one way or the other.

Perhaps the "traditions" of educational thought and practice suggested by Jackson (1986) provided the wrong frame for our search for consistency. Jackson himself notes that there "are few, if any, instances of either purely mimetic or purely transformative teaching" (p. 129); this fact likely holds true too for the more limited frame of "progressive" and "traditional" curricular orientations against which our analyses could be measured. Still, we were not looking for "pure" instances of one orientation or the other; rather, our analyses were organized around a search for curricular orientations that are predominant, orientations that are reflected in emphases in choices and actions. Is it possible that the "traditions" that Jackson sketches so elegantly are traditions only in educational thought, and not at all in educational practice, or at least not in the practice of teaching mathematics in the United States? Thompson's (1984) case studies suggest otherwise; Thompson presents compelling evidence for the idea of these specific and distinct curricular conceptions. Thompson's study, however, provides further support for the finding that teachers may be aware of the different theoretical orientations but still think and behave inconsistently in the teaching of mathematics.

We have to consider the possibility that the lack of curricular coherence we identified, and which is also identified in Thompson's (1984) work, reflects inadequacies on the part of the research instruments rather than meaningful inconsistencies in practice. In particular, our study relied on teacher responses to questionnaires. Some of the questions and response categories were worded in ways that were problematic for us, and so it would be reasonable to assume that they posed problems of interpretation for the teachers whose views we analyzed. The language of many of the questions was highly abstract; with few concrete referents against which to make choices and judgments, it would be sensible to assume not only that the teachers responded in accord with individualistic interpretations to words or phrases with a wide range of possible meanings (similar to the cross-cultural problems of definition of terms identified by Westbury (1988) also with respect to SIMS data), but also in line with different normative and/or practical referents for different prompts within a single line of questioning. If the teachers had been probed more thoughtfully, more concretely, or more deeply, would the inconsistencies have dissolved?

Thompson (1984) argues that studies of matters such as the integration of teachers' conceptions of mathematics and mathematics teaching require "in-depth studies of an anthropological, clinical, or case study nature" (p. 126). Although we are not convinced that this is necessarily so, we need to remain open to the possibility that our findings are biased by our methods of investigation. In addition to the problems of interpretation noted above, we are not certain about the manner in which the questionnaires were presented to the teachers, and we cannot argue forcefully that the teachers responded to the questionnaire with the same degree of seriousness and care that we attributed to their responses.

Of course it is possible that teachers would have been similarly supportive of almost all agendas placed before them, and unable or unwilling to see conflicts in the points of view they expressed, whether probed through questionnaires or highly sensitive and in-depth interviews. Jackson (1968), among others, has highlighted the conceptual simplicity in teachers' talk, the tendency of teachers to approach educational affairs intuitively, and the problematic nature of conceiving of teaching as a highly rational affair. Other educators (Firestone, 1989; Short, 1983; Boyd, 1979; Kirst & Walker, 1971) have highlighted the "policy clutter"[3] with which teachers have to contend. The curricular inconsistency of the teachers analyzed for this study may be a reflection of their willingness to take at least somewhat seriously the variety of policies they confront, policies which themselves are inconsistent across levels of policy-making and over time.

A careful review of our findings suggests one further and perhaps more comprehensive interpretation. This explanation, following from the insights of Westbury (1973) and Cuban (1984) regarding constancy and change in classroom teaching, requires that we examine more carefully each of the variables and the pattern of findings in light of the distance of the variables from the practices of schooling and classroom teaching. It argues, finally, that what looks like apparent inconsistency in the teachers' views may instead be thoughtful responses to a set of issues that vary markedly in their distance from schooling most generally and classroom teaching most specifically.

Although we have identified all four variables as constituent parts of Schwab's (1970) commonplaces of teaching, and as reflecting both the aims and means of mathematics education, we could also scale the variables with regard to their connection to the activity of teaching. Teacher beliefs about the nature of mathematics itself, for example, would be viewed as abstract in the extreme, not necessarily connected at all to the activity of teaching eighth-grade mathematics. (Knowledge of the nature of mathematics does not, in and of itself, provide clear direction regarding either what to teach in eighth-grade mathematics courses or how to teach it.) Student activity would be viewed as concrete in the extreme, intimately connected with life in classrooms, although not necessarily connected at all to the nature of mathematics per se. Curricular objectives for eighth-grade mathematics, and beliefs about effective teaching strategies, fall somewhere between views of the subject matter and the nature of student activity—questions about objectives and teaching strategies call on teachers to respond abstractly and theoretically, but in light of what they know or believe to be true about the nature of mathematics (particularly for questions about curricular objectives) and the practical activity of schooling (particularly for questions about effective teaching). We have, then, a set of variables representing different distances from schooling and classroom in-

---

[3] We are indebted to David Cohen (personal communication) for both the phrase "policy clutter," and its theme of inconsistent recommendations across levels of policy making and over the course of teachers' preparation and practice.

room instruction, and, ironically, we have a set of findings regarding teachers' curricular orientations that shift systematically from "progressive" to "traditional" as the teachers move from considering the issue most distant from schooling and classroom instruction to the issue most central to schooling and classroom instruction.

Westbury (1973, 1980) and Cuban (1984) argue that the practical activity of teaching, under current and historical conditions, virtually demands from teachers a traditional orientation to classroom activity. Structurally and functionally, these scholars contend, schools and classrooms are designed to support and promote the continued transmission of traditional views and practices. In fact, they propose that traditional practices should be understood as successful solutions invented by teachers to solve problems associated with a set of goals the schools have been designed to enact and the set of conditions within which teachers have been expected to work. In this regard, then, the overwhelmingly "traditional" response to questions about student activity reveal the teachers to be unusually successful students of teaching, responding in quite logical ways to the demands and constraints they face, just as the overwhelmingly "progressive" response to questions about the nature of mathematics itself seems to reveal these same teachers to be unusually successful students of mathematics.

Responses to questions about curricular objectives and effective teaching strategies are problematic for the teachers, as they would be for any of us involved with the integration of theory and practice. Both sets of questions require teachers to think theoretically, but in light of practical activity. Further, the questions call on teachers to draw on not only what they know or believe to be true about classroom instruction, but also what they know or believe to be true about the nature of mathematics itself. In response to these sets of questions, we found that the teachers in the SIMS sample were dramatically inconsistent, frequently rating seemingly contradictory items as similarly important. We have understood these findings earlier as evidence of a lack of a coherent curricular orientation with regard to mathematics instruction. It may be more responsible, however, to understand the teachers' responses not necessarily as contradictory, but rather are signs of attempted syntheses of theory and practice, syntheses of theoretical understanding of teaching, learning, and the subject matter of mathematics with practical knowledge about the structure and function of classrooms and schools. The inconsistency discussed earlier may well reflect a lack of a coherent curricular orientation, but it may also reflect a strikingly clear and accurate representation by teachers of the different concerns brought to bear in the act of teaching in schools, and an attempt to synthesize different bodies of knowledge and respect the "eclectic" (Schwab, 1970) character of education.

While there are reasons to be cautious about our findings of curricular inconsistencies, and our various interpretations of those findings, this investigation seems nonetheless to be an important step in the service of making sense of the nature of curricula as enacted and the consequences of those curricula. The question we are left with now, after hours in search of teachers with a coherent point of view, is a 180-degree turn from where we began: What are the consequences for student engagement and achievement of teaching mathematics without a coherent point of view? What are the consequences of emphasizing simultaneously competing curricular objectives, of valuing equally teaching strategies which place dramatically different demands on students, of believing strongly in ideas about learning which turn on dramatically different philosophical orientations? How important is consistency in both the substance of instruction and the manner of presenting that substance? What are the most important variables across which teachers need to be consistent if they are to be effective?

And, if teachers do need to be theoretically coherent in their thinking and their action in order to be most effective, how best might we encourage such consistency? Are researchers and policy makers best advised to frame their questions and ideas for reform within the limitations embedded in schooling and classroom instruction as it is currently understood, helping teachers become more efficient and effective with "traditional" practices as Cuban (1984) suggests? Or is the future of education better served by encouraging dramatically new thinking about the structures and functions of schools and the technology of teaching that Westbury (1973) argues for so passionately? Either choice asks us to predict an uncertain future for the profession of teaching and, most importantly, for the students to be served by tomorrow's teachers.

REFERENCES

Boyd, W. L. (1979). The politics of curriculum change and stability. *Educational Researcher, 8*, 12–18.

Cohen, D. K. (1988). Teaching practice: Plus que ça change. . . . In P. W. Jackson (Ed.), *Contributing to educational change: Perspectives on research and practice*. Berkeley, CA: McCutchan.

Cuban, L. (1984). *How teachers taught: Constancy and change in American classrooms 1890–1980*. New York: Longman.

Firestone, W. A. (1989). Educational policy as an ecology of games. *Educational Researcher, 18,* 18–24.

Jackson, P. W. (1968). *Life in classrooms.* New York: Holt, Rinehart & Winston.

Jackson, P. W. (1983). The reform of science education: A cautionary tale. *Daedalus, 112,* 143–166.

Jackson, P. W. (1986). *The practice of teaching.* New York: Teachers College Press.

Kirst, M. W., & Walker, D. F. (1971). An analysis of curriculum policymaking. *Review of Educational Research, 41,* 479–509.

Lazerson, M., McLaughlin, J. B., & McPherson, B. (1984). New curriculum, old issues. *Teachers College Record, 86,* 299–319.

Leder, G. C., & Gunstone, R. F. (1990). Perspectives on mathematics learning. *International Journal of Educational Research, 4,* 105–120.

Romberg, T. A., & Carpenter, T. P. (1986). Research on teaching and learning mathematics: Two disciplines of scientific inquiry. In M. Wittrock (Ed.), *Handbook of research on teaching* (3rd ed.). New York: Macmillan.

Schwab, J. J. (1970). *The practical: A language for curriculum.* Washington, DC: National Education Association.

Schwab, J. J. (1973). The practical 3: Translation into curriculum. *School Review, 81,* 501–522.

Short, E. C. (1983). Authority and governance in curriculum development: A policy analysis in the United States context. *Educational Evaluation and Policy Analysis, 5,* 195–205.

Thompson, A. G. (1984). The relationship of teachers' conceptions of mathematics and mathematics teaching to instructional practice. *Educational Studies in Mathematics, 15,* 105–127.

Tyler, R. W. (1949). *Basic principles of curriculum and instruction.* Chicago: University of Chicago Press.

Walker, D. F., & Schaffarzick, J. (1974). Comparing curricula. *Review of Educational Research, 44,* 83–111.

Westbury, I. (1973). Conventional classrooms, "open" classrooms and the technology of teaching. *Journal of Curriculum Studies, 5,* 99–121.

Westbury, I. (1980). Schooling as an agency of education: Some implications for curriculum theory. In W. B. Dockrell & D. F. Hamilton (Eds.), *Rethinking educational research.* London: Hodder & Stoughton.

Westbury, I. (1988). How should we be judging the American high school? *Journal of Curriculum Studies, 20,* 291–315.

4

Is the United States Really a Low Achiever in Math? The SIMS Findings Re-Examined*

Ian Westbury

College of Education
University of Illinois at Urbana-Champaign
Champaign, IL

It is impossible to read either popular or professional accounts of the state of American schooling or recent developments within U.S. mathematics education and not see references to the fact of an achievement gap between schools in the United States and schools in Japan and other countries. Here, for instance, are two examples. The first is from Stigler, Lee, and Stevenson's (1990) influential analysis of mathematics achievement in Japan and China:

> The fact that Japanese middle and high school students outscore American students on tests of mathematics achievement has been known for at least [the] twenty years [since the IEA First International Mathematics Study]. The most salient results to emerge have been the outstanding performance of Japanese students and the mediocre performance of American students.

* An abbreviated version of the argument presented in this chapter was published in 1992 as Comparing American and Japanese achievement: Is the United States really a lower achiever, in *Educational Researcher*, 21 (5), 18-24.

I am grateful to Corinna Ethington of the Memphis State University and Karen Gold of ETS for reading an earlier version of this chapter and suggesting that the line

The second example is from the 1992 *President's Budget*:

> Results from the Second International Mathematics Study, which obtained achievement test results from eighth graders in 20 countries and from students in their final year of high school in 15 countries, showed that U.S. students performed poorly in every grade and every aspect of mathematics tested.

Such reiteration of the findings of IEA studies, and recently the SIMS findings in particular, in the context of the decade-long public debate about the quality of American public education, has played a central role in creating and justifying widespread discouragement about the schools (Lerner, 1982, 1991). And, invariably, the discussions have linked the "fact" of low comparative mathematics achievement in the United States to global economic competition and the apparent problems of American industry, research and development, and the fitness of the nation to meet the needs and opportunities of the 21st century. Such arguments have provided part, if not all, of the overt rationale for what is now a decade-long movement for school reform, improved teacher education, and national testing.

In a different but related way the SIMS findings about various countries' achievement in school mathematics have been used to make a case for the cultural and economic prowess and potential of Asian countries and societies. In such arguments school achievement becomes another manifestation of Japanese, and to a lesser extent Asian, *exceptionality* as economic and cultural systems. One outcome of this has been the emergence of a veritable research industry seeking to describe and explain this exceptionality (see, for

of analysis seemed profitable. Walter Doyle and Stephen Willoughby of the University of Arizona, Reba Page of the University of California, Riverside, Jürgen Baumert of the Institut für die Pädagogik der Naturwissenschaften at the University of Kiel, Germany, and Peter Roeder and Kai Schnabel of the Max-Planck-Institut für Bildungsforschung, Berlin, provided invaluable opportunities to voice the argument made here at seminars they hosted at their institutions. Peter L. Glidden of the University of Illinois at Urbana-Champaign, Lauren K. Sosniak of Washington University of St. Louis, and Kenneth J. Travers of the University of Illinois at Urbana-Champaign and the National Science Foundation read earlier versions of this chapter and their comments helped me see what the argument was.

The analyses of the SIMS data presented in this chapter depended heavily on the public-access SIMS database developed as part of the University of Illinois at Urbana-Champaign *SIMS Database Enhancement Project*. This project was supported by a grant from the National Science Foundation, NSF SPA 87-51425, Ian Westbury and Kenneth J. Travers, coprincipal investigators. The analyses reported in the first part of this chapter were made possible by support provided by the Research Board of the University of Illinois at Urbana-Champaign. Needless to say, I am grateful to these agencies, who would not necessarily endorse the conclusions or interpretations presented here.

example, DES, 1988; Lynn, 1988; Stigler & Stevenson, 1991; White, 1987).

SIMS is important in all such arguments because it, along with other recent IEA studies, is one of the few large-scale assessment studies based on national samples that compare achievement cross-culturally, and SIMS *did* seem to find (and so confirm) a gap between U.S. and Japanese achievement. Figure 4.1 presents one version of the SIMS findings (Crosswhite, Dossey, Swafford,

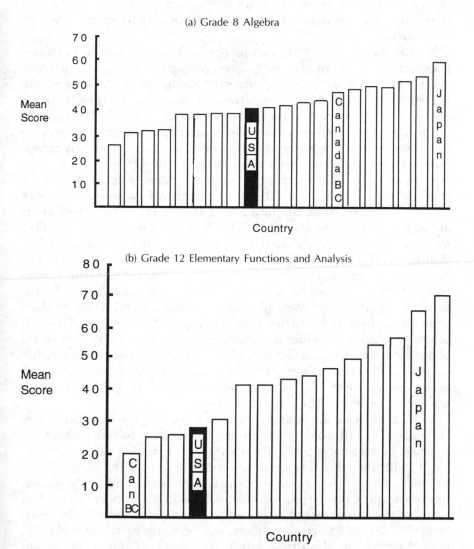

FIGURE 4.1   U.S. Mathematics Achievement in International Context

(Adapted from Crosswhite, et al., 1986, p. 167, p. 362. Used with permission of The Board of Trustees of the University of Illinois.)

McKnight, Cooney, Downs, Grouws, & Weinzweig, 1986), and it is presentations like this one that lie behind the kinds of concerns that I have been describing. While the interpretation that is implicit in such presentations of the results of SIMS has been contested by some (e.g., Rotberg, 1990), the critical dissenting voices have been few, with the consequences that I have been sketching—that in recent years few studies within educational research have been given the role that SIMS has had in public and professional discussion—in terms of both the significance of the findings that they have yielded and the public policy implications that have flowed from them.

In this chapter I want to review the findings of SIMS at both the Population A and Population B levels as they bear on two different issues. First, I want to re-examine the comparative ranking of the United States and Japan to argue that no easily sustainable case exists in the study's data for an achievement gap with the implications that have been so much talked about. My argument will be based on some methodological considerations central to any cross-national comparisons and a reanalysis of the U.S. and Japanese data in the light of these considerations. I have selected Japan for this analysis because it is the achievement of Japanese students that has seemed to lie at the core of the much of the discussion about U.S. achievement. Second, I will address what is to my mind the most problematic issue that has emerged from SIMS, but one that has received virtually no attention in the public discussion of the study—the relatively small proportion of the U.S. age cohort who complete the sequence of courses in the high school that make up the mathematics program. In that discussion I will draw on data from the full set of countries that participated in the Population B study to argue that while there may be no reason to be concerned about how well the schools teach and students learn their mathematics in American schools, there *are* serious questions to be asked about the numbers of students who drop out of the U.S. mathematics sequence *before* the Grade 12 year.

In both of these arguments I will be stressing the significance of the neglected but analytically necessary variable of curriculum. In the case of my analysis of U.S. and Japanese mathematics achievement I will show that *when curriculum differences are factored into an analysis*, the performance of the U.S. teachers and students can be seen as quite comparable to that of Japan. The implication is that many of the inferences about, on the one hand, the inefficiency or lack of quality of American schools, teachers and instructional practices fade as, on the other hand, do claims of Japanese exceptionality, at least insofar as this can be inferred from school achievement in the content areas I will be examining, algebra at the Population A level and elementary functions and analysis (calculus) at the Population B level. In my analysis of what I will term *retentivity* I will emphasize the place of the curriculum in creating a pattern of *distribution of mathematics learning* in the United States that is, to put the best light on it, disturbing.

UNITED STATES AND JAPANESE ACHIEVEMENT IN SCHOOL MATHEMATICS

Before developing my arguments about U.S. and Japanese achievement, I will review the database I will be drawing on for the analysis I will report by recapitulating very briefly the description of SIMS offered in the Introduction. I will emphasize here only the details of the U.S. and Japanese studies.

Both the U.S. and Japan SIMS studies were based on representative national samples of schools and classes at two grade levels: Population A, consisting of students in the grade in each country at which the modal age was 13 years, or (the design option selected by Japan) the grade in which the curriculum being covered most closely matched the curriculum implicit in the SIMS test instruments; Population B, students in the terminal grade of the school system who were taking the most advanced mathematics courses routinely offered within the secondary school system. In the case of the Population A study, the grades selected for testing were Grade 8 in the U.S. (mean age: 169 months) and Grade 7 in Japan (mean age: 163 months). Both countries' studies were longitudinal at the Population A level. Table 4.1 presents the national population definitions for the two countries at both the Population A and Population B levels.[1]

---

[1] It must be noted that in the case of the Population A study, the Japanese national committee made some significant modifications of the internationally recommended design. For reasons associated with the timing of the Japanese study and the schedule for developing the instruments, the Japanese Population A study did not use the standard SIMS longitudinal test forms but, instead, the cross-sectional instruments for end-of-year testing and a specially developed test made up from 60 items from the cross-sectional SIMS pool for the beginning-of-year testing. This Japanese posttest contained 40 items classified within the study as *algebra* whereas the U.S. posttest contained 32 algebra items; 30 items were common to both posttests. The Japan pretest contained 14 algebra items whereas the U.S. pretest forms contained 32 algebra items. For the analysis of achievement to be reported here only the items common to both studies were used: The posttest analysis is based on the 30 *algebra* items included in both studies; The pretest and growth analyses are based on the 13 items common to both countries studied. It should be noted, however, that the profile of results does not change significantly as different item sets are analyzed.

TABLE 4.1
United States and Japan: National Population Definitions

Population A

United States: All students in Grade 8 in mainstream public and private schools. For the majority of students this is the second year of secondary school.

Japan: Students in Grade 7, the first year of lower secondary school, in public schools and national schools. Students in private schools and special schools for the handicapped were not included (i.e. under 5 percent of the age cohort).

Population B

United States: Students in mainstream public and private secondary schools who are enrolled in a mathematics course having as its prerequisite the standard sequence of mathematics courses: *Algebra I, Geometry,* and *Algebra II.*

Japan: Students in Grade 12 of full-time upper secondary schools, public, national and private, who are studying mathematics as a substantial part (more than five hours per week) of the general course or the science–mathematics course.

The Analysis: Rationale

The 1974 *Standards for Educational and Psychological Tests* of the American Psychological Association (American Psychological Association, 1974, p. 25) defines the psychometrically fundamental concept of *validity* in terms of "the appropriateness of the inferences from test scores or other forms of assessment." As Madaus (1983, p. 34) notes, "The 1974 committee saw various methods of validation, but all of them required a definition of what was to be inferred from the scores and data to show that there was an acceptable basis for such inferences." In the case of the SIMS data as conventionally interpreted, the basis of such inference is what is in effect a consensual international definition of Grade 8 and Grade 12 "mathematics" operationalized in terms of an item pool that represented an international consensus on what students at these grade levels might be expected to know; the actual performance of students on the SIMS tests is then used to evaluate accomplishment vis-à-vis this highly abstracted criterion. We need to note that this structure of inference does not ask whether or not students in one or another country were taught the material on the SIMS test battery (that is, it does not examine the overlap of the SIMS test with what was taught as a basis for an argument that links what was actually taught and what was learned in the schools of a given country; Leinhart, 1983).

This structure of inference may be appropriate for some purposes, but we must also recognize that it is a truism of educational evaluation that students know what they have been taught, do not know what they have not been taught, and tend to know what they know in direct relationship to the amount of time spent teaching it. It is (perhaps) useful under some circumstances to ignore this truism—as is the case in Figure 4.1. However, for most purposes the more important question is not whether students have learned some abstracted (and arguable) body of internationally consensual content but, rather, how well they have been taught (or how well they have learned) the material included in their curriculum—whether that be the specific *intended* curriculum of a country or the actual *implemented* curriculum of a country's classrooms. I believe that it is how well students are taught and how well they learn in the actual curriculum of U.S. schools that lies behind the contemporary concern about the quality, or efficiency, of the American school and teacher force, behind concerns about the quality of American culture as it effects children and youth, and behind claims of Japanese educational exceptionality. When all is said and done, we have to assume that the claim of those who have drawn on the SIMS finding to criticize the quality of American schooling is that the achievement findings of SIMS and similar surveys reveal major problems or accomplishments in the efficiency and effectiveness in American schooling vis-à-vis Japanese (and other) schools.

We can see the significance of this issue of curricular validity for assessing the U.S. findings from SIMS by noting the differences between the curricula in algebra of the four course types offered to U.S. eighth graders and the single Grade 7 course taught in Japan. Figure 4.2 presents a profile of teacher reports of the time devoted to the coverage of topics from the international generalized Population A curriculum by teachers in these courses. There is a substantial difference between the U.S. course types in the emphasis given algebra. It is only the U.S. algebra course type that has a profile similar to Japan's course. The same kind of difference in the content of the curricula is also seen at the Population B level (see Table 4.2); while the Japanese course (like most Population B courses internationally) is heavily focused on the calculus, most American students take a course that does not give significant attention to the calculus. In the following discussion I will pick up the implications of these differences in the curricula of Japan and the United States for the assessment of American students' achievement in the SIMS content domains of Population A algebra and Population B elementary functions and analysis.

Results: Population A Algebra

Posttest Cumulative Learning.   As I have already indicated, SIMS identified four Grade 8 curricula/course types in the United States as compared to the one curriculum/course prescribed for Japan's Grade 7 classes. Table 4.3 presents the number of classes offering each of these curricula in the U.S. sample as well as present-

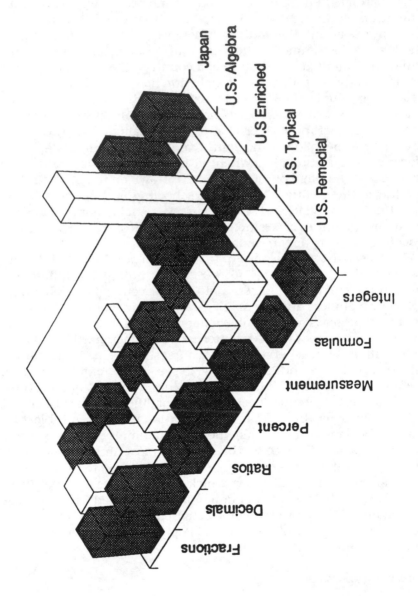

FIGURE 4.2 United States (Course types) and Japan: Time Spent on Math Topics: Periods in Grade 7/8 Year

TABLE 4.2
Coverage of *Elementary Functions and Analysis* (Calculus)
at Grade 12 Levels

	N	Mean Coverage of Calculus Items in SIMS Item Pool[1]
United States		
Precalculus classes	199	44%
Calculus classes	57	83%
All classes	256	51%
Japan	256	89%

[1]The SIMS Population B item pool contained 46 calculus items.

TABLE 4.3
Number and Percentage of Classes in Grade 8
Course Types in U.S. Sample

Course Type	N	Percent of Sample	Coverage %
Remedial	30	10.9	37
Typical	174	63.9	64
Enriched	31	11.3	78
Algebra	38	10.9	88
All Classes	273	100.0	66

ing the mean number of items in the SIMS algebra content domain which the teachers of these different course types identified as being covered by their classes.

Given such differences in the patterns of coverage of the SIMS algebra domain in these Grade 8 course types, what happens when U.S. achievement is disaggregated by course type? Figure 4.3 and Table 4.4 presents such a disaggregation for class-level posttest (end-of-year) scores extended to include the parallel posttest achievement for Japan—and shows a striking pattern. The mean posttest achievement for algebra of enriched and algebra classes is broadly similar to that of Japan. It is the remedial and the large number of typical classes where algebra receives relatively less or little attention that achieve at a much lower level. There is, however, one obvious objection to this interim conclusion. The students enrolling in U.S. algebra and enriched classes are a selected group within the U.S. eighth grade cohort. On the other hand the analysis I reported above draws on the total Japanese sample. Any finding of similarity of outcomes is, therefore, entangled with an aptitude effect. In order to

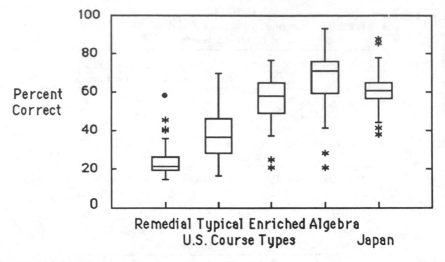

FIGURE 4.3   United States and Japan: Posttest Achievement in Population A Algebra
(*Note*. In boxplots like those found in Figures 4.3, 4.4, and 4.5, the length of the box, the rectangle bounded by the "hinges," represents the proportion of the distribution which falls between the 25th and 75th percentiles. The line across the box represents the median. The length of the "whiskers" represents the min and the max or the adjacent outermost value,

$$1.5 \times (\text{pctile}_{75} - \text{pctile}_{25}),$$

if this is less than the min and the max. The * and the • represent extreme values.

disentangle aptitude and curriculum coverage as possible sources of achievement a subgroup of classes in the top quintile of achievement on the Japan pretest (all items; $N = 60$) was pulled from the sample and the posttest achievement of this group compared to that of U.S. enriched and algebra classes. Table 4.5 presents the results of this analysis. It is clear that this analysis does not change the

TABLE 4.4
End-of-Year Achievement in Algebra in Population A Year,
United States and Japan

	N	Mean p-value	S.D.	Min	Max
United States					
Remedial classes	30	25	10	14	58
Typical classes	179	38	12	17	69
Enriched classes	33	56	13	20	76
Algebra classes	38	67	15	20	93
All classes	280	42	17	14	93
Japan	211	60	7	37	87

TABLE 4.5
Algebra Posttest Achievement: Students in U.S.
Grade 8 *Algebra* and *Enriched* Classes and Top
Quintile of Japanese Classes

	N	Mean p-value	S.D.
United States			
Algebra classes	38	67	16
Enriched classes	33	56	13
Japan	42	68	6

standing of the U.S. algebra and Japanese classes. It seems then that the lower overall achievement profile of the U.S. Population A sample when compared to the profile for Japan is overwhelmingly an outcome of major differences between the curricula of the two countries. When curricula in the two countries are similar, there is essentially no difference in the performance of U.S. and Japanese students and, by implication, of both the school system and teachers, at the Population A level. We can also note that there is nothing in these findings that requires us to invoke either instructional or cultural variables unique to Japan to understand Japanese achievement.

Growth.   As Wolfe (1989) notes, posttest scores represent *cumulative learning* prior to a point of testing and do not measure the effects of any specific instruction in, say, a class or a national grade level. Gain (growth) scores, on the other hand, permit an assessment of the quality and/or efficiency of instruction as this is represented in the "learning" that takes place between a pre- and posttest.

Figure 4.4 and Table 4.6 present raw gain scores (posttest minus pretest) by U.S. course type and the parallel gain score for Japan. (Because of the differences between the item pools for the two countries' tests, the 13 algebra items on the Japan pretest were used to develop pretest scores for the two systems; posttest scores were derived from the items which were common to both countries.) The results suggest that in the Population A year at least significant learning takes place only in Japan—although there are what might be interpreted as curriculum-related differences in learning in the U.S. Grade 8 year when algebra and enriched classes are compared to remedial and typical classes.

It would appear, therefore, that one cross-national finding that is not readily predictable given the marked curricular differences be-

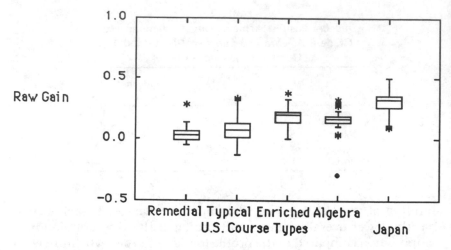

FIGURE 4.4   United States and Japan: Raw Gain (Posttest minus Pretest) in the Grade 7/8 Year.

tween U.S. Grade 8 mathematics classrooms and those of Japan's Grade 7 classes is the clear gain in algebra knowledge ("learning") seen among Japanese students. However, we can ask if this is also a likely outcome of curricular differences between Japan and the United States Grade 8 algebra students, for example, are typically enrolled in a pre-algebra class in Grade 7 and might be expected to have covered some algebra in the Grade 7 year. This is not the case with Japan's Grade 6 elementary school curriculum. This possibility is significant because it is a consistent finding within SIMS that the greatest "learning" takes place on newly learned material (Muthén, Chapter 11). The significant growth in Japan when compared to the United States seen in Figure 4.4 might then be an artifact of a

TABLE 4.6
Growth in *Algebra* Knowledge During Population A Year

	N	Mean Growth	S.D.
United States			
Remedial classes	25	4	7
Typical classes	144	8	9
Enriched classes	27	18	8
Algebra classes	29	16	11
Japan	211	31	7

curricular difference of this kind. This possibility cannot be addressed as directly as we might like because of the limitations of the SIMS data but two tentative approaches to it are available.

In the course of the SIMS data collection teachers completed an opportunity to learn (OTL) questionnaire in which they were asked to indicate whether or not the content underlying each item on the SIMS end-of-year cognitive instrument being completed by their students had been taught to their classes, and when—"this year" or "before this year." Table 4.7 presents the results of an analysis of the responses of U.S. and Japanese teachers to the OTL questions. The responses suggest that while there are major differences between U.S. course types, there is only a slight difference in the curricular structure of Japan's Grade 7 classes and U.S. Grade 8 algebra classes. In both cases the bulk of the algebra items are reported to be covered in the Population A grade. There does seem, on the basis of these representations of the curriculum, to be a case for Japanese exceptionality vis-à-vis the United States when it comes to the kind of efficiency in instruction that results in effective learning.

However, we also need to consider such findings in the light of pretest achievement. Although U.S. algebra teachers claimed that little or no algebra content had been covered prior to the Grade 8 target grade, the beginning-of-year pretest scores of U.S. algebra students suggest that they had learned much more algebra in Grade 7 than had Japan's Grade 6 students (see Figure 4.5 and Table 4.8). If we can take pretest achievement as a robust proxy for both the extent and the period of coverage of algebra prior to the Population A year in the two countries, Figure 4.5 suggests a different picture of the U.S. curriculum than that indicated by the U.S. teacher responses to the OTL questionnaire (see also Flanders, Chapter 2). In

TABLE 4.7
Coverage of Items in SIMS Population A *Algebra*

| | Mean Number of Items Covered[1] | |
	Before Pop A Year	In Pop A Year
Japan	1	23
United States		
Remedial classes	0	11
Typical classes	.5	20
Enriched classes	.5	25
Algebra classes	2.5	26

[1]The Japanese item pool in *Algebra* contained 40 items. The U.S. item pool in *Algebra* contained 32 items.

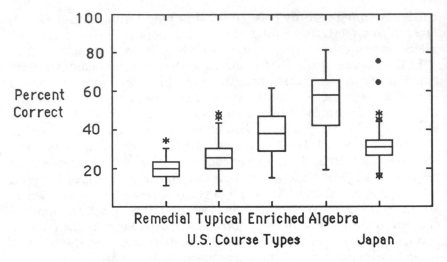

FIGURE 4.5 United States and Japan: Pretest Achievement in Grade 7/8 Algebra

other words, the hypothesis remains open that Japan's growth is indeed an artifact of the Japanese curriculum, not a result of more effective instructional practices or contextual factors in Japanese society or culture. At best we can say that the case that the Japanese superiority as seen in Grade 7 growth scores is an artifact of a different curriculum is not proven—and remains open as a distinct and plausible possibility.

Results: Elementary Functions and Analysis

As I have already noted, the Grade 12 curriculum in the United States is very different from the curriculum of most other countries. In the years before World War I an academic mathematics curricu-

TABLE 4.8
Pretest Achievement on Common Items ($N = 13$)
in Population A *Algebra*

	N	N Missing	Mean p-value	SD
United States				
Remedial classes	25	5	20	5
Typical classes	144	35	28	7
Enriched classes	27	6	39	10
Algebra classes	29	9	55	13
Japan	211	2	31	6

lum that culminated with the calculus emerged in Europe; by the 1930s, this had become the standard curriculum for most upper secondary mathematics education in most countries. However, this early 20th-century reform of the mathematics curriculum was not picked up in the United States in this prewar period despite the earnest efforts of its many American advocates. Indeed, the idea that the calculus might even be a part of the high school curriculum did not become a possibility in the United States until the 1950s and, even then, the dominating reform aspiration for the curriculum centered on the notion that a precalculus course might be the culminating experience in the high school for college-bound science and engineering students—with the implication that the calculus might be then routinely taught to college freshman. It was only in the 1960s and 1970s that calculus began to be taught in some American schools as an advanced elective.

When the SIMS surveys were undertaken in the early 1980s only 20 percent of the U.S. Population B cohort was taking a calculus course. As a result, it must be concluded that calculus component of the SIMS test battery (46 out of 136 items in the pool) was quite inappropriate for at least 80 percent of the classes in the SIMS U.S. sample (see Table 4.2). In the light of this context, it seems reasonable to conclude that the only issue of real interest is the achievement of American calculus classes when compared to other countries.

My goal in this section of this chapter is to undertake a comparison of Japanese Population B class-level posttest achievement and the achievement of U.S. calculus classes with the goal, again, of focusing on the consequences of opportunity to learn (that is, the curriculum) as a determinant of American achievement. As in my analysis of the Population A data, the question I will be addressing is the role of different curriculum in producing different patterns of achievement and the implications of an answer to that question for claims, on the one hand, of profound inefficiencies in the American educational system and, on the other hand, of Japanese exceptionality at the Population B level.

Table 4.9 and Figure 4.6 present the results of an analysis of the aggregated class-level achievement of American precalculus and calculus classes along with Japanese Population B classes in the SIMS elementary functions and analysis content domain. The expected lack of match between the curriculum of the precalculus classes and the 46 calculus items in the SIMS test pool is obvious in these findings. We do see, however, a narrowing of the gap between the achievement of U.S. calculus classes and Population B classes in Japan—although there is still a significant overall difference in

TABLE 4.9
United States and Japan: Posttest Achievement
in *Elementary Functions and Analysis*

	N	Mean *p*-value	S.D.
United States			
Precalculus classes	195	24	10
Calculus classes	57	48	14
All classes	252	29	15
Japan	207	69	20

achievement (21 percentage points over the domain) between classes in the two systems. But we also need to note that, as seen in Table 4.10, this gap in achievement varies across topical areas within elementary functions and analysis becoming, for example, narrower in the SIMS subdomain of differentiation (5 percentage points) and wider in the subdomains of limits and continuity (28 percentage points) and applications of integration (30 percentage points).

To what extent can these differences in performance be attributed to curriculum? Let us consider, first, the overall differences between both the *extent* of coverage and the *period* of coverage of the content underlying the SIMS items in Japanese and U.S. classes. Table 4.11 presents the results of an analysis of the period of coverage of items

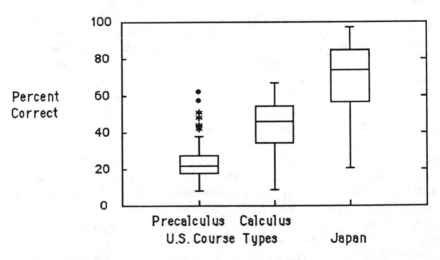

FIGURE 4.6   United States and Japan: Posttest Achievement in Grade 12 Elementary Functions and Analysis

TABLE 4.10

Population B Achievement (% correct) in Subtopics within SIMS
Elementary Functions and Analysis **Content Domain**

Subdomain	N	Japan	U.S. (*Calculus Classes*)
Elementary Functions	4	73	49
Properties of Functions	4	87	71
Limits and Continuity	4	65	37
Differentiation	4	68	63
Applications of the Derivative	10	63	41
Integration	6	66	50
Techniques of Integration	2	69	50
Applications of Integration	5	64	34
All items	43	69	48

in the calculus domain as these were reported by teachers on the OTL questionnaire as well as the findings on the total number of items being reported as covered "prior to" or "in" the Population B year. Both U.S. and Japanese teachers reported similar levels of overall coverage on the items, but in the case of the United States 35 items (of the 38 covered) were taught in the Grade 12 year whereas in the case of Japan only 18 (of 40 covered) were taught in Japan's Grade 12 year and 24 items were taught prior to the Grade 12 year. In other words, the U.S. teachers reported that they attempted to cover the whole domain in the Grade 12 year and their responses to the OTL questionnaire suggest that they give a more or less even-handed emphasis to every subdomain within the calculus content area (see Table 4.12). This finding suggests that instruction in U.S. Grade 12 calculus classrooms (at least insofar as the curriculum implicit in the SIMS calculus items is concerned) is structured very differently to that of Japan and moves much faster over this subject matter than does the Japanese curriculum.

TABLE 4.11

Japan and United States (*Calculus classes*): Coverage of Items (*N* = 46)
in SIMS *Elementary Functions and Analysis* Content Domain

	Mean Number of Items Covered		
	Total	Before Grade 12	In Grade 12
Japan	41	24	18
United States *Calculus* classes	38	4	34

TABLE 4.12

Coverage of Subtopics within *Elementary Functions and Analysis* Content Domain, United States (*Calculus* classes) and Japan

Topic	N Items	Total Coverage		Coverage Prior to Grade 12 year		Coverage in Grade 12 year	
		Japan	U.S.	Japan	U.S.	Japan	U.S.
Elementary Functions	11	10.1	9.4	8.3	2.5	2.1	6.4
Properties of Functions	4	3.8	3.9	3.4	1.0	1.3	2.9
Limits and Continuity	4	3.7	3.5	1.2	0.0	2.8	3.1
Differentiation	4	3.5	3.4	0.6	0.1	3.3	3.7
Application of the Derivative	10	9.1	8.0	4.6	0.0	4.9	8.5
Integration	6	5.1	5.2	1.8	0.0	3.8	5.9
Techiques of Integration	2	1.7	1.5	0.7	0.0	1.3	1.8
Applications of Integration	5	3.8	3.5	3.2	0.0	2.2	4.0
All items	46	40.7	38.4	23.8	4.3	17.9	34.7

Such findings offer a way of understanding the range of differences in achievement across subdomains between the two countries' Grade 12 students. Differences in the rate of coverage can be presumed to interact with the difficulty of the topics within the domain. American students learn well, and American teachers teach well (to the extent that "well" is seen in terms of Japan's performance) that content that can be appropriately taught and learned in the first phase of instruction in the calculus (for example, differentiation). When more time for mastery is required than that available in a packed year (for example, for mastery of integration), they do less well. Japan's students master such "more difficult" material because they have more time for their learning—as a result of the ways in which their curriculum is structured.

Implications of the Argument So Far

The analysis I have presented suggests that the overall difference between Japanese and U.S. achievement is a predictable consequence of different curricula. When U.S. teachers teach a curriculum that parallels that of Japan, U.S. achievement converges with, and in the case of the U.S. Grade 8 algebra classes matches, that of Japan. In other words, the SIMS findings from Japan and the U.S. as I have interpreted them here offer no basis for claims of any superiority/inferiority of Japanese mathematics instruction vis-à-vis U.S. mathematics instruction. What we do see are major differences in the curricula of the two countries' schools, differences which result in readily interpretable and predictable differences in both aggregate achievement and "learning."

There is a set of larger questions circling around this observation—and around comparative research projects like SIMS—that becomes important as we think not only about the specific findings of the study but also about the kind of study SIMS represents. What are such comparative studies seeking to do, and, in particular, what meaning does a claim of "high" or "low" achievement, etc., of one country or school system versus another have? Are such claims ever "useful" in the context of research as policy analysis?

As Przeworski and Teune (1970) observe, from the viewpoint of the comparativist, "country" is a name for a social and cultural system which conceals as much as it reveals; in their words,

> The goal of comparative research is to substitute *names of variables* for the *names of social systems* such as Ghana, the United States, Africa, or Asia. . . . When medical scholars discovered that the rate of heart attacks is lower in Japan than in the United States, they . . .

replaced the names of social systems? [i.e., "Japan"] by a variable, arguing that the incidence of such attacks depends on the consumption of polysaturated fats. (pp. 8–9, emphasis added)

As comparativists have pursued the implications of the project Przeworski and Teune (1970) outline they have developed and formalized both the implicit logics of cross-national or cross-regional comparison and a sense of what a comparative project should, might, or can yield. Thus, Castles (1988) writes in the context of a comparative analysis of public policy making that:

In seeking to locate the nature of national distinctiveness, there is a temptation to make a premature shift to a level of specificity at which differences are inherently more salient than possible similarities with other nations. In terms of the logic of comparative analysis, such an analytical move is always illegitimate unless it is preceded by an attempt to exhaust the explanatory potential of higher order similarities between group of nations. *It is always necessary to examine the possibility that the phenomena we observe are the consequences of features that nations have in common before attributing them to national singularities.* (p. 38, emphasis added)

Indeed, for Castles (1989) "country" as a variable in an comparative argument is only salient as one thinks about the puzzles of "cases" that are, to use his term, "underdetermined" by the findings of a cross-national, comparative analysis of the kind discussed by Przeworski and Teune (1970) and Castles (1988).

In the light of such models for cross-national studies, it is paradoxical as one considers the standard interpretation of SIMS that it is the IEA studies which have shown the fundamental salience of the higher order variable curriculum (defined in terms of the opportunity to learn a set of topics) for levels of achievement when seen cross-nationally (see, for example, Comber & Keeves, 1973; Kifer, 1989; Postlethwaite, 1975). Moreover, studies undertaken within the United States have reinforced the insights that emerged initially from the IEA studies to argue that it is the distribution of curriculum coverage within and between schools, classes and students that is the principal direct determinant of achievement. Coverage is the variable that mediates the effects of such contextual variables as social class, gender, ethnicity, school expenditure levels, teacher qualifications and experience, and the like on school achievement (Barr & Dreeben, 1983; Bidwell & Kasarda, 1980; Gamoran, 1987). The curriculum is, from this perspective, the core component of the structured process of schooling, and it is schooling and the ways in which it is distributed between students that actually produces the effects of schools.

> The effects of schooling are produced by students' instructional experiences. These experiences are constrained by the framework within which schooling occurs, but they are highly varied within schools and even within tracks. . . . For example, some authors have argued that at least part of the reason for manifest sex and ethnic differences in high school mathematics achievement is that females and Hispanics enroll in fewer academic mathematics courses. . . . Tracking and course-taking together account for substantively significant differences in school achievement. (Gamoran, 1987, pp. 137–138, 153; emphasis added)

Unfortunately the approach to the analysis and interpretation of the SIMS data that is implicit in such prescriptions and explicit in analyses of sociologists and political economists who work within cross-national contexts has not, to this point, been part of the widely cited U.S. analyses of the SIMS data (e.g., McKnight, Crosswhite, Dossey, Kifer, Swafford, Travers, & Cooney, 1987) or of the popular discussion of the meaning of the SIMS findings for American schooling. Instead, the dominant analytic and explanatory approach has been the one that Castles (1989) has castigated as "inappropriate" and "illegitimate." The result has been interpretations of the results of the study that focus on national singularities and not on features of school systems that are common across all countries and which may be deployed in different ways. Thus, we have seen a single-minded focus in the discussions of the SIMS study of the "singularity" of either the low U.S. global achievement or high Japanese overall achievement that the study seemed to reveal—and in each case there has been an immediate move to invoke potential country-specific factors to explain this finding. The analysis that I have presented here suggests that there is little or nothing to explain about the comparative achievement in mathematics of the U.S. and Japanese school systems beyond the differences each country has institutionalized in the scope of their curriculum coverages. From this curriculum-centered point of view the differences in achievement between Japan and the U.S. which have occasioned so much interest are simply the inevitable by-products of the historically embedded decisions which each of these countries have made about what schools should teach to what groups.

RETENTIVITY

My analysis of the U.S. and Japanese mathematics achievement data suggests an optimistic story about the performance of the U.S. school system. In this section I want to explore a different aspect of the outcomes of U.S. mathematics instruction—one that is less encouraging! I will be considering the *retentivity* of students in both the U.S. and other countries' mathematics teaching "systems." The form of the analysis I will offer reflects Castles's (1989) concern for the anomalies and puzzles which emerge from comparative analysis. However, while I will be exploring one such puzzle, I will continue to invoke the logic of analysis that Castles urges on comparativists by seeking to bring a seeming singularity within a structure that subsumes cases within a framework of higher order variables. The discussion centers on the numbers of students (the proportion of the age cohort) that enroll in mathematics classes in the last year of secondary school—with the focus being on the comparatively small proportion of the age cohort (given the character of the curriculum) found in U.S. Grade 12 classes.

Table 4.13 reports the basic data, and the issue, I will be concerned with. The table shows that while the proportion of the age cohort enrolling in U.S. Grade 12 mathematics classes (both calculus and noncalculus classes) is modal when seen in international perspective, the proportion of the grade cohort (all students in a national Grade 12 or equivalent class) is smaller than that found in many other countries (most of which enroll a smaller proportion of their age cohorts than does the U.S. in full-time education and training). At the same time, however, U.S. Grade 12 curricula are less demanding in the scope and intensity of their coverage of advanced school mathematics than are the curricula of most, but not all, SIMS systems. The consequence is that we can classify the U.S. as a low coverage/low retentivity system (see Table 4.14).

What are the consequences for the "standing" (or more precisely the "yield") of the U.S. mathematics education "system?" Looked at from the point of view of coverage and aggregate achievement on the SIMS Population B cognitive test, the U.S. system resembles school systems like Hungary, the Canadian provinces of British Columbia and Ontario, and Scotland, which also combine relatively low coverage of the curriculum embedded in the SIMS Population B item pool with the predictable low levels of achievement. But in contrast to those systems in which a less demanding curriculum is associated with high levels of retentivity, the United States has a less demand-

TABLE 4.13
SIMS Population B: Retentivity in Advanced School Mathematics
as a Percentage of Age Cohort

Country	Pop B/age cohort	Students in education and training/age cohort
Belgium (Flemish and French)	10	60
British Columbia	30	82
England and Wales	6	56
Finland	15	59
Hong Kong	8	17
Hungary	50	50
Japan	12	92
New Zealand	11	43
Ontario	19	49
Scotland	18	57
Sweden	12	42
USA	13	82

Source: Travers and Westbury (1989): Table 3.7.1.

TABLE 4.14
The "Yields" of Mathematics Education in the SIMS Systems

	Retentivity	
High	14[1]	Low
Finland		Belgium (Flemish and French)
		England and Wales
		Japan
		New Zealand
		Sweden
Coverage (73)[2]		
British Columbia		Israel
Hungary		United States
Ontario		
Scotland		
Low		

[1]Mean retentivity in advanced mathematics.
[2]That is, mean coverage of the SIMS "curriculum"; percentage of total Population B item pool reported by teachers as taught.
Source: Travers and Westbury (1989): Table 6.3.2.

ing Population B curriculum than most countries and only modal retentivity in its most advanced school mathematics classes. In the trade-off between retentivity, coverage and achievement, the United States finds itself in what might be thought of as the worst of all possible worlds: coverage and achievement are not being "sacrificed" in favor of retentivity, or higher rates of enrollment in advanced mathematics, as seems to be the case with the other systems with Population B curricula like that of the United States; on the other hand (and conversely) the United States is not sacrificing retentivity on the altar of high levels of achievement and coverage. In other words, the United States seems not to be maximizing any of the benefits that might be associated with the tradeoffs found across the other SIMS systems between high retentivity or high achievement/coverage.

Is there a way of understanding this seemingly anomalous position of the United States? This is a question about the flows of students through the curriculum sequence in mathematics and was not a central issue investigated by SIMS. However, some studies undertaken within the SIMS framework do suggest some provocative and intriguing hypotheses that seem well worth further research.

The central question posed by Table 4.14 is: Why does Population B (advanced mathematics) retentivity differ among systems? This question is answered, in part, by both course-taking requirements and the cultural assumptions surrounding subjects in the curriculum. These two factors often offer the simplest explanation of the differences we see in Table 4.14. For example, in Hungary all terminal year students in academic secondary schools were required at the time of SIMS to take a course in advanced mathematics; thus, 100 percent of the grade cohort and 50 percent of the age cohort were enrolled in Population B. Within the pattern of the sometimes extreme differences created by such frames, retentivity tends to be an outcome of the size of the pool of students within the part of the school system that offers direct access to an academic mathematics program, and, particularly, by the number of women in that pool (Travers & Westbury, 1989). But there is also the factor of the curriculum. As the report of the Cockcroft Committee on the teaching of mathematics in England and Wales, *Mathematics Counts* (1982) notes:

> Very many pupils in secondary schools [in England and Wales] are being required to follow mathematics syllabuses whose content is too great and which are not suited to their level of attainment. Efforts to

introduce pupils to as much of the examination syllabus as possible result in attempts to cover the ground too fast for understanding to develop. The result is that very many pupils neither develop a confident approach to their use of mathematics nor achieve mastery of those parts of the syllabus which should be within their capacity. (pp. 132–133)

As *Mathematics Counts* goes on to observe, although the comprehensivization of English secondary schools in the 1960s and 1970s increased the number of students being exposed to mathematics (as distinct from arithmetic) in the early secondary grades, there were no concomitant changes in the scope of the "academic" syllabuses that these many "new" students in secondary schools were required to cover, the result of a straight transfer of the traditional elite-preparatory grammar school curricula into the new mass-terminal comprehensive school. These curricula had been developed 40 or more years earlier on very different assumptions about the aptitudes of those who might (and should) be studying mathematics in the school. We can speculate that one consequence of this restrictive internal "frame" around school mathematics has been the preservation of the sociocultural characteristics of advanced school mathematics in English schools across these 40 years. It seems likely that this is indeed the case (Travers & Westbury, 1989).

Can we generalize the hypothesis being offered by the Cockcroft Report? Might the curriculum variable of pace, which *Mathematics Counts* identifies, account for at least some of the characteristics of flows through mathematics programs, and thus the retentivity and yield, of systems in general? As we have seen, it is the curriculum that instantiates on a day-to-day basis many of the structures, and much of the culture, of the larger milieus that surround and penetrate the schools. And there is a significant body of research suggesting that pace is indeed a critical variable determining success in school learning.

For the study I am reporting, SIMS National Committees were asked to indicate in which grade in their country's (intended) curriculum the content underlying each of the 39 items in a test-like instrument was taught.[2] The items on the instrument covered the

---

[2] I need to emphasize that this argument and the data on which it is based must be seen at this point as suggestive rather than definitive. The responses of countries to the questionnaire that was used to map the overall structuring of the curricula reflect the *intended* rather than *implemented curriculum*: Throughout the SIMS analyses, it has been emphasized that the implemented does not always mirror the intended curriculum. Likewise, the sample of the

scope of upper elementary and secondary mathematics through Population B (Hirstein, 1980). Figure 4.7 presents the findings for *high-coverage countries* (defined in terms of the proportion of the SIMS Population B item pool that teachers reported covering in their responses to the OTL questionnaire). The shaded columns in the histograms report the number of items in the set indicated as taught in each of the indicated grades and the white columns report the mean coverage in each grade for all high-coverage countries. The histograms are ordered in terms of retentivity.

We can interpret the shaded columns in Figure 4.7 as a reflection of the pace of the curriculum in the various grades of each country's curriculum. The height of each column represents the *absolute pace* (that is, the number of items to be covered) in each grade while the relative difference in the height of each adjacent column defines disjunctions in pace across years. The white columns offer a basis for a comparison of the patterns between countries.

Let us begin with a discussion of the curricula of the high-coverage and achievement countries described in Figure 4.7. An inspection of the individual histograms suggests that lower retentivity within this set of countries is associated with:

1. *higher paced early years* in the overall mathematics program,
2. *disjunctions* (marked differences) in the rates of coverage, or pace, between years, disjunctions we may suspect are associated with critical decision points for students as they consider whether or not to persist with later course taking in mathematics.

Conversely, higher retentivity countries tend to:

1. *even out* their rates of coverage and pace over the curriculum sequence,
2. *delay* the introduction of substantial amounts of material until later in the sequence, and

---

curriculum represented in the questionnaire was necessarily very limited and may or may not be representative of any system's overall program. But these qualifications say no more than the reality that this investigation was a pilot study that has yielded some significant possibilities for further research which might be undertaken—research which requires, by its nature, a comparative perspective but which could have profound implications for the ways in which we think about the U.S. mathematics curriculum.

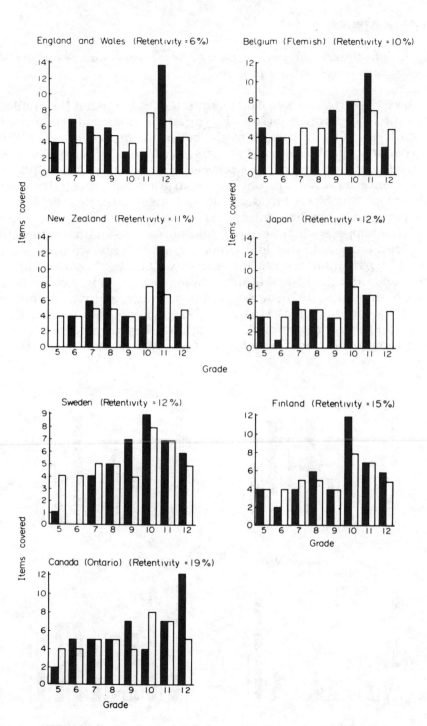

FIGURE 4.7 Population B High-Coverage Countries: Curriculum Pace

3. *minimize difference* in pace between years—at least in the early stages of the program.

Looking across the set of histograms it does seem that the profiles of content deployment across the years in a program is associated with levels of retentivity in mathematics in the last grade in the secondary school. And as I have suggested, the Cockcroft Report's suggestion of an interaction between pace, mastery, and student confidence does show a way in which a causal linkage between these, on their face, quite disparate notions of a curriculum profile and retentivity might come about.

What happens when we apply this approach to an analysis of the United States and other low-coverage areas? Figure 4.8 presents a set of curriculum profiles for British Columbia, Ontario, Israel, Scotland, and the United States. These places are more of a mixed bag than are the high-coverage regions, with retentivities ranging from six to 50 percent. Moreover, there is a significant difference between the upper pair of places, the United States and Israel, and the lower set, British Columbia, Ontario, and Scotland, with their

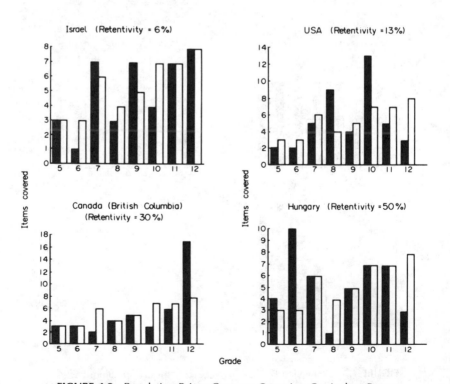

FIGURE 4.8   Population B Low-Coverage Countries: Curriculum Pace

(in context) very high retentivities. I will focus my discussion here on Ontario, British Columbia, and the United States as cases that should, on their face, be similar in both their school and larger cultures.

The profile of the British Columbia curriculum (Population B retentivity, 30 percent) suggests that the overall program has a flat, "undemanding" structure with few disjunctions in rates of coverage between grades before Grade 12. The Ontario curriculum (Population B retentivity, 19 percent) has a similarly flat structure except for the disjunction between the province's (elementary school) Grade 8 year—where half of the schools were typically taught by non-specialist teachers at the time of SIMS—and the (first high school and specialist-taught) Grade 9 year. There is, again, a marked increase in coverage occurring in the terminal year (Grade 13). In contrast, the U.S. curriculum (Population B retentivity, 13 percent) has several marked disjunctions in pace as well as more demanding absolute levels of coverage in several of the grades than is seen in either British Columbia or Ontario. The implication would be that in British Columbia and Ontario, with their slower paced, less spiked programs, the pressure on students as they move through the program is less than is the case in the United States. In particular, Canadian students do not experience the high-coverage, fast-paced introductions to algebra and geometry that are the hallmarks of the U.S. college-preparatory sequence. As we all know, it is the experience that students have with these courses which all too often determines who persists with mathematics in the United States.

What is important for our purposes in this study is the role of the curriculum that emerges—if not definitively, certainly suggestively. The form and character of a curriculum, and thus the frame that the curriculum becomes, would seem to be a significant determinant of retentivity across both high- and low-achievement countries. To the extent that retentivity is an important, and as I suggested under-emphasized, problem of the U.S. mathematics education "system" when seen in international context, this conclusion is a significant one. My next task is to consider what this central place that the curriculum has assumed in both of the analyses that I have reported here might mean.

CONCLUSION

This chapter considered two aspects of the "yield" of mathematics instruction in U.S. schools. In the first part, we considered the patterns of achievement that seem to emerge from the SIMS testing and, in particular, the commonly reported finding that U.S. achievement is, to use Stigler, Lee, and Stevenson's (1990, p. 1) word, "mediocre" when compared to that of many other countries, and particularly Japan. In the second part we considered "yield" in terms of retentivity, the proportion of the age cohort who persist with school mathematics through to the Grade 12 level. Here again the performance of the U.S. system might more accurately be regarded as mediocre; educational systems in Ontario, British Columbia, and Scotland, which also have the kind of low-coverage/low achievement mathematics program found in the United States, have many more students who persist with their learning of mathematics to the terminal year in secondary school than the United States does. And although the level of retentivity in the United States is similar to that of Japan, that country, along with most of the countries that participated in SIMS, asks its students to complete a program that is much more demanding than that of the United States—which results in higher levels of overall achievement.

In other words, the results of SIMS would seem, on their face, to amply support the notion that U.S. mathematics education is a low achiever. And inasmuch as Japan emerged within SIMS as a (if not the) higher achiever, the results of the study would also seem to provide still more evidence of Japan's prowess—not only as a designer, manufacturer, and seller of automobiles, but also as a social and cultural system. At least this is the conventional interpretation of the SIMS findings.

But, as Przeworski and Teune (1970) suggest, the words "country" or "nation," when they are components of an analytic discussion, tell us much less than they might seem to. These terms conceal and confound: (a) social and cultural "variables" that are common to all or most social systems, albeit that they may be differently distributed, and (b) "variables" that individually in their patterning are unique to a single social system. Thus to say, as the SIMS findings seem to say, that global U.S. mathematics achievement is "mediocre" when compared to that of, say, Japan, does not tell us why or how the pattern of achievement found in the United States comes about. Nor does it give us any basis for the understanding that we need if we are to decide if the seeming problem suggested by a first inspection of the SIMS results is a real problem or a nonproblem—or what the problem might be. It does not give us a basis for the kind of analysis that is needed if an improving intervention is to be designed.

In other words, while the embedding of what seems to be overwhelmingly clear and firm findings about something so straightforward as "country" seems to offer a basis for firm understanding, that understanding is more often than not illusory. It conceals the difference between the predictable consequences of "universals," which are distributed in different ways in different places (for whatever reason) and so vary in their impact—and the truly local (national), social, or cultural forces. It is the task of comparative research to separate out the roles of "universals" and local forces in creating, for example, one or another pattern of school achievement. This is the task I have attempted in this chapter.

The first part of the chapter explored the low overall achievement of U.S. students on the SIMS tests. We found that:

- If we compare how much overall mathematics, as defined by the SIMS test, U.S. and Japanese students learn, when we ignore the curriculum, U.S. students do fall short. But such a finding does not say that the principal reason for this is the fact that most U.S. students are being tested over content they have not been taught (see also Flanders, Chapter 2).

- If we compare how much American and Japanese students learn when they take courses that contain approximately the same content (for instance, enriched (prealgebra) and algebra classes), U.S. achievement is similar to that of Japan.

My analysis directs attention to the ways in which the "international mathematics curriculum" represented in the SIMS test is deployed in the United States, and indicates clearly that it is the curriculum that is taught in the United States that determines the "mediocre" U.S. achievement. To the extent that it was achievement on that SIMS curriculum that was being evaluated by the study, U.S. Grade 8 and Grade 12 students were not "ready for the test." In the case of Grade 8, those students who were ready did as well as their peers in most other countries.

Achievement can be thought of as one dimension of the "yield" of a school (subject) system. The other critical dimension of yield is the way in which the system distributes opportunity to learn. In the second part of this chapter I reported some findings on the proportion of the age cohorts in the countries that participated in the SIMS Population B study who persist with mathematics until the end of the secondary school (the proportions of students that the systems retained in academic mathematics classes in the last year of school). We find that the United States, almost alone among the SIMS systems, combines low coverage and achievement with (comparatively) low retentivity. In searching for an understanding of why this might be the case, we again find the curriculum emerging as a key concept. The United States seems to have, when seen in comparative context, a fast-paced curriculum that makes considerable demands on its students. Looked at across the set of SIMS countries such curricula seem to be associated with tight "frames" around students' participation in the high-status mathematics sequence(s) and restrictive assumptions about the proportion of an age cohort who can profit from learning mathematics. But in the set of SIMS countries such assumptions are typically associated with "high" levels of coverage and achievement, not with the more limited ambitions seen in the United States.

The final report of the U.S. SIMS study was entitled *The Underachieving Curriculum* (McKnight et al., 1987). In that report five "deceptive explanations" of U.S. overall achievement were canvassed and dismissed as the report argued for its thesis of an "underachieving curriculum." This chapter both highlights and extends the observations of *The Underachieving Curriculum* on the importance of the curriculum as the determinant of the patterns of achievement and participation in mathematics instruction found in American schools. It also reinforces the claim of that report that many of the "explanations" that might be, and are being, offered to account for what are seen as the problems of U.S. mathematics instruction are deceptive. We have seen, for example, that when American teachers teach a curriculum that is similar to that of Japan, American students perform as well as Japanese students. But for most U.S. Grade 8 students and for all Grade 12 students the curriculum that U.S. teachers cover is so different from that of Japan—and many other countries—that any comparison is a comparison of incommensurables.

But, at the same time as I make this claim, I must also observe that what the comparative argument represented by SIMS also does is dramatize the problematic character of the U.S. mathematics curriculum. The U.S. curriculum is structured in a very different way than are the curricula of most other countries and seem to have neither the virtues of a curriculum that trades off high coverage and achievement for high levels of participation nor the virtues of a curriculum which, while restricting access to mathematics, does produce high levels of achievement. We must ask why U.S. schools teach a curriculum that is so different from that of most other countries and that seems to optimize nothing.

What would seem to emerge from the analysis I have offered here is the conclusion that the overwhelmingly important issues that face U.S. mathematics instruction center on the curriculum and the "decisions" that the system has made—purposefully or otherwise— about *what* to teach, *how* that content should be distributed across subgroups of students, and *where* that content should be distributed across grades and courses. These questions clearly emerge from this chapter as much more significant than the questions that have dominated the discussion of secondary schooling for the past decade: How well or badly do teachers teach, and how well or badly are students learning? The question U.S. policy making around mathematics education must address, or so it would seem from the argument here, is the character of the curriculum, where that curriculum should and might be changed, and how the changes that might be adopted can be introduced in schools. What a study like SIMS can do (as I hope I have done here) is frame such discussions by explicating the consequences of one set of assumptions, and so offer a basis for a consideration of other assumptions and their possible consequences.

REFERENCES

American Psychological Association. (1974). *Standards for educational and psychological tests*. Washington, DC: Author.

Barr, R., & Dreeben, R. (1983). *How schools work*. Chicago: University of Chicago Press.

Bidwell, C. E., & Kasarda, J. D. (1980). Conceptualizing and measuring the effects of school and schooling. *American Journal of Education, 88,* 401–430.

Castles, F. G. (1988). *Australian public policy and economic vulnerability.* Sydney: Allen & Unwin.

Castles, F. G. (1989). Introduction: Puzzles of political economy. In F. G. Castles (Ed.), *The comparative history of public policy.* New York: Oxford University Press.

Comber, L. C., & Keeves, J. P. (1973). *Science education in nineteen countries: International studies in evaluation* (Vol. 1). New York: Wiley.

Crosswhite, F. J., Dossey, J. A., Swafford, J. O., McKnight, C. C., Cooney, T. J., Downs, F. L., Grouws, D. A., & Weinzweig, A. I. (1986). *Second international mathematics study: Detailed report for the United States*. Champaign, IL: Stipes.

Department of Education and Science (DES). (1988). National Curriculum Working Group for Mathematics. *Mathematics for ages 5 to 16.* London: HMSO.

Gamoran, A. (1987). The stratification of high school learning opportunities. *Sociology of Education, 60,* 135–155.

Hirstein, J. (1980). From Royaumont to Bielfeld: A twenty-year cross-national survey of the content of school mathematics. *Comparative studies of mathematics curricula: Change and stability 1960–1980.* Materialen und Studien Band 19. Bielefeld: Institut für Didaktik der Mathematik, Universität Bielefeld.

Kifer, E. (1989). What IEA studies say about curriculum and school organization. In A. C. Purves (Ed.), *International comparisons and education reform.* Alexandria, VA: Association for Supervision and Curriculum Development.

Leinhart, G. (1983). Overlap: Testing whether it is taught. In G. F. Madaus (Ed.), *The courts, validity and minimum competency testing.* Boston: Kluwer-Nijhoff.

Lerner, B. (1982). American education: How are we doing? *Public Interest,* 59–92.

Lerner, B. (1991). Good news about American education. *Commentary, 91,* pp. 19–25.

Lynn, R. (1988). *Educational achievement in Japan: Lessons for the west.* Basingstoke: Macmillan.

Madaus, G. F. (1983). Minimum competency testing for certification: The evolution and evaluation of test validity. In G. F. Madaus (Ed.), *The courts' validity and minimum competency testing.* Boston: Kluwer-Nijhoff.

Mathematics Counts: Report of the Committee of Inquiry into the Teaching of Mathematics in Schools under the Chairmanship of W. H. Cockcroft. (1982). London: HMSO.

McKnight, C. C., Crosswhite, F. J., Dossey, J. A., Kifer, E., Swafford, J. O., Travers, K. J., & Cooney, T. J. (1987). *The underachieving curriculum: U.S. school mathematics from an international perspective.* Champaign, IL: Stipes.

Postlethwaite, T. N. (1975). The surveys of the International Association for the Evaluation of Educational Achievement. In A. C. Purves & D. U. Levine (Eds.), *Educational policy and international assessment: Implications of the IEA surveys of achievement.* San Francisco, CA: McCutchan.

Przeworski, A., & Teune, H. (1970). *The logic of comparative social inquiry.* New York: Wiley-Interscience.

Rotberg, I. (1990). I never promised you first place. *Phi Delta Kappan, 72,* 296–303.

Stigler, J. W., Lee, S-Y., & Stevenson, H. W. (1990). *Mathematical knowledge: Mathematical knowledge of Japanese, Chinese, and American elementary school children.* Reston, VA: National Council of Teachers of Mathematics.

Stigler, J. W., & Stevenson, H. W. (1991). How Asian teachers polish each lesson to perfection. *American Educator,* 13–20, 43–47.

Travers, K. J., & Westbury, I. (1989). *The IEA study of mathematics 1: Analysis of mathematics curricula.* Oxford: Pergamon Press.

White, M. (1987). *The Japanese educational challenge: A commitment to children.* New York: Free Press.

Wolfe, R. G. (1989). Identification and description of opportunity to learn and growth in achievement. *Evaluation and assessment in mathematics education* (Science and Technology Education Document Series No. 32). Paris: UNESCO, Division of Science, Technical and Environmental Education.

II

SCHOOL STRUCTURES, SOCIAL STRUCTURES, GENDER, AND MATHEMATICS EDUCATION

5

What Makes for Effective Mathematics Instruction? Japanese and American Classrooms Compared

Maryellen Schaub
David P. Baker

Department of Sociology
The Catholic University of America
Washington, DC

Recently many international studies have compared academic achievement in Japan and the United States (Lapointe, Mead, & Phillips, 1989; McKnight, Crosswhite, Dossey, Kifer, Swafford, Travers, & Cooney, 1987; National Research Council, 1989). The results from such studies generally indicate that Japanese students score significantly higher than U.S. students on standardized tests of mathematics. Because the Japanese system produces such different results than the American one, a comparison of mathematics instruction in the two countries can help us understand what are the essentials for effective mathematics education.

This chapter reports on our recent study of classroom management and instructional approaches in Japanese and U.S. seventh and eighth grade classrooms (Schaub & Baker, 1991). Our study starts with the assumption that the average Japanese mathematics class is more effective in the teaching of mathematics and then attempts to explain how this occurs. As Chapter 4 in this volume suggests, there is a need to qualify the degree to which one can easily assume that all Japanese classrooms are more effective than all U.S. classrooms but even so, our study finds what appear to be clear differences in the use of effective methods in the two countries.

National differences in mathematics achievement in general, and specifically between Japan and the United States, have caused an active debate within the American educational establishment. With the hope of finding a way to quickly raise American mathematics performance, commentators have speculated on what is different about schooling in Japan and the United States that could produce such a large achievement gap. Mostly this speculation has been based on simple, single-factor explanations for this gap, such as higher paid teachers, more homework, longer school years, and so forth. In other words, it is suggested that Japan, or any other country that outscores the United States, has more of some simple single quality that can explain successful mathematics; it is further assumed that if the poorer performing U.S. system could generate more of this particular quality, then it would perform on an equal level to Japan.

There are at least two problems with this approach. First, by and large the simple answers that have been invoked have generally been shown to be wrong. For example, consider the studies summarized in Table 5.1, which compare Japan and the United States on various characteristics that have been suggested as "solutions" to the problem of more effective middle-school mathematics. None of the solutions are supported unequivocally, and most are clearly incorrect. The better performing Japanese system usually does not have more of the qualities that have been suggested as producing Japan's effective mathematics education. Japanese teachers are not better paid, better educated, or teaching to smaller classes. More than likely, Japanese middle grade students are not more intelligent or more selected than American middle grade students. Japanese students do not receive more instructional time; rather, they actually receive less than American students.[1] Classroom variation in stu-

---

[1] It is difficult to make a definite statement about this since Japanese students may receive more mathematics instruction in the earlier and later school grades.

dent social background is greater in Japan than in the United States. Japanese teachers do not assign more extensive homework in middle grades mathematics than American teachers.[2]

The second failing of the "quick fix" approach is that it has generally not compared differences in the primary activities of instruction and classroom management between Japan and the United States. Since these activities are so central to effective teaching and learning, it seems to be the best place to start to understand what produces favorable school outcomes and to look for valuable lessons from successful systems.

This chapter undertakes such a comparison. First we examine how Japanese and American middle school classrooms produce mathematics achievement. This is followed by a comparison of the classroom management and instructional techniques used in each system. Lastly, we conclude with some recommendations for the more effective teaching of mathematics that are suggested by our research.

THE PRODUCTION OF ACHIEVEMENT
IN JAPANESE AND AMERICAN CLASSROOMS

As we have suggested, a primary reason why quick fixes will not work is that they do not focus on the central activities of classroom management and instruction. It may be that the classroom processes that produce achievement are not the same in Japan and the United States. Perhaps the teaching process in the average Japanese classroom is sufficiently different from the process in the average American classroom to make any simple answers incorrect.

Observers of the two countries' school systems have begun to suggest precisely this. For instance, in a review of research on learning approaches in Japan and the United States, Holloway (1988) concludes that the Japanese stress effort as the road to academic success, while Americans stress ability (Shimahara, 1986). Numerous observational studies focused on the classroom environment in Japan and the United States have suggested that there may be important yet overlooked differences between the two

---

[2] The test of the resource hypotheses presented in Table 5.1 are specifically for middle grades mathematics and are not intended to be a statement on all differences, at all levels, between Japanese and U.S. schooling. There could be differences in resources later in schooling that support some of these hypotheses. This assessment needs to be done for other subjects and at other levels of schooling.

TABLE 5.1

Test of One-Variable Expectations of Mathematics Achievement Differences between Japanese and U.S. Middle Grades Students

Hypothesis	Indicator	Direction of Finding	Hypothesis Supported	Source
(Japan compared to the U.S.)				
Japan has smaller teacher/student ratio	Number of students per teacher	J > U.S.	No	3
Japan has better paid (and thus motivated) teachers	Annual salary	J = U.S.	No	9
Japanese teachers receive more training and are more experienced	Semesters general training	J > U.S.	No	3
	Postsecondary mathematics	J > U.S.	No	4
	Pedagody in mathematics	J > U.S.	Yes	3
	Years teaching mathematics	J > U.S.	No	8*
	Years teaching general	J > U.S.	Yes	8

Japanese students receive more schooling	Yearly number of minutes math instruction	J > U.S.	No	3,8
Japan schools a more select population of students	School retention rate until 17 years	J > U.S.	No	3
Japanese student body is more homogenous at the classroom level	Classroom variation in student background	J = U.S.	No	8
	Classroom variation in student language	J > U.S.	Yes	1
Japan spends more resources on education	Spending on all education	J = U.S.	No	5
	Spending K-12 as % GDP	J > U.S.	Yes	5
Japanese students are more intelligent	Wechsler Intelligence Scale for children	J > U.S.	Yes	2
	Wechsler Intelligence Scale for children	J = U.S.	No	6
	Battery of cognitive tests	J = U.S.	No	7

Source: 1. Garden, 1987; 2. Lynn, 1982; 3. McKnight, et al., 1985; 4. Oldham, 1986; 5. Rasell and Mischel, 1990; 6. Stevenson and Azuma, 1983; 7. Stevenson, Stigler, Lee, Lucker, Kitamura, and Hsu, 1985; 8. Second International Mathematics Study; 9. Barrow and Suter, 1986.

*Sources marked as 8 are from original analysis done by authors. See Schaub and Baker (1991) for details.

countries that could explain achievement differences (Hamilton, Blumenfeld, Akoh, & Mirura, 1988; Lewis, 1988; Sato, 1990; Schiller & Walberg, 1982; Stevenson, Stigler, Lee, Lucker, Kitamura, & Hsu, 1985; Stevenson, Stigler, Lucker, Lee, Hsu, & Kitamura, 1986; Stigler, Lee, Lucker, & Stevenson, 1982). Furthermore, the burden of these observations runs parallel to what emerges from the literature on teacher behavior (process) and student achievement (product) (see Brophy & Good, 1986, for a recent review). Thus, to take two of the variables identified in process-product research, differences in teacher management of classroom time and instructional methods between the United States and Japan might explain national differences in performance.

SIMS provides data that are well suited to examine such issues. The data set includes not only achievement scores on a standardized mathematics test but also detailed accounts by teachers of their methods of instruction and management of class time. Since full classrooms were sampled, the information about teacher management of class time and instructional methods can be directly linked to achievement for a nationally representative sample of students in each system.

We used the Japanese and U.S. data files for Population A. The Japanese sample includes data on 208 seventh-grade classrooms with as many teachers and over 8,000 students and the U.S. sample includes data on 222 eighth-grade classrooms, with as many teachers and over 6,500 students.[3] Using a percentage number-known formula to correct for student guessing (Gulliksen, 1950), we calculated a test score for each student.[4] We then aggregated individual student scores to calculate class means and estimates of classroom variation. To estimate classroom variation we use a coefficient of variation that has the advantage of correcting the estimation of dispersion of student scores for any mean difference between classrooms.

At the end of the year, teachers of the sampled classes were asked a series of questions about their management of class time for

---

[3] The SIMS national committee in each country determined which middle grade's curriculum fit the study's test. In most countries this was the eighth grade, but in Japan, the seventh grade was the best match. In the U.S. sample some classrooms were added nonrandomly for supplemental study and a small number of classrooms yielded very incomplete data; both of these kinds of classes were dropped to produce the sample of 222.

[4] The correction for guessing was calculated as follows:

a) Total score $= (\Sigma R - (\Sigma w/4))/\Sigma I$

where: ΣR = number of items correct on core and rotated form,

ΣW = number of items incorrect on core and rotated form, and

ΣI = total number of items on core and rotated form.

various teaching and nonteaching tasks during a typical week of teaching. The questions included such topics as "preparing for class," "explaining new material," "reviewing old material," "administration," and "keeping order." Teachers were also asked about their use of various instructional methods such as "lecture to the entire class," "having students work alone at their seats," "having students work in groups," and "having students take tests." Since Japanese and American teachers have different amounts of contact time with their classes, we compared the management of time across the two countries by standardizing the raw amount of minutes reported in the original responses into a percentage of time used.

PATTERNS OF CLASSROOM ACHIEVEMENT

To see what we mean by our notion of different ways of producing classroom achievement, examine Figure 5.1, which is a plot of the simple change (class mean posttest minus class mean pretest) for Japanese and American classrooms. There is a striking difference

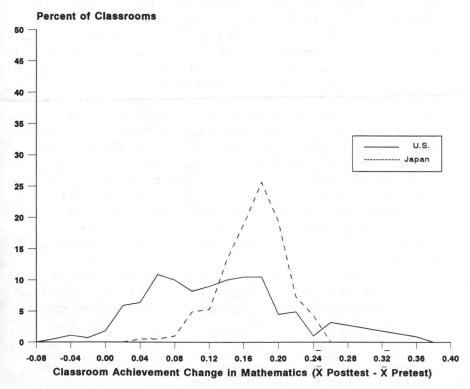

FIGURE 5.1 Distribution of Change in Mathematics Achievement in Japanese and American Classrooms

between the two distributions. Achievement gains over the school year in Japanese classrooms are all positive and the classroom scores are tightly distributed. By contrast the American gains are widely spread. At the same time there are a small number of U.S. classrooms in which students learn more overall than do their counterparts in the best Japanese classrooms.[5]

Japanese seventh-grade classes outscore American eighth-grade classes on the posttest by over 20 percentage points on average. Additionally, there is a difference in the effects of past years of schooling in the two countries. Japanese classes start the year knowing on average 40 percent of the material, while the American classes start the year knowing on average only 23 percent of the material. Also the mean class gain over the year in Japan is almost 16 percent while in the United States it is 11 percent. These differences underscore what is already well known about the differences in the effectiveness of the two school systems.

What has not been done is to consider how Japanese and American classrooms produce the pattern of outcomes that we see in Figure 5.1. We did an analysis that relates the classroom posttest mean to three dimensions of achievement. First we examined what effect incoming (beginning-of-year) mathematical knowledge of the class had on what they learned by the end of the year. It could be that some classes do not change much—in other words, the level of incoming knowledge in mathematics predicts the outgoing level. Or it could be that in other classrooms the outgoing level is not as determined by the incoming level. The second dimension is the level of variation in this incoming knowledge for each class. It is often suggested that a high degree of variation in student knowledge is a barrier to class achievement, since the teacher must teach to a variety of levels in one class. A large negative coefficient associated with this variable would indicate this kind of drag on learning. The third dimension is the degree of change in student variation from the pretest to posttest for the class. If teachers are able to reduce between-student variation over the year this may increase classroom achievement.

Since we are interested in how these dimensions of classroom achievement might differ between the two national systems we did the analysis separately for each data file.[6] The posttest mean in

---

[5] Similar results as those shown in Figure 5.1 are obtained when obviously tracked or ability-grouped U.S. classrooms are removed from the sample. This yields only a small amount of truncation of both ends of the distribution.

[6] The actual analysis estimates a regression equation that regresses the classroom posttest on the pretest, the degree of variation in the pretest and the

American classrooms was twice as dependent on the incoming level of mathematics knowledge as the posttest mean in Japanese classrooms. End-of-year achievement in U.S. classrooms is more determined by student inputs (abilities and past learning) than the end-of-year achievement in Japanese classrooms. What a class of students ends up knowing in Japan is less dependent on what they begin the year with. Thus, being a member of a class and being exposed to the instruction within it may have a greater effect on posttest score in Japan than in the United States.[7]

This is further reflected in the effect of pretest variation in the two countries. Student variation on incoming knowledge of mathematics reduces classroom posttest means more in Japan than in the United States. The overriding effect of incoming knowledge on the level of outgoing knowledge in the United States may make other influences trivial. What is hinted at here is a fundamental difference in the way achievement is produced in the two countries. Incoming variation in students' knowledge is a hinderance in Japan while between-student variation appears to have little influence on overall class achievement in the United States.

Japanese mathematics classes are better at reducing between-student variation over the school year than U.S. classes (Japan mean reduction = .982; U.S. mean reduction = .858, $t = 5.00$, $p .01$).[8] Furthermore, Japanese teachers who are most successful at reducing variation also yield higher class posttest means. In other words, the distance from the slowest learners to the fastest learners in the American classroom stays more stable over the course of eighth-grade, but in Japan it is generally reduced, while the whole class learns more mathematics. From this analysis of mathematics learning, one can begin to appreciate the effect Japanese teachers have on producing the high levels of achievement that we reported above. A question remains: *How does this difference in classroom achievement come about?*

---

change in variation from the pretest to the posttest. Added to this was a dummy variable for nation and three interaction terms. We report the rewritten equation for each country here (see Schaub & Baker, 1991).

[7] Similar results to these were found when U.S. classrooms that were obviously tracked by ability groups were removed.

[8] Classroom change in between-student variation is modified coefficient of variation, computed as:

$$\text{reduction} = 1 - \left(\frac{\text{SD posttest} - \text{SD pretest}}{\text{X posttest}} \right)$$

Larger positive values indicate greater reduction in variation.

MANAGEMENT OF CLASS TIME
AND INSTRUCTIONAL METHODS

As we have suggested, one important answer to the question comes from considering the day-to-day management of classes and the specific instructional approaches taken by Japanese and U.S. mathematics teachers. Part A of Table 5.2 presents an analysis of the management of class time by comparing Japanese and American teachers. The findings suggest that U.S. teachers prepare less, review older material more, and spend more time on keeping order and doing administrative tasks during the classroom period than Japanese teachers. Japanese teachers explain new material more, although this difference is not statistically significant. It appears that at the very least, U.S. teachers are preparing less and spending proportionally less time on instruction, and when they do instruct they spend more time than Japanese teachers on reviewing older material. When considering our results on achievement, these differences in time management approaches are consistent with prior research on teacher effectiveness (Bloom, 1976; Good & Grouws, 1975, 1977; Powell, 1980).

A similar pattern is evident in the findings on instructional methods seen in Part B of Table 5.2. Japanese teachers lecture to the class as whole more frequently, while U.S. teachers have students work alone at their seats, do group work and take tests more frequently.[9] Although some research argues no instructional method is clearly better (Anderson, 1959; Averch, Carroll, & Donaldson, 1972), these results are consistent with prior research (i.e., Bennett, Jordan, Long, & Wade, 1976; Flanders, 1970; Good & Grouws, 1975, 1977; Soar, 1973; Solomon & Kendall, 1976; Stallings & Kaskowitz, 1974).

Japanese teachers use class time to instruct the student—and all of the students—while U.S. teachers use class time for an array of activities which may or may not involve mathematics instruction. United States teachers tend to use instructional methods that are less oriented to teaching to the entire class than Japanese teachers. However, the lower mean class variation on incoming knowledge in Japan may make whole class instruction more effective and easier to do. We also found that the best U.S. classes in terms of increased learning over the school year tended to exhibit class management and instructional patterns similar to Japanese classes.

---

[9] The use of class time for noninstructional activities by U.S. teachers is paralleled by a similar finding that U.S. students spend more time outside of class during school for various noninstructional reasons (Stevenson et al., 1986).

TABLE 5.2
Comparison of Japanese and U.S. Teachers' Management of Class
Time and Instructional Methods

	Japan $\bar{X}$	U.S. $\bar{X}$	t-Ratio
A. Management of class time:			
Preparing for class	28.76	21.00	3.70**
	(23.63)	(18.13)	
Explaining new material	43.10	41.97	.50
	(23.10)	(23.30)	
Reviewing old material	22.41	26.05	2.30*
	(16.30)	(16.30)	
Administration in class	6.28	7.68	1.97*
	(4.70)	(9.30)	
Keeping order	8.85	12.21	2.31*
	(14.30)	(15.60)	
B. Instructional Methods (amount used):			
Lecture to entire class	41.43	36.09	2.96**
	(17.60)	(19.30)	
Students work alone at desks	31.23	42.40	5.17**
	(15.50)	(24.00)	
Students work in groups	8.66	14.11	3.25**
	(10.30)	(22.40)	
Taking tests	11.09	17.57	6.96**
	(9.80)	(9.20)	

Note: N: Japan = 208; U.S. = 222; data in parentheses are SDs.
*$p \leq$ 05
**$p \leq .01$.
Source: Schaub and Baker (1991).

Lastly, we examined whether these differences in the management of class time and instructional methods are associated with higher mathematics achievement. Table 5.3 shows that the pattern of teaching that is more evident in Japan increases class mathematics achievement, while the pattern that is more evident in the U.S. decreases class achievement. For example, time spent on explaining new material and lecturing to the whole class raises post-test means, while reviewing older material, keeping order, and having students work alone or in small groups lowers achievement. The only exception to this pattern is that time spent on administrative tasks is associated with higher achievement and U.S. teachers engage in these activities more than Japanese teachers.[10] We also

---

[10] Under this category in the SIMS questionnaire are a mixture of activities from taking roll to setting up equipment. It is unclear to us why these should necessarily result in higher class achievement.

TABLE 5.3
OLS Regression of Class Posttest Means on Teachers' Management of Class Time and Methods of Instruction in Japan and the U.S. Combined

	Unstandardized Coefficient	SE
Management of class time:		
Preparing for class	.03	.04
Explaining new material	9.41**	3.43
Reviewing old material	-8.77*	4.76
Administration	10.63*	5.37
Keeping order	-37.36**	10.13
Instructional methods:		
Lecture to entire class	8.39*	4.24
Students work alone at desks	-11.91**	3.83
Students work in groups	-9.23**	4.06
Taking tests	9.54	7.94
Adjustment for mean differences (1 = Japan, 0 = U.S.):		
Country	20.18**	1.61
Constant	34.64**	2.43
R^2 ($F = 28.00$)	.44	

Note: $N = 430$. Model is trimmed because interaction terms were not significantly different from zero and their addition to the model did not change the size of the main effects. Also, the pattern of main effects remained the same after various controls for prior class achievement were added to the equation.
*$p \leq .05$.
**$p \leq .01$.
Source: Schaub and Baker (1991).

found that the pattern of management of classrooms and instruction most prevalent in Japanese classrooms also produces achievement gains in U.S. classrooms that use these approaches.

CONCLUSION

In light of these results, what can we now say about the differences shown in Figure 5.1? And further, what lessons do these results have for improving mathematics in the United States?

First it is clear that there are differences in the way achievement is produced in the average Japanese classroom and the average U.S. classroom. Japanese teachers produce more growth in mathematics learning; they are less restricted by the level of knowledge and ability of incoming students. United States teachers are more restricted by the level of knowledge of incoming students. Achievement in U.S. classes is less sensitive to between-student variation. Japanese teachers who reduce variation among students in a class are successful in producing higher achievement.

As one possible explanation for this difference we examined patterns of management of class time and instructional methods. The patterns that we find illustrate in a concrete way how two systems of schooling can produce different levels of learning. Japanese teachers organize their classrooms and use their time to impart new material in a fashion that seems to be conducive to student achievement. United States teachers use this type of classroom organization less.

The different ways in which Japanese and U.S. teachers approach instruction can also explain the differing dimensions of classroom achievement that we find. Achievement in U.S. classes is more dependent on the incoming knowledge of student than is the achievement of Japanese classes. This finding makes sense in the light of the differences in instruction and management of class time between the two countries. Manipulating the learning environment so that all or most students gain new knowledge can lower the association between pre- and posttest scores; students can be changed. This apparently happens more in Japan than in the United States. There is less changing of students in the average U.S. classroom; the student's input is more predictive of the student's output.

A similar argument can be made about the reduction of achievement dispersion within classes in the two systems. Our results indicate that Japanese teachers uniformly reduce between-student variation in achievement. The mean reduction of between-student variation in American classes is smaller. Again this is predictable from the differences in instruction and management of class time that we observe. Japanese teachers teach more often to the entire classroom while U.S. teachers tend to use instructional methods that are directed toward the individual student (such as seat work or small group work). Teaching to the class as a whole is just one among several ways in which Japanese schooling reduces variation.

However, as we have emphasized, there is also evidence in our study that the most effective U.S. classrooms are similar to the Japanese pattern of classroom management and instruction. In other words, there is not a uniquely Japanese approach to effective mathematics that cannot be produced in the United States. Figure 5.1 indicates that the differences between Japanese classrooms in achievement gains are far less than between U.S. classrooms. In fact the most striking quality of the U.S. distribution is this spread—a spread of effectiveness in the teaching of mathematics. The fact that Japanese teachers use an effective model and use it more uniformly across classrooms perhaps accounts more for this system's success than does any particular cultural quality unique to Japan.

This is both good and bad news for those interested in the improvement of mathematics instruction in U.S. schools. It is good news because it suggests that more effective approaches are possible in the United States and that some teachers know this and use this approach. Effective mathematics teaching is not culturally bound. Effective teaching and learning is attainable using sound, proven, and standard methods of classroom management and instruction.

The bad news is that in the United States the reform of teaching, particularly along the lines of the basic model suggested above, poses real difficulties. The U.S. system is certainly not immune to reforms; it is just that it is difficult to incorporate the kind of reform needed in this case. There are at least two factors that work against this improvement. First, reform of U.S. schooling continually focuses and refocuses on the inequality of educational opportunity (Natriello, McDill, & Pallas, 1991), often at the expensive of effectiveness. Equity is an important standard and is a goal so thoroughly part of the U.S. system that it is hard to dislodge it. This is not to say that it should be dislodged, only that reform of inequality is a large task and often overshadows other changes. Second, when effectiveness becomes an issue of reform in the United States, as it did during the recent so-called "excellence movement," the basic suggestions for reforms that are made would actually intensify existing qualities of the U.S. system. For example, consider the recent push for greater decentralization of the management of schools and classrooms, which appears as a central plank in the excellence movement. As a system the U.S. schools are already the most decentralized of any major national system in the world today. It is hard to imagine that a reform towards greater decentralizing would do anything other than deepen the characteristics of the system currently in place. Thus, the spread of effectiveness shown in Figure 5.1 would most likely increase in a system that is further decentralized.

The pattern shown in Figure 5.1 for Japan is partly a function of a certain degree of uniformity among classrooms achieved if not by overt government centralization, then certainly by uniform control and uniformly accepted approaches and procedures. These circumstances would not necessarily be captured by further decentralization and current American proposals for reforms, based crudely on a free-market notion.

It is reasonably clear what works, and some U.S. teachers and students are currently engaged in effective mathematics learning. The challenge for the rest is to consider the costs of effective schooling and whether or not implementation is worth that effort.

REFERENCES

Anderson, R. C. (1959). Learning in discussions: A resume of the authoritarian-democratic studies. *Harvard Educational Review, 29,* 201–215.

Averch, H., Carroll, S., & Donaldson, T. (1972). *How effective is schooling? A Critical Review and Synthesis of Research Findings.* Santa Monica, CA: Rand Corporation.

Barrow, S., & Suter, L. (1986). *A comparison of teachers' salaries in Japan and the United States.* Washington DC: Office of Educational Research and Improvement U.S. Department of Education.

Bennett, N., Jordan, J., Long, G., & Wade, B. (1976). *Teaching styles and pupil progress.* London: Open Books.

Bloom, B. S. (1976). *Human characteristics and school learning.* New York: McGraw-Hill.

Brophy, J., & Good, T. (1986). Teacher behavior and student achievement. In M. C. Wittrock (Ed.), *Handbook of research on teaching* (3rd edition). New York: MacMillan.

Flanders, N. (1970). *Analyzing teacher behavior.* Reading, MA: Addison-Wiley.

Garden, R. (1987). *Second international mathematics study: Sampling report.* Washington, DC: U.S. Department of Education, National Center for Educational Statistics.

Good, T., & Grouws, D. (1975). *Process-product relationships in fourth grade mathematics classrooms* (Report No. NIE-G-00-3-0123). Columbia: University of Missouri, College of Education.

Good, T., & Grouws, D. (1977). Teaching effects: A process-product study in fourth grade mathematics classrooms. *Journal of Teacher Education, 28,* 49–54.

Gulliksen, H. (1950). *Theory of mental tests.* New York: J. Wiley & Sons.

Hamilton, V., Blumenfeld, P., Akoh, H., & Mirura, K. (1988). *Group and gender in Japanese and American elementary classrooms.* Unpublished manuscript, Wayne State University.

Holloway, S. (1988). Concepts of ability and effort in Japan and the United States. *Review of Education Research, 58.*

Lapointe, A., Mead, N., & Phillips, G. (1989). *A world of differences: An international assessment of mathematics and science* (Report No. 19-CAEP-Ol). Princeton, NJ: Educational Testing Service.

Lewis, C. (1988). Japanese first-grade classrooms: Implications for U.S. theory and research. *Comparative Education Review, 32,* 159–172.

Lynn, R. (1982). IQ in Japan and the United States shows a growing disparity. *Nature, 297,* 222–223.

McKnight, C., Crosswhite, F., Dossey, J., Kifer, E., Swafford, J., Travers, K. J., & Cooney, T. (1985). *The underachieving curriculum: Assessing U.S. school mathematics from an international perspective.* Champaign, IL: Stipes.

National Research Council. (1989). *Everybody counts: A report to the nation on the future of mathematical education.* Washington, DC: National Academy Press.

Natriello, G., McDill, E., & Pallas, A. (1990). *Schooling disadvantaged children: Racing against catastrophe.* New York: Teachers College Press, 1991.

Oldham, E. (1986). *Qualification of mathematics teachers.* Unpublished report, U.S. Department of Education, National Center for Educational Statistics, Washington, DC.

Powell, M. (1980). The beginning teacher evaluation study: A brief history of a major research project. In C. Denham & A. Lieberman (Eds.), *Time to learn.* Washington, DC: National Institute of Education.

Rasell, E., & Mishel, L. (1990). *Shortchanging education: How U.S. spending on grades K–12 lags behind other industrial nations.* Washington, DC: Economic Policy Institute.

Sato, N. (1990). *Japanese education where it counts: In the classroom.* Presented at the annual meeting of the American Educational Research Association, Boston, MA.

Schaub, M., & Baker, D. P. (1991). Solving the math problem: Exploring mathematics achievement in Japanese and American middle schools. *American Journal of Education, 99,* 623–642.

Schiller, D., & Walberg, H. (1982). The learning society. *Educational Leadership, 39,* 411–412.

Shimahara, N. (1986). The cultural basis of student achievement in Japan. *Comparative Education, 22,* 19–26.

Soar, R. S. (1973). *Following through classroom process measurement and pupil growth* (ERIC ED 106 297). Gainesville: University of Florida, Institute for Development of Human Resources.

Solomon, D., & Kendell, A. (1979). *Children in the classrooms: An investigation of person-environment interaction.* New York: Praeger.

Stallings, J., & Kaskowitz, D. (1974). *Follow-through classroom observation evaluation 1972–1973* (SRI Project URU-7370). Stanford, CA: Stanford Research Institute.

Stevenson, H., & Azuma, H. (1983). IQ in Japan and the United States: Methodological problems in Lynn's analysis. *Nature, 306,* 291–292.

Stevenson, H., Stigler, J., Lee, S., Lucker, G., Kitamura, S., & Hsu, C. (1985). Cognitive performance and academic achievement of Japanese, Chinese and American children. *Child Development, 56,* 718–734.

Stevenson, H., Stigler, J., Lucker, G., Lee, S., Hsu, C., & Kitamura, S. (1986). Classroom behavior and achievement of Japanese, Chinese and American Children. In R. Glaser (Ed.), *Advances in instructional psychology*. Hillsdale, NJ: Erlbaum.

Stigler, J., Lee, S., Lucker, G., & Stevenson, H. (1982). Curriculum and achievement in mathematics: A study of elementary school children in Japan, Taiwan and the United States. *Journal of Educational Psychology, 74*, 315–322.

6

The Effects
of Central Control
on Classroom Practice*

Peter L. Glidden

College of Education
University of Illinois at Urbana-Champaign
Champaign, IL

Two recent calls for school reform propose different solutions to the problem of low overall mathematics achievement in the United States. One solution, proposed by the U.S. Department of Education (1991), calls for national examinations for high school seniors. Another solution, proposed by the mathematical and scientific com-

* I want to thank both the Bureau of Educational Research and the Research Board at the University of Illinois at Urbana-Champaign for their support; without this help this study could not have been completed. I also would like to thank Ian Westbury for his encouragement in preparing this chapter and his extremely helpful comments on previous drafts, Howard H. Russell of the Ontario Institute for Studies in Education for explaining Ontario's Grade 13 mathematics courses, David F. Robitaille of the University of British Columbia for explaining the province's Algebra 12, James Armstrong of Educational Testing Service for explaining the AP Calculus Development Committee, and Madhavi Kantamemni and Erin Fry for their assistance in collating the data. Of course, any opinions or errors contained in this study are mine alone.

munity, calls for school districts to adopt the standards for curriculum and evaluation proposed by the National Council of Teachers of
Mathematics (NCTM) (Mathematical Association of America, 1991;
National Council of Teachers of Mathematics, 1989; National Research Council [NRC], 1989). These two calls share the ultimate goal
of improving student achievement, but they reflect different perceptions of mathematics teachers and mathematics teaching.

Proponents of national syllabi and examinations believe that the
best way to improve student achievement is to effect change from
the top down. It is accepted that syllabi and examinations pro-
foundly influence instruction by directing teachers to teach particular content for a specific level of student attainment. Therefore, if
the United States is to improve student achievement, it must give
teachers an explicit focus towards which they will teach.[1]

The mathematical and scientific community takes the opposite
view. They argue that the "New Math" reform efforts of the 1960s
demonstrated that curricula cannot be written at the national level
for adoption at the local level (NCTM, 1989; NRC, 1989). Instead,
curriculum reform must be a grass-roots effort that involves teachers from the outset; teachers act as "curriculum filters" and ultimately they decide what mathematics to teach and how to teach it
(e.g., Holmes Group, 1986; NCTM, 1989; NRC, 1989; Porter, Floden,
Freeman, Schmidt, & Schwille, 1988; Romberg, 1988).

Although both of these proposals assume that getting more teachers to teach a common curriculum (whether based on an examination syllabus or the NCTM *Standards*) is an essential component of
improving student achievement, they offer opposing approaches to
achieving that goal. Proponents of examinations claim that teachers
need to be told firmly what mathematics to teach and that they will
and can be responsive to such direction; proponents of grass-roots
reform claim that telling teachers does not work, they must understand for themselves why the mathematics is to be taught.

The potential success of one or the other of these approaches
largely depends on understanding why teachers teach what they do.
If teachers will teach particular mathematics content because only a
syllabus or external examination can focus their attention on this or
that content, then a national examination will have the effects its
proponents claim. On the other hand, if teachers—actively and
necessarily—must make their own informed, reasoned, and inde-

---

[1] It has not yet been decided whether these examinations will be standardized
examinations (curriculum-independent) or domain-referenced (curriculum-based)
examinations. This question is discussed in the last section.

pendent instructional decisions, then grass-roots reform will produce the effects its proponents claim. As a third possibility, perhaps teachers make instructional decisions for a combination of reasons. For example, teachers might follow a syllabus to prepare students for an examination, but also teach additional content based on their own judgment of what their students need or could benefit from. If so, national examinations and grass-roots curriculum reform *in tandem* would be more effective than either alone.

To investigate how a central curriculum or examination affects teachers' instructional decisions, we examine the Population B classroom process data from three of the school systems that participated in SIMS. By analyzing these data we can determine: (a) the extent to which teachers teach the same mathematics within a school system, (b) their reasons for teaching particular mathematical topics, and (c) their reasons for using particular representations of mathematical concepts. The SIMS data allow us to compare and contrast these decisions across educational systems that have central or local control of curriculum (content) and examinations (standards).[2]

CONTROL OF CONTENT AND STANDARDS

Population B

We will examine the Population B classroom process data from British Columbia and Ontario, Canada, and the United States. For British Columbia, this population was "all Grade 12 students enrolled in the course Algebra 12 in the public school system"; for Ontario, this population was "students enrolled in two or more Grade 13 mathematics courses (calculus, relations and functions, and algebra)"; and for the United States this population was "students in mainstream public and private schools who are enrolled in a mathematics course having as its prerequisite the standard sequence of mathematics courses: Algebra I, Geometry, and Algebra II" (Travers & Westbury, 1988, pp. 64–65).

British Columbia. In British Columbia, the provincial ministry of education exerts strong control over the content of Algebra 12. The ministry approves course textbooks and publishes curriculum

---

[2] It should be noted that only the United States, British Columbia, and Ontario used the Population B Teacher Classroom Process Questionnaires in their studies.

guides that specify the content in considerable detail. But although the ministry publishes and authorizes the curriculum, the committees that actually write the curriculum guides are composed almost entirely of experienced classroom teachers from the province's schools. The ministry nominates teachers to serve on these committees and it also invites the British Columbia Association of Mathematics Teachers (BCAMT) to nominate other members. Thus, although the ministry mandates the curriculum, BCAMT and classroom teachers work together to articulate what form that curriculum should take. Consequently, the curriculum guides bear not only the imprimatur of the ministry, but also the imprimatur of BCAMT and of other classroom teachers. Thus, in British Columbia the ministry, BCAMT, and mathematics teachers work together to establish clear expectations about what mathematics to teach. I will suggest later that such involvement in developing the curriculum gives teachers a sense of "ownership" of the curriculum.

British Columbia has a relatively small population (2.5 million in 1981) concentrated in two metropolitan areas, Vancouver (1.2 million) and Victoria (0.2 million), about 50 miles apart. There are on the order of 2,000 secondary mathematics teachers concentrated in a relatively small area. Thus, even though the curriculum writing committees are small (about 12 members each), the committee members represent a relatively large proportion of classroom teachers. Overall, this makes it easy for the members to communicate with each other, and justify the curriculum when necessary—the ministry is nearby, most schools are relatively close to one another, there are relatively few teachers, and those teachers know one another from involvement in BCAMT-sponsored activities or from living and working near each other.

Because the market for textbooks in British Columbia is small, few publishers produce texts for the province. At the time of SIMS, only four textbooks were approved for Algebra 12, and three of those were used by over 95 percent of the teachers. This adds to the picture that is emerging: the ministry mandates a curriculum, classroom teachers and BCAMT write the curriculum guides that articulate the curriculum, the gospel of the articulated curriculum spreads throughout the province, and a small number of ministry-approved textbooks support teaching. Yet the picture is not quite complete.

At the time of SIMS, there was no province-wide terminal examination for Algebra 12. Nevertheless, the ministry exerted significant influence on standards in a variety of ways. Until the 1970s the ministry administered school-leaving examinations. Consequently, British Columbia had a strong tradition of preparing students for external examinations, which had lingering effects on instruction at the time of SIMS. Moreover, the school-leaving examinations did not simply disappear, but were replaced by noncompulsory scholarship examinations that offered monetary grants for further education. As Travers and Westbury (1988) state, "The content of these [scholarship] examinations exerts considerable influence on the implemented [taught] curriculum" (p. 5). In addition to the scholarship examinations, the Ministry of Education also conducts province-wide assessments every four years, which include Grade 12 students.

Thus, even though there are not terminal examinations, per se, it is clear that the ministry does exert strong, albeit indirect, control of standards. The ministry not only has ample opportunity to communicate what standards it expects, it also has various ways to reward students who meet those standards and teachers who adopt them. Although the Ministry of Education does not have de jure control of standards, it does have substantial de facto control. For this study, we classify British Columbia as a system with strong central control of content and standards.

Ontario.   In Ontario, the provincial ministry of education approves all textbooks and monitors compliance with the senior guidelines, which prescribe the content of Grade 13 mathematics courses. "Since the Ministry of Education approves all textbooks used in schools and regularly monitors implementation of the guidelines, it exerts considerable influence over course content throughout the Province" (Travers & Westbury 1988, p. 9). Unlike British Columbia, Ontario does not administer province-wide examinations nor does it sponsor scholarship examinations. In Ontario, therefore, course content is controlled centrally, but standards are controlled locally.

United States.   In the United States the individual states have responsibility for education, and each state determines how much authority to delegate to local school districts. For the vast majority of Population B courses, content and standards are determined locally. Some schools do, however, offer Advanced Placement (AP) calculus courses. The syllabi for these courses are determined by the AP Calculus Development Committee, whose members include university mathematicians, secondary mathematics teachers, and staff members of the Educational Testing Service, which administers the examination. Students who pass an AP calculus examination can earn college credit.[3]

---

[3] For more detailed descriptions of all these curricula see Travers and Westbury (1988, 1989).

Because colleges and universities award credit based on the results of the AP examination, the syllabi and examinations must meet the approval of university mathematicians. Thus, although the AP Calculus Development Committee does include classroom teachers, their role is extremely limited. For AP Calculus classes, therefore, there is strong central control of content and standards, like British Columbia; but unlike British Columbia, there is virtually no teacher involvement in developing the curriculum.

The Framework for This Study

In the SIMS lexicon, "system" is used to describe an educational jurisdiction. British Columbia (represented by the code CBC) and Ontario (represented by CON) constitute two systems. For this study we extend the definition of system to distinguish U.S. classrooms that are preparing for the AP calculus examination (APC) for those that are not (NAP). As a result, in the United States there are two "systems" contained within Population B; AP Calculus classes, which teach centrally controlled content to centrally controlled standards, and Non-AP calculus classes, which teach locally controlled content to locally controlled standards.

These four systems provide a framework to investigate: (a) how consistent teaching is within each system, (b) teachers' reasons for teaching particular mathematical topics, and (c) teachers' reasons for using particular representations of mathematical concepts. Non-AP calculus classes in the United States are under local control for content and standards, the Ontario Ministry of Education controls the content of Grade 13 mathematics, and both Algebra 12 in British Columbia and AP Calculus classes have centrally controlled content and standards. Of the three systems that have central control, only teachers in British Columbia work with the central authority in developing the curriculum. The framework for this study is shown in Table 6.1.

MATHEMATICS CONTENT

Course Descriptions

Population B classroom teachers completed teacher classroom process questionnaires in up to four content areas: College [Advanced] Algebra, trigonometry, analytic geometry, and calculus. These questionnaires asked teachers to report what topics they taught, why they taught them, and why they used particular inter-

TABLE 6.1
Control of Content and Standards for Population B in British Columbia,
Ontario, and the U.S.

| | | CONTROL OF STANDARDS | |
		Central	Local
CONTROL OF CONTENT	Central	U.S. AP Calculus classes (APC) British Columbia Algebra 12 (CBC)	Ontario Grade 13 (ONT)
	Local		U.S. Non-AP Calculus classes (NAP)

pretations of mathematical concepts. (Table 6.2 gives examples of topics from the questionnaires.) We begin our analysis by considering the topics.

Taken together, the pool of topics contained in these four questionnaires was designed to fit all the systems in SIMS equally well. Of course, this means that some questionnaires fit some courses better than others, and for this study we first must determine which questionnaires fit which courses. To do this, we examine the topics on each questionnaire and determine how many of them are included in each course description. If most of them are included, then we say the questionnaire contains *principal content*. If few topics are included, then we say that the questionnaire contains *supporting content*. This distinction allows us to investigate whether teachers' reasons for instructional decisions differ for prescribed mathematics (principal content) and supplemental mathematics (supporting content).

British Columbia. In British Columbia at the time of SIMS Algebra 12 was offered in two formats: *Basic* and *Enriched*. Some of the content was the same for both formats (including complex numbers, conics and quadratic systems, exponents and logarithms, sequences and series, trigonometry, polynomial equations, and circu-

TABLE 6.2
Examples of Topics From the Population B Teacher
Classroom Process Questionnaires

College (Advanced) Algebra. (There were 31 topics in all.)
  Set Notation and Set Operations
  Synthetic Division, Rational Roots
  Complex Roots of Quadratic Equations
  Fundamental Counting Theorem (x ways) (y ways) = total ways
  Finding Conditional Probability
  Variance and Distributions
  Matrix Operations
  Groups, Fields and Their Properties
  Topics in Number Theory (Modular systems, divisibility)
Trigonometry. (There were 19 topics in all.)
  Standard position for angles with vertex at the origin
  Definition of the six trig functions from a right triangle
  Graphs of general trig functions such as $y = A \sin(Bx + C)$
  De Moivire's Theorem
  Inverses of the secant, cosecant, and cotangent functions
Analytic Geometry. (There were 14 topics in all.)
  Rectangular coordinates and the equations of a line and circle
  Parametric equations of a line in the plane
  Polar Coordinate system
  Equations of lines in 3-space
  Graphing rational functions
Calculus. (There were 21 topics in all.)
  Limit of a Sequence
  Limit of a Function
  Implicit Differentiation
  Arc Length
  Multiple Integrals

lar functions), but in the enriched format the content was taught at a higher level of sophistication. The enriched format also included topics not included in the basic format (for example, vectors in the plane, matrices and determinants, and polar coordinates).

Drawing on the course description of Algebra 12 (Council of Ministers of Education, 1981), we judge that most of the topics on the SIMS trigonometry questionnaire are included in both formats. Therefore, we say that the trigonometry questionnaire contains principal content. It is difficult to evaluate the appropriateness of the geometry questionnaire. About half the topics were included in the enriched format, but the SIMS data do not allow us to determine which classes were enriched and which were basic. Therefore, we analyze the geometry data separately. A few algebra topics were contained in both formats, but not enough to justify including the whole questionnaire. Therefore, we say the algebra questionnaire contains supporting content.

Ontario.   As already noted, Population B students in Ontario consisted of students who were taking two of the following three courses: relations and functions (CONRF), calculus (CONC), and algebra (CONA). Relations and functions includes typical pre-calculus topics such as functions, inverses, conics, trigonometric functions, and transformational geometry (Council of Ministers of Education, 1981). The trigonometry and analytic geometry questionnaires contain the principal content of this course. Calculus includes typical calculus topics such as limits, derivatives, integrals, complex numbers, and polar coordinates. The calculus questionnaire contains principal content. The other questionnaires contain supporting content.

The title of the Ontario algebra course is misleading—it is better characterized as a course in discrete mathematics. It includes topics such as: "sets, subsets, permutations, combinations; mathematical induction; binomial theorem; vectors . . . "; plus options such as "matrices and linear transformations; complex numbers, polar coordinates; groups, rings, fields; probability" (Council of Ministers of Education, 1981, p. 55). None of the SIMS classroom process questionnaires adequately reflect this content. Consequently, all the questionnaires completed by these teachers contain supporting content.

United States.   Nearly all the content of the calculus questionnaire is contained in AP Calculus.[4] Although some of the topics from the geometry questionnaire are included, they are too few in number to justify using the entire questionnaire. As with British Columbia, this questionnaire will be analyzed separately. Because there is no set curriculum for Non-AP calculus classes, all four classroom process questionnaires were judged as containing principal content.

Matching the SIMS Data to Course Content

Matching the four classroom process questionnaires to the content of these courses produces three categories of fit: principal con-

---

[4] The SIMS sample included 31 classes preparing for AP Calculus examinations. Twenty-eight classes were following the AB syllabus and three classes were following the BC syllabus. We limit our discussion of AP Calculus courses to the 28 classes following the AB syllabus because including the data from the three BC classes would complicate our interpretation of the data without significantly increasing our sample size.

tent, when most of the topics in the questionnaires are included in the course description; supporting content, when few of the topics are included; and a third category for questionnaires in between—those that cannot be classified as principal or supporting (for example, analytic geometry questionnaire for British Columbia and AP Calculus). For this third category we say that these questionnaires contain ancillary content, and we analyze them separately.

The results of matching the topics in the classroom process questionnaires to course content is shown in Table 6.3. The questionnaires are arranged from the lowest level of mathematics (algebra) to the highest (calculus). Thus, it should be noted that supporting content is prerequisite mathematics for principal content, but the same is not true for ancillary content. Ancillary content can be prerequisite or concurrent mathematics (AP Calculus) or more advanced mathematics (British Columbia). Also presented in Table 6.3 are the number of respondents completing each questionnaire.[5] In some cases (for example, algebra and trigonometry for AP Calculus) these data suggest that the questionnaire was completed only by teachers who took the time and effort to teach supporting topics.

The stage is set to investigate how central control affects teachers' instructional decisions. There is no central control of Non-AP calculus classes, there is central control of content in Ontario, and there is strong central control of content and standards in British Columbia and AP Calculus classes. Despite this similarity between British Columbia and AP Calculus, there is the important difference that B.C. teachers develop curriculum guides in collaboration with the central authority while AP teachers do not. Finally, we matched the SIMS questionnaires to the content of the different courses telling us which questionnaires contain principal course content and which do not. We now can proceed to analyze the questionnaire data.

TEACHERS' INSTRUCTIONAL DECISIONS

What Mathematics Was Taught

Each questionnaire listed several topics and for each topic teachers were asked whether it was: (a) taught as new material, (b) reviewed then extended, (c) reviewed only, (d) assumed prerequisite knowledge, or (e) neither taught nor reviewed. For this study, we

---

[5] Overall, 65 percent of Grade 13 students took Relations and Functions, 55 percent Calculus, and 28 percent Algebra (Travers & Westbury, 1988).

TABLE 6.3

Principal, Supporting, and Ancillary Course Content for Population B Mathematics Courses

Classroom Process Questionnaire	British Columbia Algebra 12 CBC	Ontario Algebra CONA	Ontario Relations & Functions CONRF	Ontario Calculus CONC	U.S. Non-AP Calculus Classes NAP	U.S. AP Calculus Classes APC
Advanced Algebra	Supporting ($N \approx 89$)	Supporting ($N \approx 54$)	Supporting ($N \approx 45$)	Supporting ($N \approx 18$)	**Principal** ($N \approx 57$)	Supporting ($N \approx 6$)
Trigonometry	**Principal** ($N \approx 92$)	Supporting ($N \approx 10$)	**Principal** ($N \approx 66$)	Supporting ($N \approx 18$)	**Principal** ($N \approx 55$)	Supporting ($N \approx 6$)
Analytic Geometry	Ancillary ($N \approx 93$)	Supporting ($N \approx 43$)	**Principal** ($N \approx 60$)	Supporting ($N \approx 15$)	**Principal** ($N \approx 68$)	Ancillary ($N \approx 17$)
Calculus				**Principal** ($N \approx 60$)	**Principal** ($N \approx 85$)	**Principal** ($N \approx 28$)

Note. Not all respondents answered all questions on each questionnaire. In these cases the number of respondents given is the average number of respondents for each questionnaire and is denoted by $\approx$ in the table.

define a topic as having been taught if it was taught as new material, reviewed then extended, or reviewed only. Otherwise, we consider the topic as not taught.

Determining what mathematics was taught is a three-step process. First, we compute the percentage of respondents who taught each topic. This gives a distribution of percentages for the topics in each system or course. We then display these distributions using box plots. Analysis of these plots tells us how well the topics on the questionnaires match what was taught. These plots are given in Figure 6.1.

As an example of how to interpret these plots, consider the box plot for principal content in British Columbia (Figure 6.1a). The top, very short whisker, tells us that 25 percent of the topics were taught by at least 98 percent of the teachers, the box tells us that 50 percent of the topics were taught by between 35 percent and 98 percent of the teachers, the bottom whisker tells us that 25 percent of the topics were taught by between 17 percent and 35 percent of the teachers, and the median line tells us that half of the topics were taught by at least 95 percent of the teachers.

The findings in Figure 6.1a suggest that central control does affect what mathematics is taught. Teachers in systems with central control of content and standards (British Columbia and AP Calculus) have higher coverage of principal content than teachers in other systems (Ontario and Non-AP Calculus). In addition to telling us what topics were taught by many teachers, these data also tell us that some topics were taught by relatively few teachers—the bottom quartiles of the distributions. The whiskers on the box plots show that even in systems with some central control, such as Ontario, teachers make individual decisions to teach particular topics.

These data also suggest that if there are common expectations for the mathematical content of a course, then teachers are more likely to teach the same topics, regardless of central control. Thus, for calculus, as opposed to many other mathematics courses, there is relative agreement among mathematicians as to which topics must be covered. Consequently, teachers for the two calculus courses report teaching most of the topics included in the questionnaire. Likewise, expectations for British Columbia's Algebra 12 course are clearly stated and widely known, so most teachers teach most topics.

The findings on the precalculus courses (Ontario relations and functions and Non-AP calculus classes) offer additional support for this observation. There is little consensus on what the content of a precalculus course should be and, correspondingly, the data show less coverage of possible topics. Although both relations and functions and calculus are taught under the same system, teachers

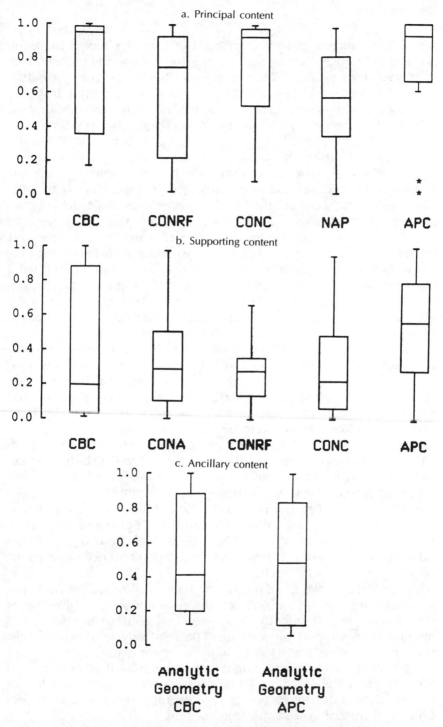

FIGURE 6.1 Distributions of Percentages of Topics Taught

report more agreement on teaching the calculus topics than the precalculus topics, thereby suggesting that coverage is independent of control. Part of this difference may be due to the questionnaires not matching the course content equally well, so we cannot draw any firm conclusions based on this evidence. Nevertheless, this finding raises an interesting question that deserves further research.

Figure 6.1b shows that the supporting content was taught much less frequently than the principal content, as we would expect. Because these questionnaires may contain some topics that are not in the various course syllabi, we must interpret these data carefully. The topics that were taught by high percentages of teachers (the parts of the box plots that extend above, say, 0.6 on the vertical scale) most likely reflect topics that are contained in the course, but happen to appear on a supporting questionnaire. However, the other topics (the portions of the box plots that extend below 0.6) tell a different story. Although these are supporting topics, there are significant percentages of teachers who chose to teach these topics. To illustrate this point, let us examine the data for AP Calculus classes in detail.

Although only six teachers chose to complete this questionnaire, they constitute almost one-quarter of the AP Calculus respondents. Thus, about one-quarter of the AP Calculus teachers believed that they taught enough algebra and trigonometry to warrant completing the two corresponding classroom process questionnaires. However, there is considerable variation between those six teachers in what topics they taught. A few topics were taught by nearly all six (the top whisker) and some topics were taught by very few (the bottom whisker). However, for about half the topics (the box), between two and five teachers elected to teach these particular topics. Thus, there was a substantial minority of teachers who taught algebra and trigonometry topics, yet within that minority there were differences in which topics were taught. These data show that a significant minority of AP Calculus teachers made independent decisions about what mathematics to teach.

Figure 6.1c shows the data for the two questionnaires that contain ancillary content. In general, the data show that these topics were taught less frequently than principal content but more frequently than supporting content. The relatively long boxes show that there is wide variation in what analytic geometry topics are taught—half the topics are taught by between about 20 percent and 80 percent of the teachers. This supports our earlier decision to classify these questionnaires as containing roughly equal proportions of principal and supporting content.

Overall, the data in Figure 6.1 suggest that teachers in systems with strong central control of content and standards (B.C. and AP Calculus classes) report teaching more of the topics than teachers in other systems. Principal content frequently was taught, supporting rarely was taught, and ancillary content was occasionally taught. This pattern supports our earlier classification scheme and provides evidence that these data reflect classroom practice.

It is important to remember that any conclusions we have made about the effects of central control are tentative. Some of the data can be explained by the expectations inherent in the content or by mismatches between the courses and the SIMS questionnaires. For some content for some systems (the prime example is supporting content for B.C.), the box plot was rather long, that is, the range of the distribution is large. How do we interpret this? Does it mean that teachers could not agree what to teach (the percentages were distributed fairly evenly within the range) or does it mean that teachers did agree what to teach (the percentages were concentrated near the extremes)? Therefore, before we can make conclusions about how central control affects teachers' decisions about what mathematics to teach, we need to investigate whether teachers taught the same mathematics.

Uniformity of Coverage

The question we now ask is, "How do different levels of central control of content and standards affect between-teacher variability on which topics were and were not taught?" To investigate this question we construct a *uniformity index*, which is the fraction of teachers who agreed either to teach a topic or not.[6] Values of the uniformity index vary between 0.50 (half the teachers taught a topic and half did not) and 1.00 (either all the teachers taught the topic or none did). We then examine the distribution of these uniformity indices for each system or course.[7] Because the uniformity index is a

---

[6] To determine the uniformity index, we computed the fraction of teachers who taught the topic and the fraction who did not. The larger of these is the uniformity index.

[7] These box plots should be interpreted in the same way as those in the last section. For example, consider the data for British Columbia as shown in Figure 6.2a. The top whisker tells us that for 25 percent of the topics, at least 98 percent of the teachers agreed either to teach them or not; the box tells us that for 50 percent of the topics, between 78 and 98 percent of the teachers agreed; the bottom whisker tells us that for 25 percent of the topics, between 63 and 78 percent of the teachers agreed; and the median line tells us that for half of the topics, over 95 percent of the teachers agreed either to teach these topics or not.

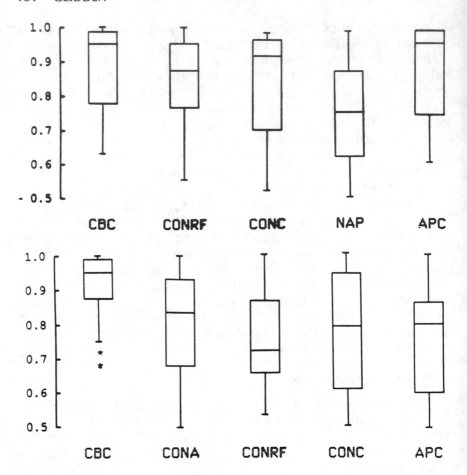

FIGURE 6.2   Distributions of Uniformity Indices for Principal and Supporting Content

function of the percentage of teachers who taught the topic, this analysis and some of the results will be familiar from the last section, but, as we shall see the uniformity index does provide a useful perspective. The box plots of the uniformity indices are given in Figure 6.2.

The data in Figure 6.2a show that there is substantial agreement about what mathematics to teach among teachers from systems with central control of content or standards (CBC, CON, and APC). Advanced Placement Calculus teachers teach the most uniformly, closely followed by British Columbia.[8] Ontario teachers exhibit

---

[8] There may be more uniformity among B.C. teachers than these data show. Algebra 12 was offered in basic and enriched formats, but respondents were not asked which format they taught. Consequently, among those teaching each format there may be greater uniformity that these data do not show.

somewhat less uniformity in the mathematics they teach (CONRF and CONC).

Non-AP calculus teachers report much less agreement about what topics to teach. There are three possible explanations for this: (a) local control of content and standards, which gives teachers more freedom to decide what to teach; (b) the fact that there are many basic types of Non-AP calculus courses; or (c) the fact that all four classroom process questionnaires were judged to represent principal Non-AP calculus course content. Regardless of the explanation, the data show that Non-AP calculus teachers disagree about what mathematics to teach.

For supporting content (see Figure 6.2b), the distributions of the uniformity indices show that there is considerable disagreement about what topics to teach, except in British Columbia. There, over 88 percent of the teachers agreed to teach or omit three-quarters (the box and top whisker) of the topics included in the algebra questionnaire (the supporting content). By contrast, Ontario relations and functions teachers (for whom the algebra questionnaire also was supporting content) displayed much less agreement.

The uniformity box plot for supporting content in British Columbia explains a result we noted at the end of the last section. The large range of supporting content taught does not reflect teachers making independent decisions; on the contrary, as the uniformity data show, there was considerable agreement among B.C. teachers on what mathematics to teach. The uniformity data for ancillary content are rather similar to the supporting data, and consequently confirm our earlier conclusions.

Overall, the teaching and uniformity data show that where there is more central control there is more agreement between teachers on what mathematics to teach. Teachers in British Columbia and AP Calculus classes (central control of content and standards) displayed the most agreement, teachers in Ontario (central control of content) displayed slightly less agreement, and Non-AP calculus teachers (no central control) displayed the least agreement. This result is consistent with Stevenson and Baker's (1991) findings on Population A (eighth grade). They found that teachers in educational systems with central control of content were more likely to teach the same mathematics than teachers in educational systems with local control.

In addition to this overall result, several other patterns emerge. The teaching and uniformity data show that British Columbia teachers exhibited significant agreement about what mathematics should be taught. Even though British Columbia does not have a school-leaving examination, it exhibited slightly more uniformity than AP Calculus classes, which do have an examination. We see the effects of the collaboration between the Ministry and classroom teachers in British Columbia beginning to emerge: The shared curriculum means that teachers know what they are supposed to teach, and the high uniformity for supporting content shows that they know what last year's teachers taught—there is no need for them to go back and cover prerequisite knowledge.

Besides showing that teachers agreed on what content to teach, the teaching and uniformity data also show that a substantial minority of teachers from Non-AP calculus classes, Ontario, and AP Calculus classes independently elected to teach particular topics. Although this result might be expected from Non-AP calculus classes for which content and standards are determined locally, it is somewhat surprising that teachers would act so independently in Ontario and AP Calculus classes. If Non-AP calculus teachers do not have a syllabus, how do they decide what to teach? Why do teachers who have a syllabus teach supplemental mathematics? We now have arrived at our second question. *Why* do teachers decide to teach the mathematics they do?

Teachers' Reasons for Teaching Mathematics Topics

Teachers who taught a particular topic were asked in the classroom process questionnaires if they did so because it was: (a) in the textbook, (b) in the syllabus or on an external examination, (c) well known to them, (d) easy to teach, (e) easy for students to understand, (f) enjoyed by students, (g) related to prior mathematics, or (h) useful for later study of mathematics. Teachers who did not cover a particular topic or use a particular interpretation were asked to indicate why not, choosing from the negatives of the reasons listed above. For example, a teacher could report that a particular topic was not taught because it was not in the textbook or it was difficult for students to understand.[9]

In order to facilitate comparisons between systems and courses, we report the mean number of times a reason was cited for teaching a topic or for not teaching a topic. For example in Figure 6.3a, "useful later" was cited about 60 percent of the time for British Columbia classes. This means that of the B.C. teachers who reported teaching a principal topic, about three-fifths of them re-

---

[9] Some of the negative reasons are not exact negations of the corresponding positive reasons. For instance, the negative of "well known" is "never considered using." Appendix A lists the exact wordings of the responses and the shortened forms used in this study.

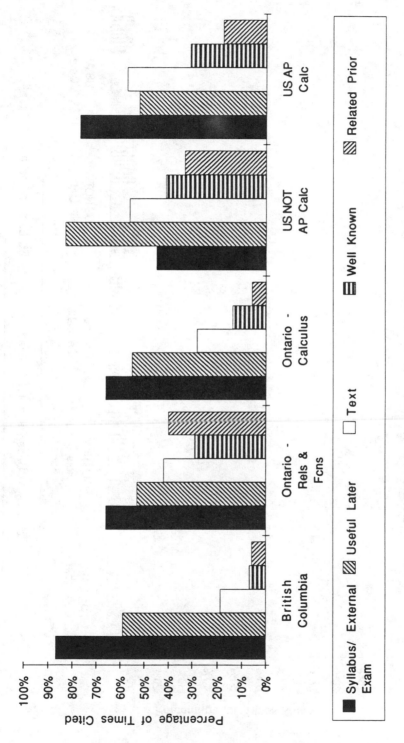

a. Reasons Most Frequently Cited for Teaching Principal Topics

FIGURE 6.3 Teachers' Reasons for Teaching Principal Content

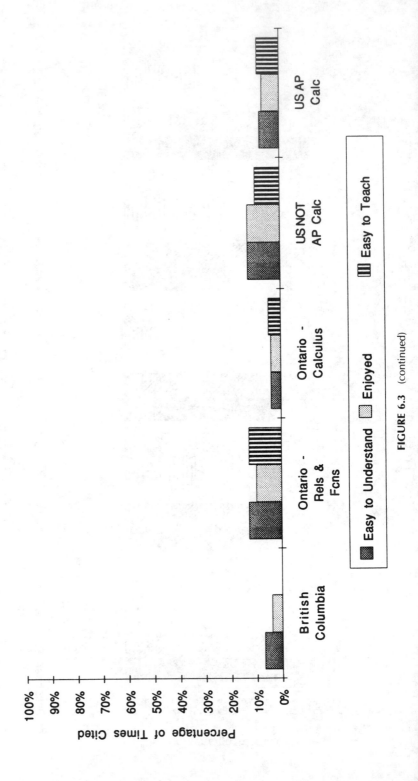

FIGURE 6.3 (continued)

ported they taught it because it was useful for later study of mathematics. The reasons are sorted from left to right, approximately in rank order.

Teachers' Reasons for Teaching Principal Content.   The most frequently cited reasons for teaching principal topics are shown in Figure 6.3a. Teachers taught topics because they were in the syllabus or on the external examination, useful later, in the textbook, well known, or related to prior mathematics. In systems with central control of content or standards (CBC, CON, and APC), the most frequently cited reason was "syllabus/external exam." The relative infrequency that "syllabus/external exam" is cited by Ontario teachers reflects only some of the effects of central control. The Ministry of Education approves textbooks in Ontario, so the frequency with which "text" is cited confounds the effects of the prescribed syllabus.

Within these data, the interaction between central and local control of content and standards begins to emerge. When there is central control (British Columbia, Ontario, and AP Calculus) teachers report that they teach topics because they are expected to. Even in Non-AP calculus classes, teachers frequently cite the textbook, a de facto syllabus, as the reason for deciding what mathematics to teach.

Teachers also Decide what Mathematics to Teach Based on Their Knowledge of Mathematics.   If we consider the reasons "useful later," "related prior," and "well known" as three dimensions of teachers' understanding of mathematics and if we add the frequencies at which each of these is cited, then in every system except British Columbia, teacher understanding is cited more frequently than "syllabus/external exam." Within these three dimensions there are differences: "useful later" was cited much more frequently than "well known" or "related prior." In fact, for Non-AP calculus classes "useful later" was the most frequently cited reason; for British Columbia and Ontario, the second most frequently cited reason. "Well known" and "related prior" are the fourth and fifth most frequently cited reason; and for AP Calculus, the third most frequently cited reasons. These data show that teachers do not teach the principal content simply because it is prescribed by the syllabus, examination, or textbook. They also teach mathematics based on their own knowledge and understanding of mathematics.

The reasons least frequently cited for teaching topics provide sharp contrast to the reasons most frequently cited (see Figure

6.3b). Teachers rarely taught content because it was easy for students to understand, enjoyed by students, or easy to teach. Although not shown, this pattern is repeated in the data for supporting and ancillary content.[10]

Teachers' Reasons for Teaching Supporting and Ancillary Content. The most frequently cited reasons for teaching supporting content are the same as those cited for teaching principal content, but "syllabus/external exam" no longer is the dominant reason (see Figure 6.4a). Teachers in Ontario algebra and calculus classes and AP Calculus classes cite "useful later" more frequently than "syllabus/external exam." In Ontario, relations and functions teachers cite "useful later" almost as frequently as "syllabus/external exam." Only in British Columbia is "syllabus/external exam" cited considerably more frequently than "useful later." If we again consider the reasons "useful later," "related prior," and "well known" as three dimensions of teachers' understanding of mathematics, then in every system except British Columbia mathematical knowledge is cited more frequently than "syllabus/external exam" as a reason for teaching supporting content.

The reasons cited by teachers for teaching ancillary content follow the pattern of the data on principal and supporting content (see Figure 6.4b). In British Columbia, "syllabus/external exam" is the most frequently cited reason, followed by "useful later." The data for AP Calculus classes tell a more complex story.

In AP Calculus classes, ancillary topics were taught for a variety of reasons: "useful later," "syllabus/external exam," "related prior," "text," "well known." However, recall our earlier result that ancillary content is taught more than supporting content, but less than principal content. For ancillary content, "syllabus/external exam" is cited more frequently than it is cited for supporting content, but less frequently than for principal content. "Useful later" is cited more frequently for ancillary and supporting content than it is for principal content.

This suggests that for AP Calculus courses, there is a direct relation between the level of mathematics and teachers' reasons for

---

[10] Some critics, particularly university mathematicians in the United States, have claimed that school teachers overemphasize making mathematics fun for students. These data show that Population B teachers did not, at least for topics included in the questionnaires. Although we cannot say for certain that they did not teach additional mathematics (for example, "taxicab" geometry or polyhedra) because it was fun for students, central control in British Columbia, Ontario, and AP Calculus classes, and the pressure to prepare students for further mathematics in all four systems makes it unlikely that they did.

teaching it. Lower level, prerequisite mathematics (supporting content) is driven by teachers' mathematical understanding; advanced mathematics (principal content) is driven by the syllabus and external examination; and middle level mathematics (ancillary content) is driven by both. This also is consistent with the hypothesis that some AP classes would have had analytic geometry the previous year while others were studying it during the current year.

Teachers' Reasons for Not Teaching Mathematics Topics. The story told by the reasons teachers cited for not teaching content is simple. Teachers most frequently cite: (a) "not in syllabus/external exam," (b) "not in text," and (c) "never considered" as reasons for not teaching principal content (see Figure 6.5a). The other reasons are rarely, if ever, cited. Although not shown, this pattern also holds for supporting content. The data for ancillary content reveals two interesting, but weak, patterns (see Figure 6.5b). British Columbia and AP Calculus teachers do not teach ancillary content (topics in analytic geometry) if it is difficult to understand or if it is not related to prior mathematics. This is consistent with our earlier assessment that analytic geometry is more advanced mathematics for British Columbia's Algebra 12 and prerequisite or concurrent mathematics for AP calculus.

Several patterns emerge from these data. Teachers do teach topics because they are in the syllabus or on an external examination. Non AP calculus teachers, who may not have a syllabus, follow the textbook as a de facto syllabus. The influence of the syllabus and external examinations extends beyond principal course content to ancillary and supporting content. Moreover, the instruments of central control (syllabus, examination, and text) are the most frequently cited reasons for not teaching particular topics. However, there is more to teacher decision making than central control.

The data also show that teachers are curriculum filters. They choose to teach mathematical topics based on their understanding of mathematics: the mathematics is useful for later study, the mathematics is well known to them, or the current topic is related to prior mathematics. A complex decision process emerges from these data. When content and standards are controlled locally (Non-AP calculus), teachers decide what to teach based on their own knowledge of mathematics, the textbook, or any syllabus they might have. If there is central control, then the syllabus or examination (or in Ontario, the text) drives teachers to teach principal content, but even so they make their own decisions about supporting and ancillary content.

Of the reasons related to teachers' mathematical knowledge, "useful later" is the most frequently cited. This raises the question of

a. Reasons Most Frequently Cited for Teaching Supporting Topics

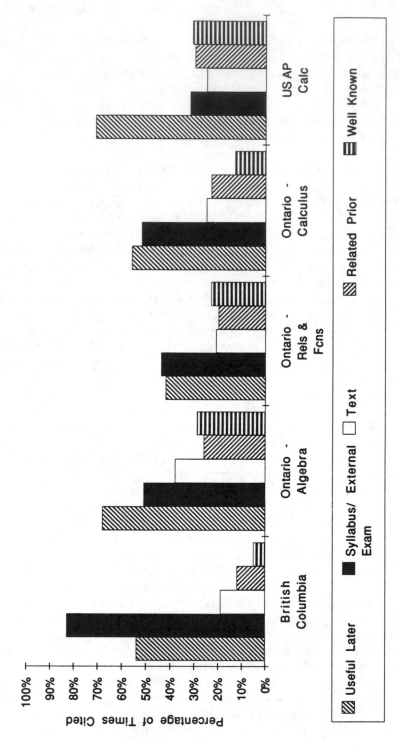

FIGURE 6.4 Most Frequently Cited Reasons for Teaching Supporting and Ancillary Content

b. Reasons Cited for Teaching Ancillary Topics

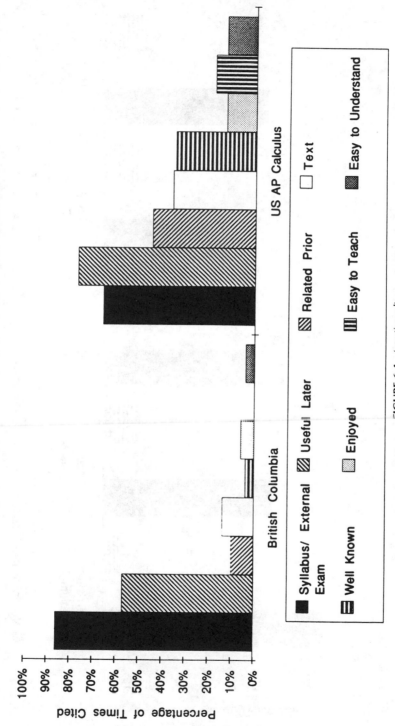

FIGURE 6.4 (continued)

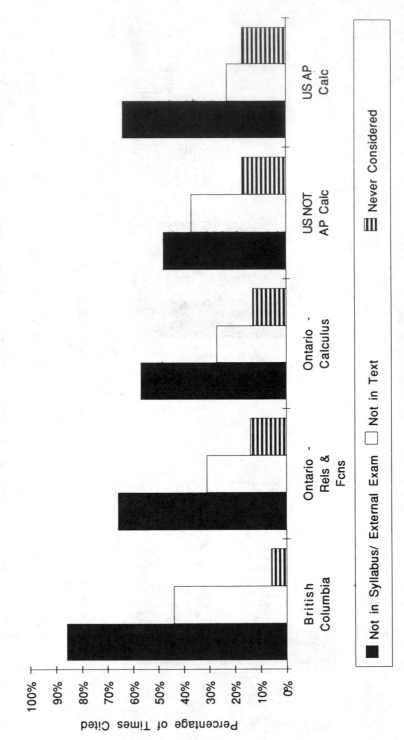

FIGURE 6.5 Teachers' Reasons for Not Teaching Content

b. Reasons Cited for NOT Teaching Ancillary Topics

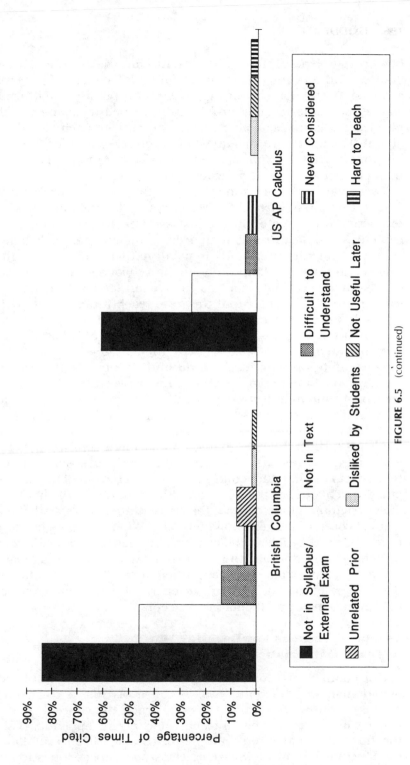

FIGURE 6.5 (continued)

how respondents interpreted "Useful for math in subsequent grades." Did they interpret it as useful for later study of pure mathematics; useful for solving applied problems in a mathematics course; useful for solving problems in applied disciplines such as physics, statistics, economics, or engineering; or useful for all of the above? The answer to this question is not essential for this study, but considering the importance teachers assign to the later usefulness of mathematics, it deserves further research.

These data also tell us more about effects of the relationship in British Columbia between the Ministry of Education and classroom teachers. We suggested in the last section that central control of content, central control of standards, and significant collaboration resulted in greater uniformity in what mathematics was taught. In this section, we see that although these teachers overwhelmingly cite "syllabus/external exam" as the reason for teaching particular content, they also report that they also teach it because it is useful later. This supports our earlier suggestion that B.C. teachers might own their curriculum—they are not teaching it only because someone tells them to, they also see why they are teaching it.

These data on why teachers do and do not teach topics have revealed some interesting relationships between the level of central control of content and standards and teachers' reasons for deciding what mathematics to teach. The data from British Columbia suggest that more uniformity of coverage can be achieved by establishing central control of standards, mandating a central curriculum, and having mathematics teachers and their professional organization articulate that curriculum in considerable detail for classroom practice. This raises the question of how much detail should be in the curriculum guide. Should the curriculum articulate the mathematical content and teaching methods? When teachers decide how to teach, do they follow the syllabus or their own judgement? We have now arrived at our third question. What reasons do teachers cite for deciding *how* to teach mathematics? To answer this question, we examine the reasons teachers cite for using particular interpretations of mathematics concepts.

Teachers' Reasons For Deciding How to Teach Mathematics

One characteristic of mathematics is that a concept can be interpreted in many different ways. Because of this, a teacher must decide which interpretation to use to teach the concept, that is, a teacher must decide how to teach the concept. Appendix B shows the three different interpretations of the logarithm function that were included in the SIMS algebra classroom process questionnaire.

Teachers who used a particular interpretation were asked on the SIMS classroom process questionnaires if they did so because it was: (a) in the textbook, (b) in the syllabus or on an external examination, (c) well known to them, (d) easy to teach, (e) easy for students to understand, (f) enjoyed by students, (g) related to prior mathematics, or (h) useful for later study of mathematics. Teachers who did not were asked to indicate why not, choosing from the negatives of the reasons listed above. (These choices were identical to those offered as reasons for deciding whether to teach particular topics.)

The data on which interpretations were used differ from the data on what topics were taught in three important ways. Only three concepts were included in SIMS questionnaires: logarithms, complex numbers, and circular functions. It is difficult to determine which interpretations actually were used. For complex numbers, teachers were asked if they used an interpretation frequently, infrequently, or not at all. For logarithms and circular functions, teachers were asked how many periods they studied each interpretation. Finally, some of the data are missing for some questions for some systems. Consequently, we limit this analysis to those British Columbia, Ontario, and Non-AP calculus teachers who answered the relevant questions and we simply report the total number of times a reason either for using an interpretation or for not using it was cited. Although this makes absolute between-system comparisons difficult, it does allow us to make relative between-system and within-system comparisons.

Teachers' Reasons for Using Particular Interpretations.
Three patterns in the data (Figure 6.6a) suggest that we can use it profitably. One is the frequency that "syllabus/external exam" is cited by teachers in British Columbia and another is the frequency that "text" is cited by Non-AP calculus teachers. We saw these patterns in the previous data on which topics were taught, and their reappearance suggest that these data can be considered as valid. The third pattern is that the overall distribution of these responses is consistent with responses to similar questions for Population A teachers in the U.S. (Glidden, 1991) and other systems (Bartels, 1991).

However, these data show that teachers use different reasons to decide how to teach mathematics than they use to decide what mathematics to teach. Teachers overwhelmingly report that they use interpretations that are "well known," "easy for students to understand," and "useful later." We saw above that teachers do not teach mathematics content to students because it is easy to under-

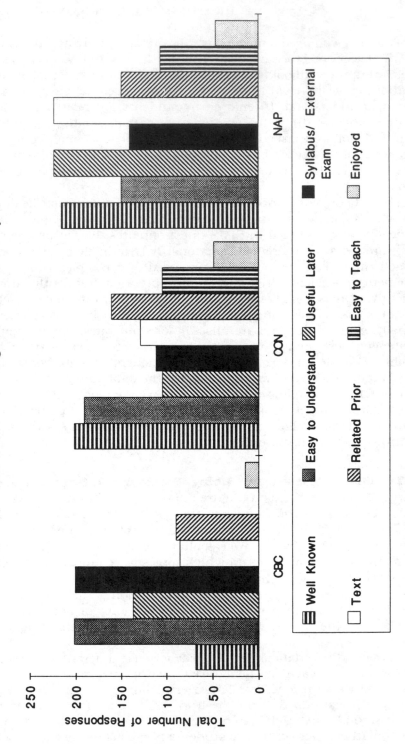

FIGURE 6.6 Teachers' Reasons For Using and Not Using Particular Interpretations

b. Reasons Cited For NOT Using a Particular Interpretation

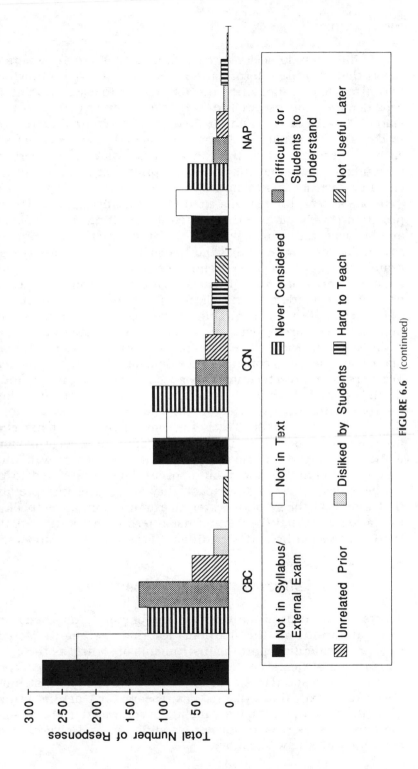

FIGURE 6.6 (continued)

stand, but they do select interpretations that are. Teachers also report that they use interpretations that are easy to teach, which is in contrast to their not citing this as a reason to teach content. If we consider the reasons "well known," "easy for students to understand," "useful later," and "related prior" as four dimensions of teachers' professional knowledge, and if we add the frequencies that each of these are cited, then in all three systems teachers overwhelmingly report that they use their professional judgment to decide how to teach mathematics.

In one aspect, the reasons cited for not using a particular interpretation closely parallel those cited for teaching topics; but from another aspect, they are completely different (see Figure 6.6b). As we saw in the data for deciding what to teach, "not in syllabus/external exam" and "not in text" exert limiting influences—they frequently are cited as reasons for not using an interpretation. Teachers also cite "never considered," the SIMS opposite of "well known." However, these data show something new: teachers do not use interpretations that are difficult for students to understand.

The data on teachers' reasons for deciding how to teach mathematics provide sharp contrast to the data for deciding what to teach. Teachers do not teach content because it is easy to understand nor do they omit it because it is difficult. However, teachers do use interpretations that are easy to understand and they do not use those that are difficult. Teachers from all three systems choose interpretations based on their professional knowledge of mathematics teaching. They choose interpretations that are well known, easy for students to understand, useful later, or related to prior mathematics. As we might expect, they do not use interpretations that are not in the syllabus, external examination, or textbook, but they also report that they do not use interpretations that are unrelated to prior mathematics or difficult for students to understand.

SUMMARY AND IMPLICATIONS

If a system has central control of content or standards, then there is more uniformity in the mathematics that is taught. Moreover, teachers frequently report the instruments of control as the reasons for teaching principal content. But even where there is local control of content and standards, teachers report the de facto instruments of control ("text" and "syllabus") as reasons for teaching principal content. In addition, the instruments of central control overwhelmingly are cited as reasons for not teaching topics. However, central control is not the whole story.

Teachers also report that they decide what content to teach based on their understanding of mathematics. They teach mathematical topics because they are useful for later study of mathematics, well known to the teacher, and related to prior mathematics. Also, teachers report that the most important factor in deciding how to teach mathematics is their own knowledge of mathematics teaching and learning. They choose interpretations that are well known to them, easy for students to understand, useful in later study of mathematics, or related to prior mathematics. They do not choose interpretations that are difficult for students to understand or unrelated to prior mathematics. Moreover, the syllabus, external examination, and textbook have little influence in deciding which interpretation to use, although they are influential in deciding which interpretation not to use.

In other words, this study suggests that deciding what mathematics to teach and how to teach it is not an either-or proposition. Teachers do teach toward an examination and they act as curriculum filters. This suggests that neither national examinations nor grass-roots curriculum reform will succeed on its own. If the mathematical and scientific community wants to promote curriculum reform, then the findings from this study suggest that they should help establish central syllabi and examinations that push teachers to teach the new curricula. By the same token, proponents of examinations must be aware that teachers do more than follow a syllabus: they also use their professional knowledge to decide what mathematics to teach and how to teach it. What does this mean for the recent proposals for school reform? How can we reconcile strong central control of content and standards with the fact that teachers filter a prescribed curriculum? British Columbia offers a possible answer.

In British Columbia, the Ministry of Education determines the syllabus for Algebra 12 and classroom teachers work with the ministry to write curriculum guides for it. As we said earlier, this gives teachers in British Columbia a sense that the curriculum is "theirs," a sense of ownership. They have a clear vision of Algebra 12 and they teach to their vision. More importantly, teachers in British Columbia share a common vision of school mathematics across grades. Because teachers follow detailed curriculum guides, students in each course receive the same or similar preparation. For instance, eleventh grade teachers teach what the curriculum guide prescribes, and consequently individual Algebra 12 teachers have little need to teach specific, prerequisite mathematics. Thus, ministry–teacher collaboration across grades produces a common vision of school mathematics as a whole.

We can say with confidence that this common vision of Algebra 1·2 is the result of ministry–classroom teacher collaboration and not solely the result of strong central control. Like British Columbia, AP Calculus has strong central control of content and standards. If a common vision resulted from only central control of content and standards, then we should have seen evidence of it in the data for AP Calculus, but we did not. Compared with British Columbia teachers, AP Calculus teachers taught a wider variety of topics for a wider variety of reasons. What differentiates these two systems is that British Columbia teachers are involved in curriculum development while AP Calculus teachers are not. Thus, although central control produces some measure of uniformity, teacher involvement in curriculum development produces a common vision.

Therefore, effective school reform in the United States would seem to require at least two components: (a) establishing central control of content and standards, and (b) directly involving teachers, NCTM, and other national and state professional organizations in writing curriculum guides for this content. But an important question follows: Should central control be exercised at the national, state, or district level?

The findings of this study suggest that control should be exercised at the state or district level, not the national level. The basis of this claim comes from our examination of British Columbia. Certain geographic features of British Columbia enhanced teachers' sense of ownership: the ministry that mandates the curriculum is nearby, there are relatively few teachers, teachers are located close to one another, teachers know one another, and a local professional organization collaborates in curriculum development. Although it might not be possible to replicate all of these conditions in every state, it is clear that none of them could be replicated if control were instituted at the national level—the United States is too vast and too populous.

This study also has implications for curriculum reform and centrally controlled examinations. Teachers cite a variety of mathematical and professional reasons for teaching content. Therefore, if new curricula include new mathematical topics, then teachers need to know more mathematics—they must learn these new topics, see how they relate to prior mathematics, and see how they are useful in later mathematics. If a new curriculum includes new interpretations of mathematical concepts, then teachers need more understanding of the didactics of mathematics—they must understand these interpretations deeply, be shown that they will promote better student understanding, and see how these interpretations are useful for later mathematics.

Although it has not been established what form the centrally controlled examinations will take, this analysis suggests a clear answer. If state or local authorities, NCTM, other national and state professional organizations, and classroom teachers work together to articulate a curriculum on which students will be examined, then the examination should be based on this curriculum. Moreover, the examination should reward students for knowing this mathematics at a deep level. Thus, it is clear that they should not be standardized, curriculum-independent tests. Examinations that can serve as models include the GCE A-level examinations in Great Britain and the Regents Examinations in New York State.

This study does not suggest what type of reward would be most effective: scholarships (as in British Columbia), college credit (as is offered for AP examinations), special diplomas (such as the Regents Diplomas that are offered in New York), or regular high school diplomas? This is not an insurmountable problem. The easiest solution is for each state to offer whatever rewards it believes will be most effective.

Thus, effective school mathematics reform is not a question of either examinations or grass-roots curriculum reform. As this study has shown, deciding what mathematics to teach and how to teach it is a complex process: teachers teach a prescribed curriculum, but as they do, they use their professional judgment to filter it. If educational reformers are to improve achievement in school mathematics, they must recognize this complexity. One way to address this complexity is by including classroom teachers in developing the curriculum. Having classroom teachers articulate what form the prescribed curriculum should take in the classroom produces a common vision for that curriculum. Because it is "their curriculum," teachers have a vested interest in teaching it and seeing their students achieve it. If we are to improve student mathematics achievement, we must recognize the central role teachers play in transmitting the curriculum.

APPENDIX A

Possible Reasons for Teaching Topics or Using Interpretations

Short Name	Question on Questionnaire
Well Known	Well known to me.
Syllabus/External Exam	Emphasized in syllabus or external exam.
Easy to Understand	Easy for students to understand.
Enjoyed by Students	Enjoyed by students.
Related Prior	Related to mathematics in prior grades.
Useful Later	Useful for mathematics in subsequent grades.
Easy to Teach	Easy to teach.
Text	Emphasized in students' text.

Possible Reasons for *Not* Teaching Topics or *Not* Using Interpretations

Short Name	Question on Questionnaire
Never Considered	Never considered using it.
Not in Syllabus/External Exam	Not in syllabus or external exam.
Difficult to Understand	Difficult for students to understand.
Disliked by Students	Disliked by students.
Unrelated Prior	Does not relate to previous study of mathematics
Not Useful Later	Not useful for further study.
Hard to Teach	Hard to teach.
Not in Text	Not emphasized in students' text.

Source: International Association for the Evaluation of Educational Achievement (1985).

APPENDIX B

Three Possible Interpretations of the Logarithm Function

Exponent Base. Logarithms are defined as exponents. Students abstract the generalization from observing, and working with, patterns such as:

$$4 \times 32 = 2^2 \times 2^5 = 2^7 = 128.$$

Here $\log ab = \log a + \log b$ is considered a restatement of $10^a \times 10^b = 10^{a+b}$.

Inverse Function Base.   A logarithmic function is defined as the inverse of the exponential function $f(x) = 10^x$.

Consider the graph of the log function. It is observed for several specific problems that the ordinate at $x = ab$ is equal to the sum of the ordinates at $x = a$ and at $x = b$. Thus $\log ab = \log a + \log b$.

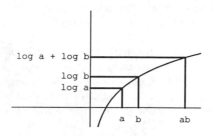

Area Under a Curve Base.   Logarithmic functions are defined in terms of area under curves of the form $f(x) = \dfrac{k}{x}$ ($y = \log x$ is associated with $k = 0.434$).

Log b is then defined as the area under the graph of $f(x)$ for $1 \leq x \leq b$. By counting squares on a fine grid paper for several specific problems, students form the generalization that the area under the curve from 1 to ab is the sum of the area under the curve from 1 to a and from 1 to b.

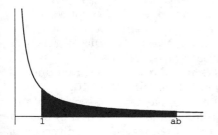 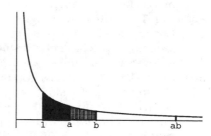

REFERENCES

Bartels, B. (1991). *The effect of experience on teachers' instructional decisions*. Unpublished paper. College of Education, University of Illinois at Urbana-Champaign.

Council of Ministers of Education, Canada. (1981). *Secondary education in Canada: A student transfer guide* (3rd ed.). Toronto: Council of Ministers of Education, Canada.

Department of Education. (1991). *America 2000: An education strategy.* Washington, DC: U.S. Department of Education.

Glidden, P. L. (1991). Teachers' reasons for instructional decisions. *Mathematics Teacher, 84,* 610–614.

Holmes Group. (1986). *Tomorrow's teachers.* East Lansing, MI: Holmes Group.

International Association for the Evaluation of Educational Achievement. (1985). *Second study of mathematics: Population B data sets.* Champaign, IL: University of Illinois at Urbana-Champaign, College of Education.

Mathematical Association of America. (1991). *A call for change.* Washington, DC: Mathematical Association of America.

McKnight, C. C., Crosswhite, F. J., Dossey, J. A., Kifer, E., Swafford, J. O., Travers, K. J., & Cooney, T. J. (1987). *The underachieving curriculum: Assessing U.S. school mathematics from an international perspective.* Champaign, IL: Stipes.

National Research Council. (1989). *Everybody counts: A report to the nation on the future of mathematics education.* Washington, DC: National Academy Press.

National Council of Teachers of Mathematics. (1989). *Commission on standards for school mathematics: Curriculum and evaluation standards for school mathematics.* Reston, VA: National Council of Teachers of Mathematics.

Porter, A., Floden, R., Freeman, D., Schmidt, W., & Schwille, J. (1988). Content determinants in elementary school mathematics. In D. A. Grouws & T. J. Cooney (Eds.), *Perspectives on research on effective mathematics teaching* (pp. 96–113). Reston VA: The National Council of Teachers of Mathematics and Lawrence Erlbaum Associates.

Romberg, T. (1988). Can teachers be professionals? In D. A. Grouws & T. J. Cooney (Eds.), *Perspectives on research on effective mathematics teaching* (pp. 224–244). Reston, VA: The National Council of Teachers of Mathematics and Lawrence Erlbaum Associates.

Stevenson, D. L., & Baker, D. P. (1991). State control of the curriculum and classroom instruction. *Sociology of Education, 64,* 1–10.

Travers, K. J., & Westbury, I. (Eds.). (1988). *Supplement to Second International Mathematics Study, Vol. I: International analysis of mathematics curricula* (ERIC ED 306 111). Champaign, IL: University of Illinois at Urbana-Champaign and International Association for the Evaluation of Educational Achievement.

Travers, K. J., & Westbury, I. (Eds.). (1989). *The IEA study of mathematics I: Analysis of mathematics curricula.* Oxford: Pergamon.

7

Gender Groupings and Improving Mathematics Achievement: Lessons From a Comparative Analysis

David P. Baker

Department of Sociology
The Catholic University of America
Washington, DC

Cornelius Riordan

Department of Sociology
Providence College
Providence, RI

Maryellen Schaub

Department of Sociology
The Catholic University of America
Washington, DC

A recent flurry of research on the effectiveness of single- and mixed-gender learning environments has led some to suggest policy changes in gender groupings as a way of improving mathematics teaching and learning in the United States. Although there are some disagreements among the U.S. studies, most agree that there can be achievement advantages, particularly for females, in single-sex schools that are not found in mixed-sex schools (Astin, 1977; Finn, 1980; Lee & Bryk, 1986; Price & Rosemier, 1972; Riordan, 1990; Tidball, 1973, 1980). Since many of these studies examine mathematics achievement, a preliminary conclusion is that single-sex schools or classrooms may be a fruitful avenue to explore for the improvement of mathematics education. However, our recently completed comparative analysis suggests that single-sex schools may not have universal positive effects across different national educational systems (Baker, Riordan, & Schaub, 1994). And what appears to happen in the very small number of single-sex schools in the United States would very likely not happen in a large-scale application of single-sex schooling in the American system.

We present an analysis to suggest that single-sex schooling, in and of itself, is not solely responsible for achievement gains. Other factors, related to the structure of a national school system, overshadow the effects of groupings—with the result that we find a mixed pattern of effects depending on the degree to which a particular gender grouping is used within a national system. Our conclusion is that the effects of gender context in schools are not universal and that there are clear reasons why this is so. This conclusion helps to solve two policy dilemmas that the U.S. research on gender groupings and achievement have suggested. The first dilemma is that a proposal to use more single-sex schooling runs counter to the historical organization of American schooling. In the United States the mixing of males and females in schools has been the dominant tradition since the beginnings of the public school system and single-sex arrangements have always been relatively rare (Tyack & Hansot, 1990). Single-sex schooling is a remnant of particular religious traditions and/or the practices of other cultural minorities that have, at times, set up schools in some opposition to the dominant public system (Baker, 1991). The desirability of coeducation is such a pervasive belief among the American majority that any attempts to increase single-sex enrollments would certainly run into heavy resistance (Riordan, 1990).

The second policy dilemma centers on the specific findings suggesting that single-sex arrangements are more helpful to females than to males. But there is some evidence that males receive some advantage in being mixed with females (Riordan, 1990). In other words, female achievement may suffer from the presence of males but, conversely, male achievement may be enhanced when males are mixed with females. This presents a problem for any policy recommendations about gender groupings in U.S. schools. Perhaps the optimal arrangement of gender grouping for males and females is contrary. A heavy investment in one type of gender grouping may come at the price of lower (or at least smaller growth in) achievement for one gender.

Given these policy dilemmas, and the recent U.S. research, we thought it useful to re-examine the effects of gender groupings on mathematics achievement from a cross-national perspective. This allows us to test an argument about whether or not gender groupings have the same effects in all systems. And if not, why not? We have recently completed such a comparative study of gender groupings using the SIMS data and our results shed light on the problems underlying these policy dilemmas (Baker, Riordan, & Schaub, 1994). Although our study did not examine the U.S. data, the American debate motivated us to design a cross-national study of the use of gender groupings and mathematics achievement. We attempted to answer two questions about gender groupings and mathematics achievement: Under what circumstances do gender groupings have the largest influence on achievement? What are the causes of this influence?

COMPARATIVE ANALYSIS OF GENDER GROUPINGS

There has been considerable research on the relative effectiveness of single and coeducational schools in other educational systems (Arnot, 1983; Carpenter & Hayden, 1987; Dale, 1974; Deem, 1984; Finn, 1980; Hamilton, 1985; Harvey, 1985; Jimenez & Lockheed, 1989; Lee & Lockheed 1990; Marsh, Smith, Marsh, & Owens, 1988; Shaw, 1980; for a complete review, see Riordan, 1990, Chapter 3). Most of this research has been confined to analyses within specific educational systems. What has been missing is a comparison of effects across national educational systems. The consequence of this noncomparative approach is that questions such as: Do gender groupings have similar effects in all systems, and Why or why not, have not been considered.

Worldwide there is considerable variation in the degree to which single-sex and mixed-sex groupings are used to organize schools. For example, in some systems, such as those found in the Republic of Ireland or some middle eastern countries, nearly all schools are single-sex, while in other countries, such as the United States, nearly all schools are coeducational. Between these extremes are a large number of national systems with varying proportions of single- and mixed-sex schooling. Generally, organizational variation has been overlooked in searching for gender-grouping effects on achievement. This variation in the proportion of single- and mixed-sex schooling has important implications for considering whether or not gender grouping has an effect on achievement. It is especially salient for broadening the theoretical perspective on gender groupings.

Since so much of the previous research on gender groupings is noncomparative, the literature on the theme has had only limited theoretical development. Many studies use little or no theory to argue why one gender grouping should produce an achievement advantage over the other; gender groupings are often studied because they are simply there or because they are related to recent searches for school effects in public and private sectors. Those studies that do draw on a theoretical perspective focus almost exclusively on an extreme micro-version of the effects of gender groupings— only the condition of segregating boys and girls or mixing them together, stripped of any other contextual influences. The common argument is that a single-sex classroom (or school) offers numerous learning advantages to students and that these advantages are diminished by the mixing of the sexes into one class. The advantages are thought to include such things as more successful role models, less gender bias in teacher–student and peer interaction, a reduction in the salience of youth culture (that is, nonacademic) values, and a greater degree of order and control. (See Riordan, 1990, for a review.) Usually these arguments suggest an advantage for females attending single-sex schools—a sort of positive "hidden curriculum" for girls—and have been developed mostly in United States and British studies where the findings generally run in this direction. One logical conclusion of this microlevel argument is that all incidents of single-sex schooling should yield an advantage in the learning of subjects such as mathematics, particularly for females. As our analysis shows, this is not supported by cross-national comparisons.

Table 7.1 summarizes a selection of studies comparing gender groupings in different countries. Although many of the studies show an advantage of single-sex groupings, not all do, and the effects vary from modest to very small. Null findings do not easily find their way into noncomparative literature, so one would expect

TABLE 7.1

Summary of Selected Studies on the Relative Academic Effectiveness of Single- and Mixed-Sex Schools[a]

National System	Grade Level	Direction of Finding		Effect Size[b]	National Sample	Study
Australia	12	Pri.	$SS_F = Coed_F$	0	No	Carpenter & Hayden, 1987
		Pub.	$SS_F > Coed_F$	.76[c]		
	9-12		$SS_F = Coed_F$	0	No	Marsh, et al., 1988
			$SS_M = Coed_M$	0		
England	8-9		$SS_F > Coed_F$	.42[c]	Yes	Finn, 1980
			$SS_M > Coed_M$	.40[c]		
Jamaica	11		$SS_F > Coed_F$	.64	Yes	Hamilton, 1985
			$SS_M ? Coed_M$	.50		
Nigeria	9		$SS_F > Coed_F$	.64	Yes	Lee & Lockheed, 1990
			$SS_M > Coed_M$	.06		
Thailand	8		$SS_F > Coed_F$	.28	No	Jimenez & Lockheed, 1989
			$SS_M > Coed_M$	−.26		
United States	1		$SS_F = Coed_F$	NA[e]	No	Price & Rosemier, 1972
			$SS_M > Coed_M$	0		
	8-9		$SS_F > Coed_F$	.25	Yes	Finn, 1980
			$SS_M > Coed_M$	.77		
	10, 12		$SS_F > Coed_F$	.12[f]	Yes	Lee & Bryk, 1986
			$SS_M > Coed_M$	.11[f]		
	10, 12		$SS_F = Coed_F$	0−.06[g]	Yes	Marsh, 1989
			$SS_M = Coed_M$	0−.06[g]		
	10, 12	whites	$SS_F > Coed_F$	.13[f]	Yes	Riordan, 1990
		whites	$SS_M = Coed_M$	−.05[f]		
		minority	$SS_F > Coed_F$	.20[f]		
		minority	$SS_M > Coed_M$	.15[f]		

Notes. [a]Studies selected . . .
[b]SS_M–$Coed_M$/SD
[c]Mean effect size over multiple achievement measures.
[d]Estimate from Robitaille and Garden, 1989.
[e]Not enough information provided to estimate effect size.
[f]Regressional effect size b_{SS}/SD_{Ach}; B_{SS} controlled for background vars., average size ($p < .05$).
[g]Standardized betas.

to find here reports of differences, but even so the effects are not uniform across all systems. Also within systems gender groupings have an effect only for certain types of students. In addition to U.S. female students, Riordan (1990) has shown that single-sex school effects are greatest among minorities (African Americans and Hispanics). These effects for minorities hold for both males and females. When effects are found for any students, they have been found in systems in which a particular gender grouping (usually single sex) is only rarely used. For example, in the United States, where most of the studies have been done and where some of the larger effects have been reported, about three percent of all secondary school enrollment is single sex. This is one of the smallest single-sex enrollments among all countries that have single-sex schooling.

To explore the conditions under which gender grouping effects occur, we did a study that compared the effects of single- and mixed-sex schools in four countries (Baker, Riordan, & Schaub, 1994). We chose systems that varied in their use of single- and mixed-sex schooling from about equal enrollment in single-sex and mixed schools to relatively small enrollments in single-sex schools. This variation, which we termed the "normative context," may help to explain why gender groupings influence achievement in some situations and not in others. It may also help to explain why there is variation in the size of effects across national systems.

THE NORMATIVE CONTEXT OF GENDER GROUPINGS AND SCHOOL EFFECTS

Our main argument is that gender groupings will have the largest effect on achievement in systems in which single-sex schooling is relatively rare, or less normative. We arrived at this hypothesis after asking several questions about the current literature on gender groupings and achievement. First, the effect of single-sex schools has generally been shown to be modest and variable across student types. This suggests that if the microclassroom processes identified as possible causes of the advantages of single-sex schools are in effect, they do not have overwhelming effects, nor do they occur for all types of students. One question is, then, why are the effects not larger and more uniform? Second, the largest positive effects of single-sex schools usually have been reported in systems in which relatively small proportions of students attend these schools. The U.S. findings on a very small single-sex enrollment are a prime example of this. A second question is, why do the size of effects of single-sex schools vary across national systems? We believe that the answer to these two questions lies in the degree to which single-sex schooling is used within a system, or the degree to which single-sex schooling is normative. We suggest that there are two reasons why the normative context of gender grouping should influence their effects on achievement. The first is the learning environment supplied by different types of schools, and the second is what students demand of different types of schools.

Since school systems are increasingly under the control of national governments, the supply of educational opportunities and the regulation of schools has become a central function of the state (e.g., Meyer & Hannon, 1979). Agencies of the state determine what happens in the classroom through such things as the regulation of curricular content (Benovat, Cha, Kamens, Meyer, & Wong, 1991), the dissemination and pace of instruction (Stevenson & Baker, 1991), teacher qualifications and inspection, achievement standards for students, and the accreditation of schools. Although states generally control schools within a national system, for a number of historical and political reasons, different types of schools that are less controlled can flourish in some national systems—in other words, even when there are forces that create a national system, numerous opportunities can exist for different types of small sets of schools.

When systems foster many small sets of special schools, the state often regulates these subgroups less rigorously. What is important about this for our understanding of gender groupings is that where there are such subgroups of schools, different educational environments are supplied by those schools. There is less standardization across learning environments. This situation can influence achievement opportunities for students in two ways. First, the resources brought to the learning environment in a set of special schools can be different from the main body of schools, thus producing a richer or poorer environment depending on the resources of the sponsors of the special set of schools. Second, to the degree that a different gender grouping (usually single sex) occurs within these special schools, the different learning environment associated with them may enhance the microeffects of gender grouping in the classroom.

Some national systems tend to limit the growth of special kinds of schools, thus creating a more controlled and uniform set of educational environments. If single-sex schooling occurs within such systems, usually larger proportions of students are enrolled and the educational environment is more similar to mixed-sex schools because the state controls these larger sets of schools. Thus, the modest effects of microprocesses are likely to be overwhelmed by this more uniform supply of schooling.

In terms of the demand for types of schools, the presence of small sets of semi-autonomous schools in a national system also influences what type of students enroll, and thus shapes what students bring to different gender groupings. The existence of different types of schools intensifies concerns over choice of school among students (and their parents); consequently, students demand different qualities from different schools. This increases between school-type differences in the kinds of students that attend a particular type of school. To the degree that gender groupings vary by school type in such a system, patterns of student enrollment will vary by gender grouping. National systems that restrict the proliferation of numerous types of schools diminish the effects of choice of school and between school-type differences in student enrollment. If different gender groupings occur in this kind of system it is less likely that patterns of student enrollment will differ across groupings.

These effects are not caused by the mere number of schools with a particular sex grouping. Rather, the conditions that allow for the existence of numerous sets of special schools (oftentimes producing small sets of single-sex schools) in a system are related to the degree to which many factors within schools are controlled by the central government. These factors reflect the degree to which, and the ways in which, formal education is politically incorporated within a nation (Ramirez & Rubinson, 1979; Stevenson & Baker, 1991). For example, the United States incorporates the control of schooling at the local community level and thus has always produced a varied set of schools, particularly at the secondary level. The U.S. state (that is, the federal government) does not actually control much of the learning environment (for example, class size, instructional methods, and classroom management) in the schools, so they are freer to generate different environments for students. Some argue that this is what produces pockets of greater school effectiveness (and greater school ineffectiveness) in the United States. In other countries the political incorporation is highly centralized within the central government; such systems tend to produce fewer small sets of schools, and also tend to control learning environments from one school to the next.

The nature of political incorporation also effects the degree to which students are presented with a choice in schooling. Special sets of schools intensify the selection of schools by students. Thus, what is supplied by a relatively small set of different schools and what is demanded by students who choose these schools can influence achievement. In some cases this may mean that the less common school types have less to offer in terms of a learning environment but offer instead other perceived benefits, such as religious training, connections to certain other special schooling opportunities, and so forth. We argue that when gender groupings are involved in both the supply and the demand for special schools, grouping effects (either positive or negative) on achievement can become prevalent. Conversely, national systems that maintain, often by official design, equal proportions of single- and mixed-sex schools, exercise more control over all schools and produce more uniformity in learning environments. Consequently, a student's choice of a particular gender grouping is perceived as less related to the quality of education that the student will receive. Therefore, issues of selection of a particular gender grouping for particular reasons is less salient.

This argument helps us understand the different patterns of effects found in the gender-groupings literature. It also helps us in solving the policy dilemmas that stem from the U.S. research. A system such as the U.S. will produce noticeable gender-grouping effects, while other systems may not. It may, therefore, not be a universally true that single-sex classrooms are better for improving achievement, even for females. Rather, it may be the case that other factors more closely related to the learning environment are associated with particular gender groupings in a system. Our study examines these arguments.

NORMATIVE CONTEXT AND GENDER-GROUPING EFFECTS

Using the SIMS Population B data we tested three hypotheses deriving from our argument about the normative context of gender groupings and achievement. First, to test our central proposal, we hypothesized that achievement levels between single-sex and mixed-sex schools will differ in countries where one kind of gender grouping is more or less common. The next two hypotheses tested our arguments about why this effect occurs. We hypothesized, second, that selective patterns of student enrollments in schools of differing gender groupings will be more evident in systems in which one grouping is relatively rare. And third, we hypothesized that the educational environment supplied by schools will vary more across gender groupings in systems in which one grouping is relatively rare.

From the countries participating in SIMS, we chose four systems that vary in the use of single-sex schooling: Flemish Belgium and New Zealand, which have close to even enrollment in single- and mixed-sex secondary schools (68 percent and 48 percent single sex, respectively) and Thailand and Japan, which have relatively low enrollments in single-sex secondary schools (19 percent and 14 percent, respectively) (Robitaille & Garden, 1989). We could not use the U.S. data because the percentage of single-sex schools is too small (about 3 percent) to make statistical comparisons based on samples of the size used in SIMS. But we already know much about the pattern of sex-grouping effects in the United States and these can be easily placed into our argument.

To test the first hypothesis we estimated the effect of gender groupings on twelfth grade mathematics achievement and compared the size of these effects across the four systems. In order to remove the likely influence of home background from these estimates, we controlled for various indicators of the student's background, such as father's occupation, mother's education level, educational aspirations, whether or not the language of instruction is the same as that used in the home, and, in some systems, public and private sectors of schools. These enhanced effect sizes, reported in Table 7.2, show the positive and negative effect on mathematics achievement as a function of learning mathematics in a single-sex classroom. A positive effect means that students in single-sex schools perform mathematics better than student in mixed-sex schools. A negative effect means the reverse. Each unit in the scores (or fraction thereof) represents a single test item.

As we hypothesized, the absolute size of the effects corresponds to the degree to which single-sex schooling is used within the national system. The effects in Belgium and New Zealand, where large numbers of students learn mathematics in single-sex schools, are close to zero and statistically significant in only one case. In Thailand and Japan, systems in which smaller numbers of students learn mathematics in single-sex schools, the effects are larger (in absolute terms) and all are statistically different from zero. For example, Thai females who learn mathematics in a single-sex school increase their achievement score by almost three test items in comparison to females in mixed-sex classes, all other relevant factors held equal. Also Thai males and both males and females in Japan who learn mathematics in single-sex classrooms learn less mathematics than do their counterparts in mixed-sex schools. (We examine the reasons for the direction of the Thai and Japanese findings below.) The analysis confirmed our argument that the association between gen-

TABLE 7.2
Difference Between Students in Single- and Mixed-Sex Schools on Twelfth
Grade Mathematics

National System	Percentage of Students Receiving Instruction in Single-Sex Schools	Effect Size Controlled by Student Background[b] (Single-Sex = 1; Co-ed = 0)	
	%	Females	Males
Belgium[a] (N = 2714)	68	−.24	−.74*
New Zealand (N = 1152)	48	.65	.18
Thailand (N = 3651)	19	2.92**	−3.21**
Japan (N = 7605)	14	−1.25**	−3.57**

Notes. [a]Belgium (Flemish) only.
   [b]Partial unstandardized regression coefficient comparing single-sex and coed, controlled by family SES, language spoken in home vs. school, students future education, and various school sectors by country. Each unit (or fraction thereof) represents a single test item.
   *$p < .05$, **$p < .001$.

der groupings and mathematics achievement is a function of the normative use of gender groupings in a national system of schools.

THE EFFECTS OF NORMATIVE CONTEXT ON SCHOOL SUPPLY AND DEMAND

The first explanation for the normative effect we examined is that in systems with small sets of single-sex schools, student selection becomes a salient part of the process. To test this we looked at whether a host of background variables could predict which students attended single-sex schools. Our hypothesis was that systems with small percentages of students attending single-sex schools will be more selective. By "selective" we mean that certain background variables will be associated with attending school; we do not necessarily mean that these schools are necessarily more selective in terms of choosing higher performing students. Examining background variables is the next best thing to having data on why a student chooses a particular school, and we inferred from this analysis which systems intensified choice of schools with different gender groupings.

As we hypothesized, in systems with equal enrollments in either type of gender grouping, student background and educational expectations do not predict which students attend a particular type of school. A student's background does not predict the choice of a single-sex school in either Flemish Belgium or New Zealand. However, in the two countries in which single-sex schools are relatively rare, background does predict a student's choice of a particular sex-grouping. In Thailand and Japan there is a clear pattern of attendance at different schools. In Thailand wealthier students and students who live in Bangkok are more likely to attend single-sex schools than mixed-sex schools. In Japan wealthier students of both sexes and students who expect to go on to attend a university enroll in single-sex schools. In other words, in Thailand and Japan single-sex schooling may be chosen by students with certain educational advantages in mind. As we discuss below, in Thailand single-sex secondary schooling for females is a route to enrollment in prestigious university programs. In Japan the situation is more complicated, but single-sex schools particularly for females, are a route to expensive but less rigorous private universities; these secondary schools are used by wealthy female students who cannot (or do not wish to) compete academically in the demanding top public universities. (See Stevenson & Baker, 1991, for a discussion of the rigors of university admission in Japan.) Such single-sex schools in Japan are socially connected to a particular set of universities.

Knowing which kind of student attends single-sex schools in Thailand and Japan helps us to understand the direction of achievement findings that we report above. In Japan the relatively small single-sex secondary sector caters to wealthy, usually female, students who wish to enter college. By comparing their own current academic abilities with entrance requirements for different universities, these students know that they will not qualify for the top universities. Single-sex secondary schools in Japan are predominantly private and are connected to a set of private universities that are expensive but less difficult to enter than the most prestigious public universities. The SIMS data does not contain information about why students choose single-sex schools, but it is a reasonable assumption that this connection is what draws a specific type of student to the single-sex school in Japan, and this is reflected in the lower performance of these students. For female Thai students who wish to pursue high-level careers in government, single-sex schools in Bangkok are the only educational route to consider (e.g., Fry 1980; Chantavanich & Fry, 1985). It is not clear to us what educational strategies are involved for Thai and Japanese males who attend single-sex schools.

We hypothesized that a second explanation behind the normative effects on achievement are the differences between learning environments provided by special sets of schools. Thus, in systems in which a particular sex grouping is rare, less control over the learning environment can cause either a richer (or poorer) environment to occur in comparison with the dominant gender grouping. In these situations the kinds of microeffects of single-sex groupings may flourish.

To test this idea we compared indicators of the quality of the learning environment in single-sex schools with the environment in mixed-sex schools. We compared 16 indicators of the quality of teachers, classroom instruction, and curriculum coverage. We compared these separately for males and females. This resulted in an analysis which is summarized in Table 7.3.

In most of these comparisons (81 of 128) there were no significant differences in the supply of resources for either single-or mixed-sex schools. In some cases, the significant differences favored single-sex schools while in other mixed-sex schools were advantaged. We predicted that most differences would occur in systems with relatively small enrollments in single-sex schooling. Moreover, we assumed that the differences in educational resources would be related to the achievement differences obtained in Table 7.1. We found that this is generally the case.

The strongest case is made by a comparison of females in New Zealand and Thailand. Among females in Thailand, the quality of teachers, classroom instruction, and curriculum coverage show seven large advantages favoring single-sex schools and only two advantages favoring coeducational schools. In New Zealand, 15 of the 16 comparisons are zero. New Zealand's female single-sex and mixed-sex schools are very similar in the educational environment supplied to students, whereas in Thailand females in single-sex schools have an advantage in educational resources.

In Flemish Belgium there are an equal number of advantages (three each) for both single- and mixed-sex schools. The effects in each school type counterbalance each other, producing no educational resource advantage and no achievement advantage (as seen in Table 7.1). Not surprisingly, in Japan we find that students in coeducational schools are supplied with more educational resources (5) than females in single-sex schools (2). This finding is consistent with Table 7.1 and our understanding of the type of students attending single-sex schools in Japan.

Thus, among females, our findings are consistent with our hypothesis. In "normative systems" (Flemish Belgium and New Zealand) there are no differential effects in mathematics achievement

TABLE 7.3

Comparison Between Single and Mixed-Sex Twelfth Grade Mathematics Classrooms on Teacher Resources, Classroom Characteristics, and Coverage of Curriculum[a]

Percent Single-Sex	Belgium (FL) 68		New Zealand 48		Thailand 19		Japan 14	
	S-Sex (male) vs. Mixed	S-Sex (female) vs. Mixed	S-Sex (male) vs. Mixed	S-Sex (female) vs. Mixed	S-Sex (male) vs. Mixed	S-Sex (female) vs. Mixed	S-Sex (male) vs. Mixed	S-Sex (female) vs. Mixed
# non-significant	10	10	14	15	6	7	11	9
# favor single-sex	4	3	1	0	4	7	2	2
# favor coeducation	2	3	1	1	6	2	3	5

[a]A total of 16 teacher and classrooms resources were compared across a school type (single/coed) for each sex in each country. Teacher characteristics included sex, age, experience, mathematics training, class preparation time, mathematics specialist or not, nonteaching duties. Classroom characteristics included size, hours of mathematics instruction per year, instruction mostly by mathematics specialist or not. Curriculum characteristics included the amount of various types of mathematics in the 12th grade curriculum.

across school type, the students are not selected, and they are provided more or less equivalent educational resources. In Thailand, where single-sex schooling is not normative, female students in single-sex schools perform significantly better than their counterparts in coeducational schools, the students are more selective (likely to demand better schooling), and the schools do in fact supply better resources. In Japan, the direction of the differences is exactly the reverse of those obtained in Thailand, but both cases confirm our hypothesis. Japanese single-sex schools for girls attract and select students who demand a less competitive educational environment and, indeed, we find that females in coeducational schools are supplied with greater resources and they outperform females in single-sex schools. These effects are in a predictable direction: Japanese single-sex schools for girls produce lower mathematics achievement than coeducational schools, and these schools supply a weaker educational environment. Japanese single-sex schools for girls cover less mathematics in their curriculum and offer less instruction.

Our hypotheses were not as strongly supported by the data on males. The results for Flemish Belgium and New Zealand, in which large numbers of males attended both single-sex and mixed-sex schools, showed no or only small achievement differences; this is in line with our hypothesis. The large negative effect of single-sex schooling for males in Thailand and Japan is less predictable from the analysis of resource differences in Table 7.3. While the direction of difference indicates that male single-sex schools in these two countries receive fewer resources, the differences are not as large as for female schools. It may also be that males receive certain benefits in mixed-sex schools in these countries. The effects of gender stratification within mixed-sex schools and its potential effects for males and females mathematics achievement needs further consideration (Riordan, 1990).

DISCUSSION

The study suggests that gender groupings do not have a consistent and uniform effect in every national system, but, rather, effects vary with the degree to which groupings are used within the national system. In systems in which both single- and mixed-sex schools are used widely, no effects on mathematics achievement, or only small effects, were found. In systems in which one gender grouping—here single sex—is relatively rare, positive single-sex effects are found in Thailand, and negative effects are found in Japan. In these systems there is also a selective pattern of student attendance in gender-grouped schools and some evidence to suggest that the educational environment supplied differs by the gender grouping of the school.

We argued that one way gender groupings influence academic achievement is through the relative prevalence of one gender grouping. Which students choose a rarer gender grouping and what they receive from this kind of school can be different from the more normative gender grouping within a national system. Small sets of special schools, even in centralized systems, may be outside the full control of government agencies, or special schools in decentralized systems may receive less state pressure to conform, thus increasing their openness to the forces of supply and demand. Single-gender schools in Thailand, Japan, or the United States are perceived (and perceive themselves) as organizations that are very different from the average school. Often this different definition is directly related to a particular issue of achievement, such as the case of lower competition in Japanese single-sex schools or elite training in Thailand or other special approaches taken in some U.S. single-sex schools. When a particular sex-grouping is a nominal characteristic of schools, as is the case for single-sex schools in Japan and Thailand, its effects on achievement can be larger than in systems, such as those in Belgium and New Zealand, in which different gender groupings are not connected to a special set of schools but are rather a large part of the national system.

What implications do these results have for proposals for the use of gender groupings to improve mathematics education in U.S. schools? First, and foremost, it seems unwise to assume that any large-scale change in gender groupings in schools would be associated with a similar large-scale change in achievement. It may be that single-sex schools do enhance mathematics achievement among U.S. students, as much of the U.S. literature suggests, but that this effect may be a function of a number of factors related to less centralized control of learning environments and the ability of students to choose schools. Furthermore, this situation may activate various microprocesses that effect achievement when students are separated by gender. Riordan (1990) has discussed these in some detail as they apply to the U.S. case. The results from our comparative analysis suggest that factors related to the normative context of school, such as selection and learning resources, can, in certain situations, overshadow the microprocesses of gender grouping. Therefore, it seems unwise to assume that more extensive use of single-sex schooling will enhance the mathematics performance for a larger number of U.S. students.

There is, however, a case to be made for the use of some special gender groupings. It may be the case that limited use of single-sex classrooms may be helpful to certain students. The more these classrooms can be made to be special, with resources and encouragement for students who attend them, the more students in them may reap additional benefits of a single-sex learning environment. Owing to the long historical tradition of coeducation in the United States, a limited use of the single-sex classrooms or school may be all that is possible.

A limited use of single-sex schooling may also avoid a possible conflict over the relative effectiveness of particular gender groupings for each gender. It may be that females gain more (or are less disadvantaged, as in Japan) in single-sex schools. The U.S. literature suggest this, although the data patterns are not overwhelmingly strong. It may be a reasonable policy to encourage special single-sex schools for American females who wish to attempt to excel in the areas of mathematics and science.

REFERENCES

Arnot, M. (1983). A cloud over co-education: An analysis of the forms of transmission of class and gender relations. In S. Walker & L. Barton (Eds.), *Gender, class and education.* Falmer, Sussex: The Falmer Press.

Astin, A. (1977). *Four critical years.* San Francisco: Jossey-Bass.

Baker, D. (1991). The politics of American Catholic school expansion, 1870–1930. In B. Fuller & R. Rubinson (Eds.), *The political construction of education: The state, school expansion and economic change.* New York: Praeger.

Baker, D., Riordan, C., & Schaub, M. (1994). *The effects of sex-grouped schooling on achievement: The role of national context,* forthcoming, 1994.

Benovaot, A., Cha, Y., Kamens, D., Mayer, J., & Wong, S. (1991). Knowledge for the masses: World models and national curricula, 1920–1986. *American Sociological Review, 56,* 85–100.

Carpenter, P., & Hayden, M. (1987). Girls' academic achievement: Single-sex versus coeducational schools in Australia. *Sociology of Education, 60,* 156–167.

Chantavanich, S., & Fry, G. (1985). Thailand: System of education. In T. Husén & T. Postlethwaite (Eds.), *International encyclopedia of education.* Oxford: Pergamon Press.

Dale, R. R. (1974). *Mixed or single-sex school: Attainment, attitudes, and overview* (Vol. 3). London: Routledge & Kegan Paul.

Deem, R. (1984). *Coeducation reconsidered*. Milton Keynes: Open University Press.

Finn, J. D. (1980). Sex differences in educational outcomes. *Sex Roles, 6*, 9–26.

Fry, G. (1980). Education and success: A case study of the Thai public service. *Comparative Education Review, 24*, 21–34.

Hamilton, M. (1985). Performance levels in science and other subjects for Jamaican adolescents attending single-sex and co-educational high schools. *Science Education, 69*, 535–547.

Harvey, T. J. (1985). Science in single-sex and mixed teaching groups. *Educational Research, 27*, 179–182.

Husén, T. (1967). *International study of achievement in mathematics*. Stockholm: Almquist & Wiksell.

Jimenez, E., & Lockheed, M. E. (1989). *The relative effectiveness of single-sex and coeducational schools in Thailand*. Washington, DC: The World Bank.

Lee, V. E., & Bryk, A. S. (1986). Effects of single-sex secondary schools on student achievement and attitudes. *Journal of Educational Psychology, 78*, 381–395.

Lee, V. E., & Lockheed, M. E. (1990). The effects of single-sex schooling on achievement in Nigeria. *Comparative Education Review, 34*, 209–231.

Lockheed, M. E., & Komenan, A. (1988). *School effects on student achievement in Africa: The case of Nigeria and Swaziland*. Discussion Paper, Population and Human Resource Series. Washington, DC: The World Bank.

Marsh, H. W. et al. (1988). The transition from single-sex to coeducational high schools: Effects on multiple dimensions of self-concept and on academic achievement. *American Educational Research Journal, 25*, 237–269.

Marsh, H. W. (1989). Effects of attending single-sex and coeducational high schools on achievement, attitudes, behaviors, and sex differences. *Journal of Educational Psychology, 81*, 70–85.

Meyer, J., & Hannon, M. (1979). *National development and the world system*. Chicago: The University of Chicago Press.

O'Kelly, C., & Carney, L. (1986). *Women and men in society* (2nd edition). Belmont, CA: Wadsworth Publishing.

Price, F., & Rosemier, R. (1972). Some cognitive and affective outcomes of same-sex versus coeducational grouping in first grade. *Journal of Experimental Education, 40*, 70–77.

Ramirez, F., & Rubinson, R. (1979). Creating members: The national incorporation of education. In J. Meyer & M. Hannon (Eds.), *National development and the world system*. Chicago: University of Chicago.

Renwick, W. (1985). New Zealand: System of Education. In T. Husén & T. N. Postlethwaite (Eds.), *International encyclopedia of education*. Oxford: Pergamon Press.

Riordan, C. (1990). *Girls and boys in school: Together or separate?* New York: Teachers College Press.

Robitaille, D., & Garden, R. (Eds.). (1989). *The IEA study of mathematics II: Contexts and outcomes of school mathematics.* Oxford: Pergamon Press.

Shaw, J. (1980). Education and the individual: Schooling for girls or mixed sex schooling—A mixed blessing. In R. Deem (Ed.). *Schooling for women's work* (pp. 66–75). London: Routledge & Kegan Paul.

Stevenson, D., & Baker, D. (1991). State control of the curriculum and classroom instruction. *Sociology of Education, 64,* 1–10.

Tidball, M. E. (1973, Spring). Perspective on academic women and affirmative action. *Educational Record, 54,* 130–135.

Tidball, M. E. (1980). Women's colleges and women achievers revisited. *Signs: Journal of Women and Culture in Society, 5,* 504–517.

Tyack D., & Hansot, E. (1990). *Learning together: A history of coeducation in American public schools.* New Haven, CT: Yale University Press.

8

Assessing the Differential Item Performance of Females in Japan and the United States

Delwyn L. Harnisch

College of Education
University of Illinois at Urbana-Champaign
Champaign, IL

Any discussion of gender differences in educational achievement and choices inevitably stimulates vigorous discussion, and frequently disagreement. This is not surprising since perceptions of sex roles have been changing, and not always evenly among people of different ages, different racial and ethnic groups, different religions, and, of course, different genders. While this makes objective reporting on such differences a difficult task, it is no less necessary.

In the choices that young men and women make, the advice they receive, and the opportunities afforded them, there is continual interplay between cultural and social expectations and educational preparation and attainment. Anticipated occupational and societal roles help shape academic interest and performance. And choices made along the way, such as not to take advanced high school courses in mathematics and science, for example, shape opportunity for further education and careers.

RESEARCH BACKGROUND

Performance differences between men and women on standardized tests may be slowly diminishing (Wilder & Powell, 1988). In many studies and tests men appear to have caught up with women on tests of verbal ability and achievement, while women are gaining on but not equaling men in mathematics. Women still lag in some aspects of spatial ability and in achievement at the top levels of mathematics. That disparities have diminished is quite evident in recent tests administered to nationally representative samples of students.

Several generalizations about gender differences regarding performance on standardized tests can be supported based on a review of the literature:

1. Many different tests given over a wide range of ages and educational levels still reveal male/female score differences;
2. The largest differences appear in tests of mathematical or quantitative ability, where men tend to do better than women, particularly in secondary school and beyond;
3. Women have tended to do better than men in many tests of verbal skills (particularly writing), but a number of studies indicate that this superiority has diminished since the early 1970s.

Many different explanations have been offered for these differences in test scores. Such explanations range from assertions of inherent biological differences between males and females, through critical assessments of differences in social and educational experiences, to the characteristics of the tests themselves. But it is clear that no single explanation captures all the variance in the differences between males and females in the quantitative domain. Patterns in course-taking, attitudes toward mathematics, differences in achievement motivation, and some characteristics of tests themselves may contribute to the differences, but fail to explain them all.

Continuing concern should be given to better understand these differences, however small they are becoming: first, substantial educational and social consequences are attached to test performance; second, individuals are psychologically affected by their success, or lack of it, on tests. For example, lower performance on mathematics tests may cause females to lower their expectations and retreat from enrolling in highly quantitative courses, and/or conclude that these fields are the province of males. It is clearly the case that these concerns deserve our attention and demand research that seeks to better understand the nature and causes of gender differences in test performance so that interventions can be properly informed.

The purpose of this chapter is to examine the extent to which item content is interacting with group membership in secondary mathematics students in Japan and the United States. Also of interest is an examination of the item characteristics associated with those item interactions that appear to provide item favorability to a particular subgroup. We also ask if these interactions are the same for the two countries examined.

EXAMINATION OF ITEM CHARACTERISTICS

Evaluation of item characteristics that differentially affect the performance of subgroups has been and continues to be of interest to everyone involved in testing. Linn and Harnisch (1981) point out that factors at the item level that result in underestimation of competence for a subpopulation have been noted since at least 1951. Several studies have been conducted to reveal differentially performing items but have not identified general item characteristics that explain differential performance by specific subgroups (Scheuneman, 1979). Tatsuoka, Linn, Tatsuoka, and Yamamoto (1988) confirmed that groups showed different performances on items with different underlying cognitive tasks when the subgroups are defined in terms of specified differences in cognitive processes involved in students' problem-solving strategies.

Logical, or judgmental, and statistical methods of evaluating items have been recommended as two procedures that should be used together to examine possible causes of differential performance (Schmitt, 1986). In this study we will be using a statistical method to examine the extent to which items are interacting with group membership. Numerous techniques have been proposed and investigated (e.g., Hulin, Drasgow, & Parsons, 1983, Chapter 5; Lord, 1980, Chapter 14; Shepard, Camilli, & Williams, 1985). More recently, several major testing companies have instituted item bias analysis procedures as part of their routine item analysis and test construction process (Berk, 1982; Holland & Thayer, 1986).

The findings from one Population B cognitive test booklet, *Form 4*, will be discussed here. The data come from the 1,999 Japanese and 1,139 American students who completed the questions found in this test booklet. Only students who had valid gender classification were examined in these analyses: 1,580 males and 419 females in Japan and 651 males and 488 females in the United States.

METHOD

The Mantel–Haenszel procedure (see Holland & Thayer, 1986) provides a chi-square test with one degree of freedom for the null hypothesis that there is no relationship between group membership and performance on the item after controlling for overall performance on the test. As applied here, groups were defined by gender classification and the total score on the one test form of the mathematics test was used as the control for gender differences. The nonparametric Mantel–Haenszel (MH) statistics for differential item performance were computed for each item by forming K 2 x 2 contingency tables for each item, where K is the number of distinct number-correct scores observed for the test. For the ith item and a given number-correct score j a 2 x 2 contingency table was constructed (see Table 8.1).

In the analysis the focal group is the females and the reference group is the males. From the above K 2 x 2 tables for a given item the following statistics were computed:

$$\chi^2_{MH} = (|\Sigma (A_j - E(A_j))| - .5)^2 / \Sigma \text{ Var } (A_j)$$

where

$$E(A_j) = (Nr_j M1_j) / T_j,$$

and

$$\text{Var } (A_j) = (Nr_j Nf_j M1_j MO_j) / ((T_j)^2(T_j - 1)).$$
$$\alpha_{MH} = (\Sigma A_j D_j / T_j) / (\Sigma B_j C_j / T_j).$$

and

$$\Delta_{MH} = - (2.35) \ln (\alpha_{MH}).$$

α_{MH} is the common odds-ratio across the K 2 x 2 tables for a given item. α_{MH} can range from zero to infinity. A common odds ratio of

TABLE 8.1
Specifications for Reference and Focal Groups
on Studied Item

Group	Score on studied item		
	1	0	Total
Reference	A_i	B_i	Nr_i
Focal	C_i	D_i	Nf_i
Total	$M1_i$	$M0_i$	T_i

one indicates that after controlling for total score, there is no differential performance on the item for students being compared by gender groups. A value of two would indicate that males are twice as likely to answer the item correctly as their matched counterparts, the females. A value of .5 would indicate just the opposite. In short, values less than 1.0 indicate that the item is relatively easier for students in the focal group (after controlling for total score), while α_{MH} values greater than 1.0 indicate that the item is relatively easier for students in the reference group. In other words, females students perform better on the average than comparable male students with α_{MH} values greater than 1.0, whereas the opposite is true for items with values less than 1.0.

The Δ_{MH} statistic simply transforms the α_{MH} statistic to obtain a measure of differential item performance expressed in terms of difference on the Educational Testing Service (ETS) delta scale (Holland & Thayer, 1985). The delta scale has a mean of 13 and a standard deviation of 4. A difference of one or more is considered large enough to be of practical significance in differential item functioning analyses conducted on ETS testing programs.

The standardized p-difference approach, D_{STD}, uses a weighting function supplied by the standardization group. The standardization approach derives its names from the standardization group. The function of the standardization group is to supply a set of weights, one for each score level, that will be used to weight each of the individual p-differences at each of the score levels before accumulating these weighted differences across score levels to arrive at a summary item discrepancy index

$$D_{STD} = \Sigma \; K_s \; [P_{fs} - P_{bs}] / \Sigma \; K_s,$$

where $[K_s/\Sigma \; K_s]$ is the weighting factor at score levels supplied by the standardization group to weight differences in performance between the focal group (P_{fs}) and the reference or base group (P_{bs}). In practice, $K_s = Nf_j$ has been used because it gives the greatest weight to differences at the score levels most attained by the focal group under study.

A flagging criterion is useful in the identification of items in need of review. In this chapter, the same flagging criterion for items is used that is currently being used by ETS researchers. Kok and Mellenbergh (1985) and Thissen and Wainer (1985) suggest that a D_{STD} of $+/-$ .05 is a reasonable cutoff for a bias effect size. Hence, only items reaching this criterion or the most extreme cases will be discussed in the next section.

RESULTS

The relative-score frequency distributions and descriptive statistics are given for the Japanese and U.S. samples of males and females, respectively, in Table 8.2. The test consisting of 17 items has possi-

TABLE 8.2
Total Score Relative Frequency Distributions and Descriptive Statistics
for Japanese and American Males and Females (Pop B SIMS—Form 4)

| Score interval | Relative Frequency | | | |
| | Japan | | U.S. | |
	Males	Females	Males	Females
17	.155	.129	.002	.002
16	.159	.098	.005	.002
15	.120	.096	.006	.002
14	.102	.088	.011	.004
13	.091	.091	.032	.008
12	.072	.079	.042	.031
11	.061	.079	.052	.029
10	.050	.072	.054	.037
9	.054	.074	.063	.055
8	.035	.062	.095	.074
7	.029	.050	.114	.148
6	.025	.045	.123	.135
5	.021	.019	.121	.135
4	.012	.012	.117	.156
3	.009	.005	.094	.094
2	.005	.002	.043	.059
1	.001	.000	.023	.027
0	.001	.000	.005	.002
Sample size	1580	419	651	488
Mean	12.92	12.08	6.70	5.98
SD	3.64	3.66	3.24	2.82

ble score intervals from 0 to 17. The percentage of the respective samples scoring at each of these score interval levels is found in Table 8.2. As is seen in the table, the distributions are more similar within country than between countries. The gender differences in the distributions are fairly similar with more of the females having lower scores than the males in both countries. In Japan, the mean for the males is 12.9 and 12.1 for the females; in the U.S. 6.7 and 6.0 for the males and females, respectively. The differences between the gender groups in Japan is significant at the .05 level $(t(1997) = 20.1)$ and also for the United States $(t(1137) = 23.4)$. The corresponding standard deviations for the males and females in Japan are 3.64 and 3.66 and for the United States 3.24 and 2.82 for the males and females, respectively. Other than the slightly smaller variability for the U.S. data, however, the total scores provide the primary basis for distinguishing between the respective gender groups for each country.

The percentage of males and females scoring at each score level are plotted in Figure 8.1 for the United States and in Figure 8.2 for Japan. As can be seen, a greater percentage of females have lower scores than the males in each country. Figures 8.1 and 8.2 also show the larger percentage of males who score in the upper range of the score distribution.

The cumulative percentage frequency distributions are plotted for the four distributions in Figure 8.3. The separation between the solid and dashed line, which represents the cumulative percentage of the respective groups that score at each score level, reveals the magnitude of the gender differences within the two countries. In both countries we see the similar trend of more females scoring at lower levels. In addition, the plot reveals the score level where the various percentage of members of a group score. For example, approximately 80 percent of the females in the United States have a score of seven or less while 80 percent of the males have a score of nine or less; approximately 15 percent of the Japanese females score seven or less while approximately 20 percent of the males have a score of nine or less.

The values of the MH statistics are presented in Table 8.3. As can be seen, α_{MH} is greater than 1.0 for nine of the 17 items in each of the data sets. The MH χ^2 values are significant at an alpha level of .05 for 15 of the 17 items in both the U.S. and Japan. Δ_{MH} is greater than one for two items in each data set and less than one for six items in Japan and for three items in the United States. Using the flagging criterion of D_{STD} which exceeds an absolute value of .05 we have three items in the Japan data set and nine items in the U.S. data set. Two of the three items in the Japan data set favor the

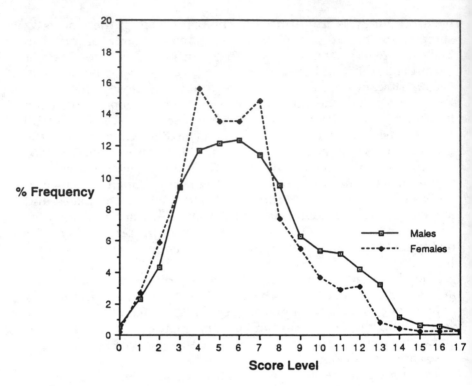

FIGURE 8.1   United States: Relative Frequency Plot for Males and Females on SIMS Mathematics Test

performance of the females while six of the nine favor the females in the U.S. In the next sections of this chapter we will examine the three items exceeding the flagging criterion for Japan and the four most extreme items for the United States. Plots of the item mean performance for the males and the females at each score level will be illustrated for the selected items with the item in its original format to the right of the figure.

Japan

Figures 8.4 and 8.5 show the items that favored the performance of females in Japan. Both of these items are representative of the trigonome ic items found on cognitive tests in advanced mathematics. The results for the item found in Figure 8.4, which asks, *Which of the following is negative* shows that over 70 percent can answer the item correctly, with the females answering it correctly 73 percent of the time compared to the 72 percent perfor-

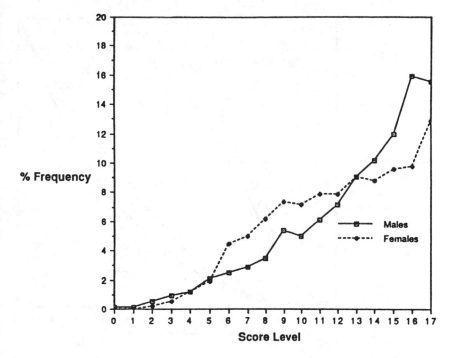

FIGURE 8.2 Japan: Relative Frequency Plot for Males and Females on SIMS Mathematics Test

mance by the males. However, when one looks at the average p-values for equivalent score values we see that the females tend to score five to ten percentage points higher for scores in the range from 8 to 15 on the test. Given these differences, is it the case that the males are less likely to understand the quadrants in which the functions are positive or negative, or is it that they are unable to decipher the mean of fractional values or radians?

The item displayed in Figure 8.5 is also from the trigonometry content area. This item focuses on an understanding of the circular function notation, the graphs of the functions and the connections between the two. The mean performance of the females on this item is at 74 percent while the males is at 71 percent. For the score range from four to 14 we see better performance (ranging from 5 to 15 percent) by females at all but one of the score levels. Both of these items basically reflect knowledge of the basic properties of trigonometric functions. It appears that females in Japan have better performance on items of this type when compared with males of equal ability. Hence, if it were decided to include more items similar

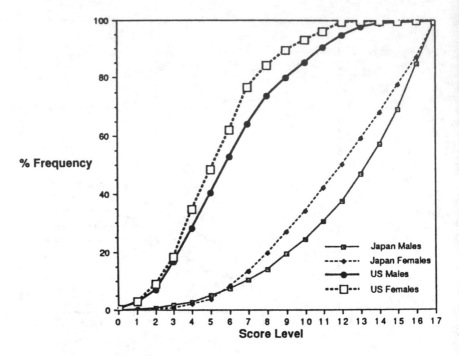

FIGURE 8.3 United States and Japan: Cumulative Percent Frequency Plot for Males and Females on SIMS Mathematics Test

to these now on the test, the expected advantage or disadvantage for students would be roughly greater than one-half of a delta scale standard deviation, depending on the type of items that were added (that is, the difference between Δ_{MH} of -1.30 and $+1.36$).

Figure 8.6 presents an item that favors the performance of males more than the females in Japan. This item deals with the general topic of differentiation and specifically with the properties of the derivative and some of its graphical representations. The mean p-values for this item show that 68 percent of the males answer it correctly compared to 50 percent of the females. When comparing members of equal ability, as shown in Figure 8.6, we see that the males score from 5 to 20 percent better than females for individuals with score values between 11 and 16. It appears that males more than females were able to understand the graphical applications of the derivative function for all values of χ. This item represents an item at the analysis level in the SIMS cognitive classification while the items that favored female performance were at the computation level.

TABLE 8.3
Summary of Mantel–Haenszel Differential Item Performance Statistics
for SIMS Items on Rotated Form 4 for Japan and the United States

(a) Japan

Item Number	α_{MH}	Δ_{MH}	D_{STD}	χ^2_{MH}
1	1.68	−1.23	−.01	20.50
2	1.80	−1.38	−.03	75.37
3	1.60	−1.09	−.06*	174.81
4	0.75	0.69	.03	47.90
5	1.34	−0.68	−.02	24.30
6	0.90	0.26	.01	8.14
7	0.84	0.41	.02	25.58
8	1.17	−0.36	−.04	20.66
9	0.69	0.86	.04	104.20
10	1.24	−0.50	−.02	15.54
11	0.95	0.12	.01	1.61
12	1.76	−1.32	−.03	66.20
13	1.67	−1.21	−.02	39.37
14	0.97	0.07	.01	0.12
15	1.74	−1.30	−.07*	64.24
16	0.56	1.36	.09**	330.79
17	0.65	1.01	.04	11.50

(b) United States

Item Number	α_{MH}	Δ_{MH}	D_{STD}	χ^2_{MH}
1	1.69	−1.23	−.05*	182.20
2	1.30	−0.62	−.05*	70.98
3	0.95	0.12	.01	2.02
4	1.41	−0.81	−.07*	85.73
5	0.82	0.47	.04	35.89
6	0.95	0.12	.00	0.36
7	1.23	−0.49	−.02	13.75
8	0.67	0.92	.04	40.21
9	0.53	1.47	.12**	483.75
10	1.08	−0.19	−.02	4.54
11	0.38	2.28	.15**	350.45
12	1.69	−1.23	−.10*	229.83
13	1.74	−1.29	−.10*	387.70
14	0.81	0.48	.06**	40.54
15	1.12	−0.28	−.03	10.48
16	1.26	−0.55	−.05*	44.87
17	0.76	0.65	.04	36.25

*indicates performance favoring females and ** for males

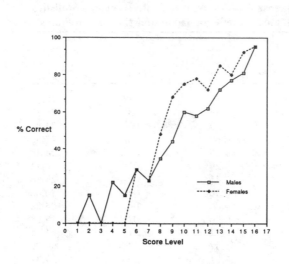

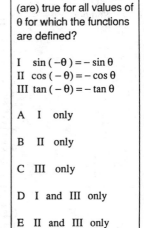

Which of the following is negative?

A $\sin \dfrac{5\pi}{12}$

B $\sin \dfrac{5\pi}{8}$

C $\tan \dfrac{5\pi}{6}$

D $\tan \dfrac{5\pi}{4}$

E $\cos \dfrac{5\pi}{3}$

FIGURE 8.4   Japan: Summary of Item Performance for Males and Females at Each Score Level (Item 3—SIMS Form 4)

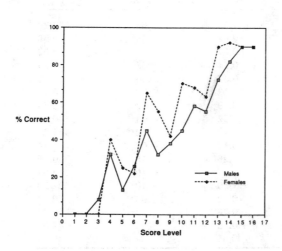

Which of the following is (are) true for all values of θ for which the functions are defined?

I $\sin(-\theta) = -\sin\theta$
II $\cos(-\theta) = -\cos\theta$
III $\tan(-\theta) = -\tan\theta$

A   I   only

B   II   only

C   III   only

D   I   and   III   only

E   II   and   III   only

FIGURE 8.5   Japan: Summary of Item Performance for Males and Females at Each Score Level (Item 15—SIMS Form 4)

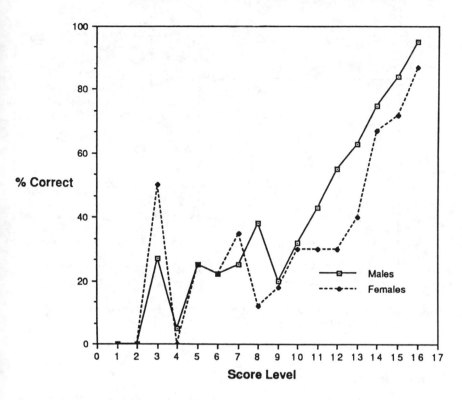

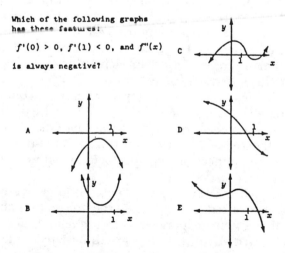

FIGURE 8.6 Japan: Summary of Item Performance for Males and Females at Each Score Level (Item 16—SIMS Form 4)

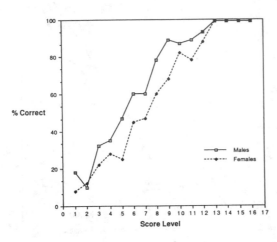

The speed of an object increases uniformly at a rate of 10% per second. At a given time, its speed is 10.00 meters per second. Three seconds later, its speed will be

A   11.10 meters per second

B   12.10 meters per second

C   13.00 meters per second

D   13.31 meters per second

E   40.00 meters per second

FIGURE 8.7   United States: Summary of Item Performance for Males and Females at Each Score Level (Item 9—SIMS Form 4)

United States

The items favoring the performance of males in the United States are presented in Figures 8.7 and 8.8. Both items are in a story-type format. The item represented in Figure 8.7 requires basic operational knowledge of percents. The basic content of this item overlaps with the statements often found in elementary physics textbooks that discuss the speed and acceleration of objects. The average performance for males on this item was 60 percent compared to 42 percent for the females. As shown in Figure 8.7, the performance is clearly favoring the males throughout the score distribution in the range of 5 to 10 percent. This item requires a set of understandings often found in an application-type problem as defined by the SIMS cognitive classifications.

The item shown in Figure 8.8 reflects another application-type problem with the content representing the area of probability. From an analysis of the item responses to this question along with the opportunity to learn about it, it appears that many students are not familiar with how to deal with probability items extending beyond a simple event. The mean p-values are 28 percent for the males and 12 percent for the females. Basically, the performance on this item is the lowest of all items on the test for the females and also at a level far below the chance level of performance. From Figure 8.8 one can

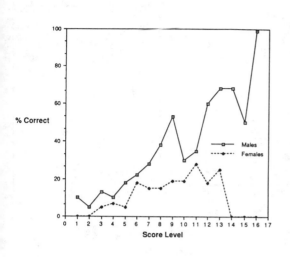

A warning system installation consists of two independent alarms having probabilities of operating in an emergency of 0.95 and 0.90 respectively. Find the probability that at least one alarm operates in an emergency.

A   0.995

B   0.975

C   0.95

D   0.90

E   0.855

FIGURE 8.8   United States: Summary of Item Performance for Males and Females at Each Score Level (Item 11—SIMS Form 4)

see the extent to which the males find this application item much easier throughout the range of test scores.

The two items which favored the performance of females are given in Figures 8.9 and 8.10. Both items are classified as computation. The item in Figure 8.9 was an equation that involved rational expressions in a classic partial fraction model. The mean performance for the females on this item was 43 percent compared to 39 percent for the males. From the plot in Figure 8.9 approximately 5 to 20 percent more of the females are answering the item correctly for individuals with score values from 5 to 13.

On the complex number item shown in Figure 8.10 one can see the favorable performance of the females in the lower end of the score range, from 3 to 7. Females answered this item correctly 62 percent of the time compared to 56 percent for the males. This item deals with a straightforward operation on complex numbers.

CONCLUSION

The consistent finding among all the items favoring the females is that they are at the SIMS cognitive level of *computation* while the items that favor the males tend to be at higher cognitive levels, *application* and *analysis*.

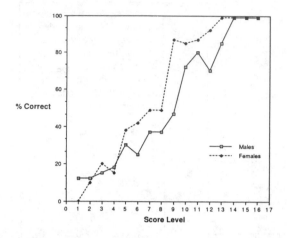

$$\text{If } \frac{x-1}{x^2+3x+2} = \frac{P}{x+1} + \frac{Q}{x+2}$$

then

A $P = -2, Q = 3$

B $P = -3, Q = 2$

C $P = -1, Q = -2$

D $P = 2, Q = -3$

E $P = 3, Q = -2$

FIGURE 8.9 United States: Summary of Item Performance for Males and Females at Each Score Level (Item 12—SIMS Form 4)

Although the results of this study are limited to only one Population B test form, they are highly consistent and unequivocal. They demonstrate the extent to which the lower level cognitive items, which focus on the computation operations, favor females more frequently than the males. It also demonstrates that the higher order operations favor the performance of the males in both Japan and the United States. In the Japanese sample it is interesting to

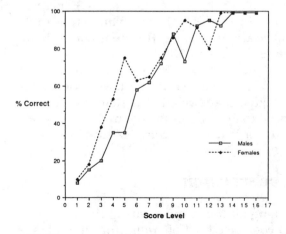

The complex number

$(1 + i)^2$ is equal to

A   0

B   2

C $2i$

D $1 + i$

E $2 + 2i$

FIGURE 8.10 United States: Summary of Item Performance for Males and Females at Each Score Level (Item 13—SIMS Form 4)

note that the items that focused on the trigonometric operations were more favorable to females while the analysis of differentiation item was more favorable to males. In the U.S. sample it appears that the items that favored straightforward computation or operations were more favored by females while items that were given in a story-problem format and focused on applications and analysis were more favored by the males. What is interesting to note from this study is the extent to which the knowledge of the cognitive problem types are consistently found to be associated with a particular group. For example, the computation problems are favored by the females while the application and analysis items are favored by the males.

The results suggest that we need to understand the more relevant instructional and cognitive variables that cause DIF for the two groups examined here. The results provide information that the items interact differently with group membership within U.S. and Japanese cultures. None of the extreme items identified with DIF were overlapping between the two study samples.

REFERENCES

Berk, R. A. (Ed.). (1982). *Handbook of methods for detecting test bias.* Baltimore, MD: John Hopkins University Press.

Holland, P. W., & Thayer, D. T. (1986). *Differential item performance and the Mantel–Haenszel procedure.* Paper presented at the annual meeting of the American Educational Research Association, San Francisco, CA.

Hulin, C. L., Drasgow, F., & Parsons, C. K. (1983). *Item response theory: Application to psychological measurement.* Homewood, IL: Dow Jones-Irwin.

Ishizaka, K. (1981). *Mathematics achievement of secondary school students—Second international mathematics study: National report of Japan: Vol. I.* Tokyo, Japan: National Institute for Educational Research [Translated version of original report].

Kok, F. G., & Mellenbergh, G. J. (1985). *A mathematical model for item bias and a definition of a bias effect size.* Paper presented at the Fourth European Meeting of the Psychometric Society and the Classification Societies, Cambridge, England.

Linn, R. L., & Harnisch, D. L. (1981). Interactions between item content and group membership on achievement test items. *Journal of Educational Measurement, 18,* 109–118.

Lord, F. M. (1980). *Applications of item response theory to practical testing problems.* Hillsdale, NJ: Erlbaum.

Robitaille, D. F., & Garden, R. A. (Eds.). (1989). *The IEA study of mathematics II: Contexts and outcomes of school mathematics.* New York: Pergamon Press.

Scheuneman, J. A. (1979). A method of assessing bias in test items. *Journal of Educational Measurement, 16,* 143–152.

Schmitt, A. P. (1986). *Unexpected differential item performance of Hispanic examinees.* Paper presented at the annual meeting of the National Council on Measurement in Education, San Francisco, CA.

Shepard, L., Camilli, G., & Williams, D. M. (1985). Validity of approximation techniques for detecting item bias. *Journal of Educational Measurement, 22,* 77–105.

Tatsuoka, K. K., Linn, R. L., Tatsuoka, M. M., & Yamamoto, K. (1988). Differential item functioning resulting from the use of different solution strategies. *Journal of Educational Measurement, 25,* 301–319.

Thissen, D., & Wainer, H. (1985). *Studying item bias with item response theory.* Paper presented at the Fourth European Meeting of the Psychometric Society and the Classification Societies, Cambridge, England.

Travers, K. J., & Westbury, I. (1989). *The IEA study of mathematics I: Analysis of mathematics curricula.* New York: Pergamon Press.

United States National Coordinating Center. (1986). *Second International Mathematics Study: Detailed report for the United States.* Champaign, IL: Stipes.

Wilder, G., & Powell, K. (1988). *Sex differences in test performances: A survey of the literature.* New York: College Board Publications.

III

NEW
METHODOLOGIES
FOR RESEARCH
IN MATHEMATICS
EDUCATION

9

Conceptual and Statistical Problems in The Study of School and Classroom Effects: An Introduction to Multilevel Modeling Techniques

Damian P. Murchan*

St. Mary's National School
Ashbourne, County Meath
Ireland

Finbarr C. Sloane**

Department of Curriculum & Instruction
College of Education
University of Illinois at Urbana-Champaign
Champaign, IL

* This chapter is the result of many interactions between the authors. Consequently, we decided that our names would be listed alphabetically.

** The invaluable editorial assistance of Kurt Tooley is gratefully acknowledged.

Because research and theory building in the social sciences is so intimately related to the use of statistical models, the commensurability of the available statistical models and the research contexts in which they are applied is crucial. Minimally, research models are composed of two overlapping and commensurable submodels: (a) the conceptual or theoretical submodel, and (b) the statistical submodel. The theoretical submodel is a simplification of and approximation to a more complex concept or social system; theoretical models provide precise views of the world and they allow us the means to infer from observed data to unobserved phenomena of interest (King, 1989). On the other hand, the statistical submodel is a formal representation of the process by which a social system produces output. The basic goal is to learn about the underlying process that generates output and, consequently, the data under study.

The two submodels overlap in such a way as to produce a working research model: theoretical submodels, as simple conceptual guides, help us build intuition and ask questions; statistical submodels help us answer these questions empirically. In this fashion the two submodels buttress each other, thereby allowing the research model as a whole to work. And, clearly, the lack of applicable, workable, and commensurable statistical models to help clarify, test, modify, and explain theory frustrates researchers in their attempts to understand and explain research contexts. Unfortunate though it may be, past research on school effects has been seriously affected by the incommensurability of submodels to each other, and to the research contexts in which they are applied.

Some of the issues associated with this problem will be discussed in this chapter. In particular, we outline three dilemmas: (a) the problems associated with the aggregation of data, (b) the unit of analysis problem, and (c) the notion that schools are hierarchically organized. Rather than treat these problems individually, as others have (see, for example, Bryk & Raudenbush, 1989), we will use a historical approach in an effort to demonstrate the interaction between conceptualization, design, and analysis; in this way we hope to develop a context for multilevel modeling techniques. We will then describe the resolution of these problems through the application of a multilevel modeling technique, the hierarchical linear model (HLM). An empirical example will then be introduced; this example will highlight key student and family background characteristics associated with eighth-grade mathematics achievement in U.S. classrooms. Finally, the future of school effects research will be discussed in the light of the multilevel approach. Throughout we hope to demonstrate the advantages of multilevel models relative to more traditional models: comparative conceptual richness, superior fit to data, and enhanced analytic power.

THE COLEMAN REPORT:
CONTEXT FOR THE DEVELOPMENT
OF MULTILEVEL MODELS

In 1966, James Coleman and his colleagues reported that "schools bring little to bear on a child's achievement that is independent of his background and general social context" (p. 352). Although the original report was published "with little publicity and no fanfare" (Madaus, Airasian, & Kellaghan, 1980, p. 28), the *Coleman Report* was soon hailed as "literally of revolutionary significance" (Heyns, 1978, p. 1314).

What was so special about this study? First, the *Coleman Report* was the first study of its kind: a state-of-the-art educational survey amassing and analyzing a huge and rich data set; this, along with the expectation that "school effects" were out there and would be easy to find and quantify, combined to make Coleman et al.'s (1966) conclusion unbelievable, improbable, unappealing, and unpopular to most educational researchers. The report's conclusion was simply mind-boggling and, if correct, "revolutionary" indeed. The problem was very few educational researchers could believe that the *Coleman Report* was right.

At the time of Coleman's study, it was difficult to find fault with the data so researchers attacked the findings on methodological grounds.[1] And there were indications that something was wrong: subsequent research using similar models failed to produce consistent correlations between student achievement and such variables as pupil–teacher ratio, the credentials, experience, and salary of teachers, quality of facilities, quality of administrators, and average yearly expenditure per pupil. Thus, a recent survey of 187 studies of school effects by Hanushek (1989) revealed troubling discrepancies in terms of both consistency and plausibility; studies only sporadically found teacher education (12 percent of the studies), teacher

---

[1] As researchers began to ask better theoretical questions about schools, and the process of schooling, then the quality of the *Coleman Report* data also came under scrutiny. For example, the data set does not allow the researcher to link students to their respective teachers. Consequently, it is impossible to ask whether different instructional settings affect student achievement.

experience (36 percent), teacher salary (22 percent), expenditures per student (25 percent), and facilities (16 percent) to be significantly associated with achievement; and strangest of all, of the 18 percent that found teacher–pupil ratio to be significantly associated with student achievement, half indicated that the more pupils per teacher, the better the students' achievement. Moreover, sizeable positive correlations between school achievement and school expenditures disappeared when this relationship controlled for individual student differences in family background and other relevant inputs. The improbability (or unbelievability or unpalatability) and inconsistency of results produced by the *Coleman Report*, its replications, and much subsequent research in education and related fields provoked a critical methodological review.

Those attempting to either replicate or empirically question the *Coleman Report*'s conclusions took many different approaches. First, some questioned the order in which chosen variables were entered in the regression model. It was argued that individual- and school-level variables were not independent of each other (that is, they were collinear), and because individual-level variables were entered before their school-level counterparts, there was little variance left for these latter variables to explain (Bowles & Levin, 1968; Hanushek & Kain, 1972; Michelson, 1970; Wiley, 1976). As a result, the effects of schools were systematically underestimated. Some recommended remedying the overlap by distributing the variance symmetrically (Beaton, 1974; Mayeske, 1974; Wisler, 1974), whereby the variance between one block of variables is allowed to overlap with that of another block. However, as Wiley (1976) points out, this technique does not solve the problem of high collinearity among the variables.

Another method of analyzing schools effects involved the aggregation of individual measures to the school level and then using the school as the unit of analysis. This may be acceptable in investigating phenomena that occur at only one level; say, for example, at the school level (Bidwell & Kasarda, 1980; Haney, 1980). But results obtained from analyses conducted at one analytic level cannot be generalized to other levels (Burstein, 1980; Haney, 1980). Relationships modeled on data that have been aggregated to a higher level (for example, classroom or school) have enhanced correlations relative to the same relationships modeled at the individual level. This happens because much of the variation that occurs within units has been removed by aggregation. Robinson (1950) demonstrated this "ecological fallacy" in his classic paper on the relationship of race and IQ. Robinson showed that at the national level, race and IQ were correlated at .95, while at the state level the correlation drops to .77;

at the individual level the relationship drops to a mere .20. Obviously, inferences made at the national or state levels would be inappropriately applied to individuals.

Relationships based on aggregated school-level data are similarly misleading if applied to individual students within schools. As Burstein (1978a, 1980) points out, these differences occur for a number of reasons: (a) students are assigned to schools in a nonrandom manner; (b) disaggregated measures change their meaning when aggregated; (c) aggregated variables are generally measured more reliably than individual variables.

Given such dilemmas, researchers were in a difficult position. No one really knew what to do. Some investigators (see, for example, Haney, 1980) suggested that analyses should be conducted at both the individual and school levels, while inferences should be made only at the level of aggregation appropriate to the question under study. (An associated dilemma, the change of variable meaning upon aggregation, will be discussed later.) The heart of this strategy was the hope that the results from both analyses would converge. Although this approach initially seemed reasonable, it was soon realized that it skirted rather than dealt with the problem of aggregation bias: unfortunately, convergence need not and usually does not occur. Consequently, what to do in cases of nonconvergence remained an open question (Haney, 1980) in that research conducted in this fashion resolves neither conceptual nor methodological uncertainties.

The *Coleman Report*'s use of school-level variables to predict individual-level outcomes was singled out as the primary methodological flaw of the study. Coleman failed to account for aggregation bias, and, as a result, the analyses underestimated or even precluded the possible effects of schools (Bidwell & Kasarda, 1980; Burstein, 1980; Madaus et al., 1980). Subsequent research revealed the exacting conceptual price of aggregation, the conceptual effect of aggregation bias—the use of aggregated school-level variables to predict individual outcomes inadvertently forces researchers to assume that all individuals within a school are identically effected by school-level characteristics (Madaus et al., 1980; Raudenbush & Bryk, 1986). This assumption is often simply wrong in that even simple material resources at the school level are generally applied differentially to students (Madaus et al., 1980). The empirical consequence is that the variance in the treatment that individuals receive becomes relatively large when compared to the variance of the school-level characteristics and is treated as error; the school-level characteristics then appear to have little effect on students.

A conceptual problem described by theoretical sociologists was also related to the analytic problems found in the *Coleman Report's* analysis. Understanding of this conceptual problem would lead to the conclusion that the problem, far from being restricted to the analysis, was endemic to the data. Coleman was trying to measure the effects of schools on schooling without having measures of the effects of schools as they operated at the individual level. A school's effect on individuals should be described or modeled by underlying processes occurring on individuals within schools (Barr & Dreeben, 1983; Bidwell & Kasada, 1980) rather than as an input/output based model focusing on "product." Stated in terms of the data themselves, the *Coleman Report* used school-level variables such as the number of books in the library, the amount of funds spent per student, the types of courses that were offered in a school as inputs, and individual achievement scores as outputs to infer something about a process.

In terms of production versus process models, the data of the *Coleman Report* were thus flawed because the ways in which resource allocation at the school or district level effected individual students was not measured. If resources do have an effect on achievement, then resources applied differentially within levels should result in differential achievement within each level. This interest in "process phenomena" is reflected in Burstein's concept of studying phenomena at the lowest possible unit: only by documenting the process by which school-level resources are applied at the individual level could the process by which schools effect individuals possibly be measured and modeled.

Of course, the notion of process also suggests that measures other than those of the *Coleman Report* must be incorporated in the analysis of any educational process. Constructs such as the time spent on tasks, the quality of the teaching, the climate (or context) of the school, and the influences of a student's peers must all be studied in order to more accurately measure and model the ways in which schools effect students (Barr & Dreeben, 1983; Bidwell & Kasarda, 1980; Heyns, 1986). Consequently, the measures employed in the *Coleman Report* must be considered poor proxies for the ways in which schools effect their students (Madaus et al., 1980).

This recognition of the nature of the inadequacies of the *Coleman Report's* statistical underpinning (statistical submodel) and its associated conceptual framework (theoretical submodel) forced researchers to reconceptualize education as an inherently multilevel process requiring multilevel methodologies (Barr & Dreeben, 1983). Unfortunately, however, this conceptual realization was well ahead of the technical know-how required to analyze data modeled in a nested, hierarchical fashion: the lack of appropriate statistical and computing techniques deprived researchers of the statistical submodels that they needed and left researchers in a dubious twilight, living between a repudiated past and a dimly seen future. Burstein (1980, p. 162), in considering this dilemma, noted that the "specification of appropriate analytical models essentially subsumes" conceptual, design, and measurement issues relating to multilevel data, and, as such, the study of schools.

To summarize: Coleman and his colleagues set out to investigate school effects with a research model utilizing ordinary least squares (OLS) regression techniques; the results produced seemed, to most, hard to believe. Subsequent critical review of OLS regression techniques revealed a number of problems; researchers were forced to abandon the old techniques and their attending conceptual framework in favor of a new conceptual framework that explicitly came to grips with the multilevel structure of the process of education. At this point, however, the whole process screeched to a halt in the face of the lack of statistical submodels capable of analyzing nested data. An interim period began during which an effort to develop appropriate multilevel, analytic submodels was undertaken.

While Burstein (1978b) recommended studying phenomena at their lowest possible level, and Haney (1980) recommended choosing one specific level of analysis, measurement issues often prevent a single-level or lowest-level analysis. Therefore, techniques that address the multilevel nature of the data are required for educational research. Although theoretical sociologists had recognized this issue conceptually, Burstein (1980), following on the earlier work of Cronbach (1976), was one of the first to address the issue methodologically. Burstein recommended running separate regressions within each group (for example, a school), and then estimating the effects of group-level characteristics on the regression coefficients. The technique had the advantage of allowing the relationship between individual characteristics to be considered unique for each group. Further, the variance being predicted by the group-level characteristics was only that of the regression coefficients of the first equation, with the noise from within school variance no longer effecting the group-level equation. The technique allowed modeling of the interaction between levels that had been described by the theoretical sociologists. The second advantage, described more directly in Burstein and Miller (1979), was that the regression coefficients could represent relationships between characteristics of individuals in addition to base-level achievement; the variance in the slopes from the within-schools equation could be viewed as outcomes to be modeled by between-school differences. This captured the notion of modeling "slopes as outcomes."

Yet Burstein's model was still incomplete. The primary problem lay in the fact that the regression coefficients from the first equation to be modeled in the group-level equation were themselves only estimates. The coefficients carried the natural variance of the parameter they were estimating, as well as that of the error that was a result of the regression equations from which they were estimated. Therefore they were highly variable, and the results of any attempt to predict them would be attenuated.

This is not a problem if all the coefficients were estimated from groups with large sample sizes (and correspondingly small variances), but becomes a problem as some coefficients need to be estimated from small groups, or groups of greatly unequal size, as is often the case in educational research.

Advances in statistical thinking and computing in the last decade (see Rubin, 1989) have allowed social science researchers to make the significant leap from Burstein's OLS-based "slopes as outcomes" model to more rigorous multilevel models (Murchan, 1991; Raudenbush, 1988). In 1986, Raudenbush and Bryk suggested a "maximum likelihood" empirical Bayes approach, thereby rectifying the following problems associated with Burstein's "Slopes-as-Outcomes" model:

1. OLS regression coefficients are generally estimated with large error. This lowers our capacity to find the effects of between-group factors.
2. Slopes associated with each unit vary in their reliability as a function of within-unit sample size. Consequently, if we are interested in modeling the effects of between-group factors, each slope needs to be weighted in proportion to its estimated accuracy.
3. Confounding occurs at two levels: the within-unit and between-unit levels. Thus, the model chosen must be able to deal with the special variance-covariance structure associated with the coefficients being estimated.
4. Variability in the estimated slope coefficients needs to be broken into two separate components: parameter variance and sampling variance. This is vitally important because only the parameter variance has meaning in terms of school effects.

Raudenbush and Bryk (1986) entitled their approach "Hierarchical Linear Modeling" (HLM). The HLM program (Bryk, Raudenbush, Seltzer, & Congdon, 1988) employs an empirical Bayes technique along with the EM algorithm. This technique allows one to estimate the true variance of the parameter, as well as the noise within each group. The estimate from that group is then weighted by the ratio of the true variance over the total variance for that parameter, and a new estimate for that group is formed by taking the product of this ratio and the current estimate and adding the result to the product of one minus this ratio times the average estimate: Here the original estimate of β is weighted such that it becomes the more stable estimate β^*, where β^* equals $\{(\beta(\lambda) + (1-\lambda)$ (average estimate of all the β's)$\}$, and λ is the reliability of β. Thus, when λ is close to one (i.e., when β is very reliable) the new estimate of β, β^* is β itself. However, when β is unreliably measured the new estimate of β, β^* is closer to the grand mean (the average estimate of all β's).

There are several advantages to the use of this technique. First, one can estimate model parameters even for groups with relatively little data. Second, the overall variance of the parameters to be estimated at the group level is reduced by the weighting scheme (known as shrinkage) such that estimates of group-level effects that are not attenuated by the extra error term associated with the OLS estimation in Burstein's model are obtained. Conceptually, the effect is to say that there is something that all schools have in common, and those schools that we know little about will be closer to the model of the average school than our original estimate would indicate. This result dovetails neatly with the argument that there is something common to all schools, which constitutes the "institution" of school (Meyer, 1987).

MULTILEVEL MODELS: A CLASSROOM EFFECTS EXAMPLE

Multilevel regression invokes two distinct operations. The first operation is to model the variability in, for example, student mathematics achievement as a function of student-level variables. This process yields a set of parameters for each classroom. In the context of the specific SIMS[2] example used in this chapter, the particular

---

[2] The SIMS study is a particularly rich source of data; see Garden (1987) and Travers and Westbury (1989).

parameters we are interested in estimating and controlling for at the student level include the effects of prior student achievement in mathematics (*Pretest*), the minority status of students (*Minority*), and student socioeconomic status (*SES*). Henceforth, we will refer to this within-classroom model and models of this type as Level-1 models.

In the second operation, the parameters estimated at the first level become outcome variables to be predicted by classroom-level variables. We will refer to the between-classroom model as a Level-2 model.

In our empirical example, we will explore the effects of: (a) average prior classroom achievement (*Average Pretest*); (b) average socioeconomic status by classroom (*Average SES*); (c) opportunity to learn as a classroom measure (*OTL*); (d) teacher experience (*Experience*); (e) proportion of certified mathematics specialists in a school (*Proportion Specialist*); (f) whether the classroom is mixed ability or not (*Mixed Ability*); and, (g) the geographic location of the school (*S-W City*), on the within-class slopes.[3,4]

When the Level-1 and Level-2 models are well specified, the resultant parameters afford the researcher an accurate index of the relative contribution of the specific between-classroom variables to the variability of the within-classroom parameters. In this example, the HLM procedure allows the analyst to estimate the contribution of the Level-2 variables to the possible variability in the Level-1 predictors, which here include prior achievement (*Pretest*), minority status (*Minority*), and socioeconomic status (*SES*).

Results

Inferences made from cross-level OLS analyses are plagued with conceptual and methodological difficulties. This study set out to incorporate more appropriate multilevel modeling of the data using empirical Bayes estimates provided by the computer program HLM. The unconditional model calculated the total variance in posttest mathematics scores across U.S. classes to be 51.85. More than half of this variance, some 57 percent, was found to be between classes,

---

[3] On final cleaning of the data set, we had an operational sample size of 4,595 students. This represented 95 percent of those students on whom cognitive data were available. Deletion of a case was typically due to excessive missing data on key variables contained in the SIMS student questionnaire. This criterion eliminated 16 out of 225 classes.

[4] More information with respect to variable construction is available in Appendix B.

with 43 percent being within classrooms.[5] This result indicates that the contribution of classroom-level variables is considerably larger than within-class variables. The estimate of the grand mean of posttest scores over all 209 classes is 19.21. Parameter variance among the mean mathematics scores for each class was 49.29. A test of the null hypothesis that there was no significant variability among the means was rejected with a χ^2 value of 6047.5 with 208 degrees of freedom. This indicated that the variability among the intercepts from the separate regressions for each class is "real" and needs to be modeled using between-class variables.

The final within-class model included three predictors: prior student achievement (Pretest), minority status (Minority), and individual socioeconomic status (SES). In this final Level-1 model, the three independent variables were centered around their class means, in order to facilitate the interpretation of the intercept, β_{0j}. The results of the Level-1 analysis are presented in Table 9.1.

The results presented in Table 9.1 suggest that Pretest and SES are positively (and significantly, $p<.01$) associated with posttest scores. Minority students achieve significantly lower scores than their White or Asian classmates. A one unit increase in pretest score is associated with an increase of .69 of a point on the posttest with the effect of Minority and SES held constant. Similarly, a one unit increase in SES is associated with an expected increase in posttest score of .39 of one point, with Pretest and Minority status held constant. Finally, non-Asian minority students are expected to score 1.19 points lower than nonminority students. Due to the centering process, the intercept of 19.20 can be interpreted as the adjusted mean score for each class.

The figures in the bottom of Table 9.1 indicate the amount of variability in the slopes across classes. For each set of slopes a χ^2 test was used to test the null hypothesis of no variability across classes. The Pretest slopes exhibited variability (χ^2 statistic of 321.46 with 162 degrees of freedom, p-value less than .001), suggesting that the relationship between prior achievement (Pretest) and end of year achievement (Posttest) differed from class to class. However, the null hypothesis of no variability could not be rejected for the Minority

---

[5] In their study of these data, McKnight, Crosswhite, Dossey, Kifer, Swafford, Travers, and Cooney (1987) found the variance across classes to be less than 50 percent. The discrepancy can be reconciled with the realization that the 57 percent found here includes variation attributable to schools, estimated to be approximately 10 percent by McKnight et al. (1987). Consequently, this result is in keeping with expectations for an educational system with a clear-cut tracking policy.

TABLE 9.1
Randon Regression Model for U.S. Population

Parameter Estimates	Effect[a]	S.E.	t-ratio
Class Mean Achievement (r = .98[b])	19.20	.49	38.79**
Pretest Slope (r = .34)	.69	.02	32.30**
Minority Slope (r = .09)	−1.19	.24	−4.85**
Student SES Slope (r = .09)	.39	.12	3.37*

Residual Parameter Variance	Estimate[c]	d.f.	χ^2	p
Student-level Variance, σ^2	21.65			
Mean Achievement	50.13	162	6811.00	.000
Pretest Slope	.05	162	321.46	.000
Minority Slope	1.35	162	184.07	.113
Student SES Slope	.34	162	186.02	.095

*p < .01,   **p < .001
All within-class variables centered around their class means.
[a] Maximum likelihood estimate of the average main effect of Level-1 predictors on student posttest achievement.
[b] Reliability of the estimated parameter calculated as the ratio of true parameter variance to total observed variance.
[c] The variance in within-class parameters unexplained by class predictors.

and SES slopes. It is possible, therefore, to assume that common slopes across classes reasonably summarizes the association between Minority, SES, and the outcome under study, student mathematics achievement measured by the posttest. Consequently, we constrained the variability in these slopes to zero, thereby reducing the number of random effects to be modeled in future analyses. That is, as the slopes exhibited no random variation, we estimated the slopes as though they were fixed.

Recognizing that there was significant variation across classes in their intercept and Pretest slopes, we decided to model this variation. In doing so we specified a model that includes seven Level-2 predictors: (a) Average Pretest, (b) Average SES, (c) Opportunity-to-Learn (OTL), (d) teachers' years experience teaching mathematics to eighth-graders (Experience), (e) the proportion of certified mathematics teachers on the mathematics faculty (Proportion Specialists), and dummy variables indicating (f) the school's policy regarding mixed-ability classes (Mixed Ability), and (g) whether the school/class was located in a city in the South or Western United States (S-W City).[6] To improve linearity, the log of the variable Experience

---

[6] As HLM cannot deal with missing data among the between-level variables, standardized scores were used for the variables OTL and Proportion Specialists. Any missing data for these variables were set to the mean over all classes.

was used. As all other predictors were found to be linear, no other transformations of the data were required. Results from this analysis are presented in Table 9.2.

The information provided in the upper part of Table 9.2 suggests that a one-unit increase in Average Pretest is associated with an expected increase in the average mathematics achievement of the class (Average Posttest) of almost one point. A one-unit advantage in Average SES is associated with an expected increase of 2.59 points on the average achievement of a class. Mixed-ability classes, likewise, seem to be associated with higher average achievement than tracked classes, the regression coefficient indicating a 1.20 point advantage, whereas class average scores in cities located in the south or west of the country are expected to be 1.46 points lower.

TABLE 9.2
Estimated Effects of Selected Class-level Variables on the Mean
and Distribution of Math Achievement: 3 Within-class Predictors

Parameter Estimates	Effect[a]	S.E.	t-ratio
Class Mean Achievement (r = .87)[b]			
Base	4.89	.81	6.04**
Average Pretest	.95	.05	19.00**
Average SES	2.59	.63	4.11**
Opportunity to Learn	.59	.20	2.95*
Mixed-Ability Class	1.20	.51	2.35*
Teacher Experience	.47	.20	2.35*
S-W City	−1.46	.65	−2.25*
Pretest Slope (r = .37)			
Base	.69	.02	34.50**
Proportion Specialists	−.06	.02	−3.00*
Minority Slope[c]			
Base	−1.13	.22	−5.14**
Student SES Slope[c]			
Base	.38	.12	3.17*

Residual Parameter Variance	Estimate[d]	d.f.	χ^2	p
Student-level Variance σ^2	21.95			
Mean Achievement	7.20	202	1592.90	.000
Pretest Slope	.04	207	434.03	.000

*p < .01,   **p < .001
All within-class variables centered around their class means.
[a] Empirical Bayes estimate of the fixed effect of class-level predictor on within-class parameters, across 162 classes used in the calculations.
[b] Reliability of the estimated parameter calculated as the ratio of true parameter variance to total observed variance.
[c] The residual variance associated with this parameter was set to zero.
[d] The variance in within-class parameters unexplained by class predictors.

Coefficients for all class variables predicting mean class achievement are significant at $p<.05$. Therefore, barring any serious problems with the fit of the model, we can reject the hypothesis that those variables have no effect on mean achievement.

As seen in the random regression model (Table 9.1), the Pretest slopes exhibited variation across classes. One class-level predictor, Proportion Specialists, was used to model variability in this relationship and was found to be a significant predictor of slope variability, a one-unit increase in the Proportion Specialists being associated with a .06 decrease in Pretest slope. This interesting finding indicates that having greater concentrations of certified mathematics teachers among schools' mathematics teachers "flattens" the Pretest slope. This is important as it suggests that teachers fully certified to teach mathematics enhance the performance of lower achieving students.

The bottom part of Table 9.2 summarizes the adequacy with which the random parameters from the Level-1 model (mean mathematics achievement and pretest slope) have been explained using Level-2 predictors. The χ^2 test evaluates the hypothesis that variability remaining among the intercepts can be attributed to nothing more than sampling variance. The value of 1592.9, with 202 degrees of freedom indicates that such an hypothesis is untenable. Similarly, the null hypothesis is rejected for the Pretest slopes. It seems that some explainable variance is left in both parameters, because, even after taking into account the effect of various predictors, the intercepts and slopes still vary.

Just what variables would reduce the residual variances further is unclear, as various exploratory regressions failed to yield any additional significant predictors. From Table 9.3 we see that the reduction in variability associated with student-level variance and mean class achievement is 41.5 percent and 85.6 percent, respectively. Consequently, our final model accounts for much but clearly not all of the variability in these two slopes. Unfortunately, the variables we included are not as strongly associated with the Pretest slope.[7] In this, the HLM technique is probably revealing some of the

---

[7] An important consideration in any causal model is just how much of the variance (in the outcome of interest) the model explains. The unique features of multilevel analysis do not engender estimation of one succinct coefficient of determination such as the R^2 used in OLS estimation. Such a figure runs counter to the logic of multilevel regression, a procedure that in effect estimates as many R^2s as there are random parameters to be modeled. It is possible within this framework to obtain meaningful estimates of the reduction in parameter

TABLE 9.3
Percent Reduction in Parameter Variance Achieved Using Final Model

Parameter	Original Variance	Final Variance	Percent Reduction[a]
Student Variance[b]	37.537	21.947	41.5
Mean Achievement[c]	50.115	7.198	85.6
Pretest Slope	.047	.044	6.4

Some rounding error present in calculations.
[a] Precent Reduction = [1 − (Final Variance/Original variance)]
[b] Original student variance, σ^2, is calculated using the unconditional (or oneway random effects ANOVA) model.
[c] Original variance for Mean Achievement and Pretest parameters calculated using random regression model, using only three within-class predictors, with Minority and SES fixed, that is, not based directly on Table 9.1, where all effects are random.

same sorts of inadequacies in the SIMS data that plague data from the *Coleman Report*. In short, this common "inadequacy," if real, probably reflects the level of emphasis on "product" common to both data sets. The continued use of unilevel statistical submodels that fail to reflect the multilevel nature of the relationships under study not only misestimates relationships, but also encourages a pervasive conceptual misrepresentation of the objects under study; the conceptual understanding of schooling as a deep, inherently multilevel process is consequently seriously compromised.

In sum, we hope that this empirical example serves to demonstrate the power of the HLM technique and to encourage researchers not already familiar with these techniques to reconsider educational problems from a multilevel perspective. Further, the results of our empirical investigations of these data with multilevel techniques reinforces the general impression that empirical studies are hindered by the quality of data collected initially for unilevel studies; this shortcoming of the data themselves is almost certainly a product of study design that was, in turn, a product of the lack of viable and salient statistical submodels to fit the nested structure of educational data.

---

variance achieved by the Level-2 model presented in Table 9.2. This is achieved by expressing the amount of parameter variance (e.g., the variability in the intercepts and Pretest slopes) which remains after the introduction of the Level-2 predictors. One minus this proportion is the proportion of the parameter variance that has been reduced. The raw figures and percent of variance reduced are presented in Table 9.3.

THE IMPORTANCE OF HIERARCHICAL LINEAR MODELS IN RESEARCH ON CLASSROOM AND SCHOOL EFFECTS

HLM as a modeling tool has four main advantages:

1. Clearly, any approach that sensibly incorporates different organizational levels—while avoiding the violation of regression assumptions regarding the independence of errors—is a positive move forward for research on schools and schooling. As Raudenbush and Bryk (1986) point out, retaining the individuality of students, classrooms, and schools focuses analyses on key sociological units in and of themselves. Consequently, by modeling our data in a multilevel manner we avoid the much documented "unit of analysis" problem that plagued research on nested data structures since it was originally recognized as a problem in sociological research (Robinson, 1950).

2. The ability of HLM techniques to estimate effects across the many organizational structures associated with schooling opens up conceptually appealing possibilities that cannot be explored using more traditional (ordinary least squares regression) methods. Not only can the average outcome level for different groups be modeled using variables that are controlled for and modeled in turn at a second or even a third level if need be, but, more importantly, the structural relationships within and between groups can be modeled as a function of classroom- and school-level variables. Consequently, a particularly useful blend of quantitative and ethnographic methods becomes possible: retaining the individuality of classrooms allows the quantitative inclusion of "exemplary" classes that, though frequently the subject of ethnographic research (Rutter, Maughan, Mortimore, Ouston, & Smith, 1979), have historically been excluded as unstable, ungeneralizable statistical outliers. HLM and similar models allow quantitative research to blend together with the ethnographic research that has become known as "exemplary schools research"—research driven by a desire to document under what conditions specific school practices are successful. Recent findings indicate that multilevel approaches including "exemplary schools" generate samples that are more stable over time and, hence, offer greater range and generalizability simultaneously.

3. HLM and similar models, through the decomposition of covariance components, offers both increased explanatory power and a concomitant ability to evaluate the success of such explanations—using HLM, we gain an enhanced ability to ascertain how much of

the explainable has been explained. One of the problems associated with Burstein's early investigations in OLS-based slopes-as-out-comes models was the inability of this technique to decompose variance components across units in the slope parameters. Slope variance consists of parameter variance (true variability) and sampling variance (variability due to error). Failure to separate sampling variability from parameter variability is disabling because the true variability is then misestimated. Decomposition of variance components allows us to evaluate both the methodological soundness of our studies and our degree of success in explaining or describing the "real" relationships of true variability as manifest in parameter variance. Thus, a Level-2 model that explains only a small percentage of the observed variance may in fact be explaining a very large percentage of what is really explainable—if the parameter variance happens to be small relative to the sampling variance. However, conventional statistical methods cannot separate parameter from sampling variance. Consequently, prior research on school and classroom effects utilizing conventional statistical methods have most likely underestimated the power of group-level variables.

4. Finally, the estimation of within-unit parameters is enhanced by the use of the empirical Bayes or generalized least squares methods underlying most of the currently available multilevel computer programs. On the assumption that within-unit regression is fundamental to answering the types of questions that are of interest to educational researchers and policymakers, the focus shifts toward methods which ensure that the microlevel regression parameters are estimated as precisely as possible. HLM is one such method.

In short—as we have shown empirically—this analytic framework accurately reflects the type of data we collect when we study schools, and, as such, we may entertain the hope of finally developing and empirically testing richer theoretical models.

SUMMARY AND CONCLUSIONS

Since the mid-1960s, policymakers have made many efforts to use large-scale surveys to obtain evidence about the quality of schools and schooling locally, nationally, and internationally. These include the *Equality of Educational Opportunity* (Coleman et al., 1966) and its reanalyses (e.g., Averch, Carroll, Donaldson, Kiesling, & Pincus, 1972; Bowles & Levin, 1968; Cain & Watts, 1970); the IEA studies (e.g., Comber & Keeves, 1973; Husén, 1967), *High-School and Be-*

yond and such large-scale evaluations as *Project Follow-Through* (Stebbins, St. Pierre, Proper, Anderson, & Cerva, 1977), and the *Sustaining Effects Study* (Carter, 1984).

Many of these studies have failed to obtain reasonable evidence of significant school, classroom, or teacher effects. These daunting results have been attributed to overlapping methodological and conceptual errors. Burstein, Linn, and Capell (1978) and Burstein and Miller (1978) support Cronbach's (1976) assertion that the principal flaw in these studies lies in the failure to understand and deal effectively with the complexities that arise from the multilevel character of the data. Burstein, Miller, Cronbach, and others (e.g., Keesling & Wiley, 1974; Raudenbush & Bryk, 1986; Wiley, 1976) stress that multilevel statistical models are needed to analyze the multilevel organizational structures we know to exist in schools.

As Raudenbush (1988) points out, traditional linear models, on which most researchers rely, require the assumption that subjects respond independently to educational programs. In fact, education is a multilevel enterprise where the assumption of independence is regularly broken. More specifically, students are nested with teachers within classes, classes and teachers are nested within schools, and schools are nested within school districts. Furthermore, as in the teaching of reading, students may be nested in an even smaller unit than classrooms, instructional groups. Hence, students do not necessarily act independently of each other. On the contrary, the hierarchical nature of instructional processes encourage some form of dependence. Realistic models should reflect this organizational reality.

In response to this need several methodologists—Burstein (1976, 1978), Burstein, Linn, and Capell (1978), Burstein and Miller (1978), and Mason, Wong, and Entwistle (1983)—have suggested that the within-group slopes from the regression of the individual dependent variable on the individual explanatory variables are indicators of within-group processes; that is, slopes from within-unit models can be used as outcomes to be modeled by between-unit differences.[8] Conceptually, differences in slopes across groups can reflect substantive educational effects. For example: (a) The slope of achievement on initial ability should be flatter in a classroom that uses mastery learning as compared with the slope in a classroom

---

[8] Many multilevel modeling programs now exist. Programs such as *BMPD5V* (Schluchter, 1988), *GENMOD* (Mason, Anderson, & Hayat, 1988), *ML2* (Rabash, Prosser, & Goldstein, 1989), and *VARCL* (Longford, 1988) generally incorporate the same basic strengths as the *HLM*.

where an individually structured program is used; and (b) Classrooms where written materials are emphasized should have higher within-group slopes of achievement on initial reading ability. If such slope effects are present, the method of analysis should identify them and enable the investigator to assess their importance.

Fortunately, as outlined in this chapter, statistical models now exist that allow educational researchers to empirically evaluate just such variability in slopes. Unfortunately, however, few educational researchers have used these methods. In fact, until quite recently, these statistical submodels have been outside the mainstream of educational research, being the focus of methodologists and other statisticians only. The time has now come for these models to cease being of interest solely to methodologists and statisticians; it is time to evaluate the quality of these statistical models when used to address real questions in the sociology of education. Interestingly, a group of researchers is doing just that.[9] One such example is seen in Chapter 10 where Gamoran contrasts two incommensurable conceptual approaches to the study of school effects (interactive and additive approaches). Without the use of such multilevel tools as the HLM, such work would be impossible.

In conclusion, school effects research has been hampered by the lack of calculable and commensurable statistical models. Theoretical developments have consequently gone unevaluated due to this mismatch between educational data and analytic tool. Fortunately, many of the statistical problems associated with the estimation and analysis of hierarchically nested data structures have been overcome. We now await with interest the applications of multilevel modeling principles and procedures, not in simulation studies, but in the detailed analysis of extensive bodies of educational data.

APPENDIX A
MATHEMATICAL DESCRIPTION
OF THE HIERARCHICAL LINEAR MODEL

Here we specify the hierarchical linear model used in our empirical example. We will employ the notational format provided by Bryk et al. (1988).

---

[9] The interested reader is referred to the work of the research group at the Centre for Educational Sociology at the University of Edinburgh, Edinburgh, Scotland.

The Level-1 Model follows:
let,

$$Y_{ij} = \beta_{jo} + \beta_{j1}X_{ij1} + \beta_{j2}X_{ij2} + \beta_{j3}X_{ij3} + r_{ij} \qquad (1)$$

where;

Y_{ij} is the mathematics achievement score for Student i in Class j.

X_{ijk} are the Level-1 predictors for Student i in Class j. Specifically, prior student achievement (Pretest), student minority status (Minority), and student socioeconomic status (SES).

β_{jk} are Level-1 regression coefficients that characterize the structural relationships within classroom j.

What sets these coefficients apart from those yielded by conventional OLS procedures is that they are allowed to vary across classrooms, a crucial factor in attempting to explain parameter variance using classroom-level structural predictors.

r_{ij} represents random error usually assumed to be normally distributed with mean zero and constant variance, for,

$i = 1, \ldots, n_j$ students within class j;

$j = 1, \ldots, J$ classes, and

$k = 1, \ldots, K$ independent variables in the Level-1 model
(here K runs from 1-3).

Note. Prior to inclusion in the Level-1 model, the individual student values X_{ij1} to X_{ij3} are typically centered around their means. This is achieved by subtracting the mean of the each classroom from each observation. In this way, β_{0j} can be construed as the achievement of a pupil in Class j who has average background characteristics, thereby making the parameter β_{0j} readily interpretable.

Maximum likelihood procedures are used in estimating these microlevel, or Level-1 parameters (Mason, Wong, & Entwistle, 1983). This procedure yields a value of β_{0j} for each classroom in the sample. The centering techniques employed imply that this coefficient can also be interpreted as the average achievement of Classroom j adjusted for the background characteristics of its students.

In the Level-2 model variables measured at the classroom and teacher level are used to predict between-classroom differences in the within-classroom slopes. To clarify the example below, we use just two classroom-level predictors, average prior achievement (Average Pretest), and average socioeconomic status (Average SES).

The Level-2 Model Follows:

$$\beta_{0j} = \gamma00 + \gamma01W_1 + \gamma02W_2 + U_{ij} \qquad (2.1)$$
$$\beta_{1j} = \gamma10 + \gamma11W_1 + \gamma12W_2 + U_{ij} \qquad (2.2)$$
$$\beta_{2j} = \gamma20 + \gamma21W_1 + \gamma22W_2 + U_{ij} \qquad (2.3)$$
$$\beta_{3j} = \gamma30 + \gamma31W_1 + \gamma32W_2 + U_{ij} \qquad (2.4)$$

where,

$\beta_{0j}, \ldots, \beta_{3j}$ are Level-1 random coefficients associated with the intercept and the variables Pretest, Minority, and SES, respectively.

$\gamma00, \ldots, \gamma32$ are the Level-2 coefficients and are associated with the variables Average Pretest and Average SES, respectively. These coefficients are estimated as fixed effects, and the Level-2 model is consequently considered a fixed effects model.

W_1 and W_2 are the Level-2 predictor variables Average Pretest and Average SES.

$U_{0j}, \ldots, U_{3j}$ are the Level-2 random effects.

Note. The HLM model assumes that the covariation between the random components of the Level-1 and Level-2 models is zero.

APPENDIX B
DESCRIPTION OF VARIABLES IN THE STUDY

Student-Level Variables

Posttest. 40-item Population A "core" test covering arithmetic, algebra, geometry, probability and statistics, and measurement. Number correct score

Pretest. Pretest version of posttest.

Student SES (SES). Standardized composite SES scores calculated as the mean of standardized scores on father's education, mother's education, father's occupation, and mother's occupation.

Minority. Dummy-coded dichotomous variable indicating minority ethnicity.

1 = American Indian, Black, Mexican/Chicano, Puerto Rican/Latin American, or other.

0 = White or Asian.

School-Level Variables

Average Pretest. Average pretest score of students in class on core test. Aggregated from student scores.

Average SES. Average SES score of students in class. Aggregated from student SES.

Mixed Ability Class. Dummy-coded dichotomous variable indicating heterogeneous grouping for Population A mathematics in the school: 1 = mixed-ability or heterogeneous grouping: 0 = homogeneous grouping based on general or mathematics ability.

Teacher Experience. Years spent teaching mathematics to eighth grade students.

Proportion Specialists. Proportion of officially certified, or otherwise fully qualified, mathematics teachers on the school's mathematics faculty.

Opportunity to Learn (OTL). Composite score of degree to which content underlying each item on the mathematics test was taught during the year. Content for each item rated by teacher as being: 1 = Not taught, not assumed; 2 = Taught as new content; 3 = Reviewed, then extended; 4 = Not taught, assumed known. Composite score = Average over the 40 items.

Strata

E-C City	*East or Central / SMSA* City*
E-C Suburb	East or Central / SMSA Suburb
E-C Rural	East or Central / Rural
S-W City	South or West / SMSA City
S-W Suburb	South or West / SMSA Suburb
S-W Rural	South or West / Rural
Private	All regions, private school.

*SMSA = U.S. Census Bureau, Standard Metropolitan Statistical Area.

Notes on Variable Construction

Data in the SIMS study were gathered on the individual student, classroom, school, and national levels. The outcome measure used in the present study was a composite number-correct score indicating students' attainment on the 40-item core test for the U.S. The *KR-20* reliabilities of the posttest and pretest were .91 and .88, respectively. Scores on the pretest were included as covariates at the individual student level.

A composite measure of student SES was formed from the standardized scores of parents' occupation and education. Equal weighting was given to each of these variables. Measures of home support and home attitude to mathematics were also included.

An "encouragement" composite was formed from students' responses regarding their parents' attitudes to mathematics: Do your parents think mathematics study is important? Do they encourage you to study mathematics?

A "family help" question asked students how frequently their families actually helped them with mathematics.

Variables covering students' gender, race, age, home language, and future educational aspirations were also included in preliminary models. Other variables provide information on the hours per week spent by the student on homework for all subjects, on homework for mathematics, and the amount of tutoring, if any, the student received outside of school each week. Data were also gathered from school principals and teachers. As the focus of this study was on the classroom unit, these variables, and some aggregated student variables were treated at the classroom level. Such variables included unweighted average SES of the class (based on individual-level SES values aggregated to the classroom level), average pretest score of the class, whether the class was of mixed ability or not, class size, whether the school was public or private, amount of time devoted to mathematics in the school's curriculum each week, teacher emphasis on problem solving, and teacher demographics (age and years experience as a mathematics teacher). An opportunity-to-learn (OTL) composite was formed from questions asking teachers to rate the emphasis they placed in their teaching on the content required to answer each of the mathematics test items during the school year.

REFERENCES

Averch, H., Carroll, S. J., Donaldson, T., Kiesling, H. J., & Pincus, J. (1972). *How effective is schooling: A critical review and synthesis of research findings* (R-956-PCSF/RC). Santa Monica, CA: The Rand Corporation.

Barr, R., & Dreeben, R. (1983). *How schools work*. Chicago: The University of Chicago Press.

Beaton, A. E. (1974). Multivariate commonality analysis. In G. W. Mayseke, A. E. Beaton, C. E. Wisler, J. Okado, & W. M. Cohen (Eds.), *Technical* supplement to a study of the achievement of our nation's students. Washington, DC: U.S. Department of Health, Education, and Welfare.

Bidwell, C. E., & Kasarda, J. D. (1980). Conceptuallizing and measuring the effects of school and schooling. American Journal of Education, 88, 401–430.

Bowles, S., & Levin, H. (1968). More on multi-collinearity and the effectiveness of schools. Journal of Human Resources 3, 393–400.

Bryk, A. S., & Raudenbush, S. W. (1988). Methodological advances in analyzing the effects of schools and classrooms on student learning. In E. Z. Rothkopf (Ed.), Review of research in education (Vol. 15). Washington DC: American Educational Research Association.

Bryk, A. S., & Raudenbush, S. W. (1989). Toward a more appropriate conceptualization of research on school effects: A three-level hierarchical linear model. In R. D. Bock (Ed.), Multilevel analysis of educational data. San Diego: Academic Press.

Bryk, A. S., Raudenbush, S. W., Seltzer, M., & Congdon, R. T., Jr. (1988). An introduction to hierarchical linear modeling: Computer program and users' guide (Version 2.0). Chicago: University of Chicago.

Burstein, L. (1976). Assessing the differences of between-group and individual regression coefficients. Paper presented at the annual meeting of the American Educational Research Association, San Francisco, CA.

Burstein, L. (1978a). Analyzing multilevel educational data: The choice of an analytic model rather than a unit of analysis. Paper presented at the Winter Measurement and Methodology Conference: Center for the Study of Evaluation, University of California, Los Angeles, CA.

Burnstein, L. (1978b). Assessing differences between group and individual-level regression coefficients. Sociological Methods and Research, 7, 5-28.

Burstein, L. (1980). The analysis of multilevel data in educational research and evaluation. Review of Research in Education, 8, 158–233.

Burstein, L., Linn, R., & Capell, F. J. (1978). Analyzing multilevel data in the presence of heterogeneous within-class regressions. Journal of Educational Statistics, 3, 347–383.

Burstein, L., & Miller, M. D. (1978). Alternative analytic models for identifying educational effects: Where are we? Paper presented at the annual meeting of the American Educational Research Assocation, Toronto.

Burstein, L., & Miller, M. D. (1979). The use of within-group slopes as indices of group outcomes. Paper presented at the annual meeting of the American Educational Research Association, San Francisco, CA.

Cain, G. G., & Watts, H. W. (1970). Problems in making policy from the Coleman Report. American Sociological Review, 35, 228–242.

Carter, L. F. (1984). The sustaining effects study of compensatory and elementary education. Educational Researcher, 13, 4–13.

Coleman, J. S., Campbell, E. Q., Hobson, C. J., McPartland, J., Mood, A. M., Weinfeld, F. D., & York, R. L. (1966). Equality of educational opportunity. Washington DC: U.S. Government Printing Office.

Comber, L. C., & Keeves, J. P. (1973). *Science education in nineteen countries. International studies in evaluation* (Vol. 1). New York: John Wiley & Sons.

Cronbach, L. J. (1976). *Research on classrooms and schools: Formulation of questions, design, and analysis.* Occasional paper. Stanford, CA: Stanford Evaluation Consortium.

Garden, R. (1987). *Second IEA mathematics study: Sampling report.* Washington, DC: Office of Educational Research and Improvement, U.S. Department of Education.

Haney, W. (1980). Units and levels of analysis in large-scale evaluation. *New Directions for Methodology of Social and Behavioral Science, 6*, 1–15.

Hanushek, E. A. (1989). The impact of differential expenditures on school performance. *Educational Researcher, 18*, 45–62.

Hanushek, E., & Kain, J. F. (1972). On the value of equality of educational opportunity as a guide to public policy. In F. Mosteller & D. Moynihan (Eds.), *On equality of educational opportunity.* New York: Vintage Books.

Heyns, B. (1978). *Summer learning and the effects of schooling.* New York: Academic Press.

Heyns, B. (1986). Educational effects: Issues in conceptualization and measurement. In J. G. Richardson (Ed.), *Handbook of theory and research for the sociology of education.* Westport, CT: Greenwood Press.

Husén, T. (Ed.). (1967). *International study of achievement in mathematics* (Vols. 1 & 2). Stockholm: Almqvist & Wiksell.

Keesling, J. W., & Wiley, D. (1974). *Regression models for hierarchical data.* Paper presented at the annual meeting of the Psychometric Society.

King, G. (1989). *Unifying political methodology: The likelihood theory of statistical inference.* Cambridge, England: Cambridge University Press.

Longford, N. T. (1988). *VARCL: Software for variance component analysis of data with hierarchically nested random effects (Maximum Likelihood).* Princeton, NJ: Educational Testing Service.

Madaus, G., Airasian, P., & Kellaghan, T. (1980). *School effectiveness: A reassessment of the evidence.* New York: McGraw-Hill.

Mason, W. M., Anderson, A. F., & Hayat, N. (1988). *Manual for GENMOD.* Population Studies Center, University of Michigan.

Mason, W. M., Wong, G. M., & Entwistle, B. (1983). Contextual analysis through the multilevel linear model. In S. Leinhardt (Ed.), *Sociological methodology.* San Francisco: Jossey-Bass.

Mayeske, G. W., Wisler, C. E., Beaton, A. E., Weinfeld, F. D., Cohen, W. M., Okada, T., Proshek, J. M., & Tabler, K. A. (1974). *A study of our nation's schools* (DHEW Publication No. (DE) 72-142). Washington, DC: U.S. Department of Health, Education, and Welfare.

McKnight, C. C., Crosswhite, F. J., Dossey, J. A., Kifer, E., Swafford, J. O., Travers, K. J., & Cooney, T. J. (1987). *The underachieving curricu-*

lum: Assessing U.S. school mathematics from an international perspective. Champaign, IL: Stipes Publishing Co.

Meyer, J. W. (1987). Implications of an institutional view of education for the study of educational effects. In M. T. Hallinan (Ed.), *The social organization of schools: New conceptualizations of the learning process.* New York: Plenum.

Michelson, S. (1970). The association of teacher resourcefulness with children's characteristics. *Do teachers make a difference?* Washington, DC: U.S. Department of Health, Education, and Welfare.

Murchan, D. P. (1991). *Traditional and multilevel estimation of classroom effects on mathematics attainment in the U.S. and France.* Doctoral dissertation, Cornell University.

Rabash, J., Prosser, R., & Goldstein, H. (1989). *ML2: Software for two-level analysis. Users guide.* London: Institute of Education, University of London.

Raudenbush, S. W. (1988). Applications of hierarchical linear models in educational research: A review. *Journal of Educational Statistics, 13,* 85–116.

Raudenbush, S., & Bryk, A. S. (1986). A hierarchical model for studying school effects. *Sociology of Education, 59,* 1–17.

Robinson, W. S. (1950). Ecological correlations and the behavior of individuals. *American Sociological Review, 15,* 351–257.

Rubin, D. B. (1989). Some applications of multilevel models of educational data. In R. D. Bock (Ed.), *Multilevel analysis of educational data.* San Diego: Academic Press.

Rutter, M., Maughan, B., Mortimore, P., Ouston, I., & Smith, A. (1979). *Fifteen thousand hours.* Cambridge, MA: Harvard University Press.

Schluchter, M. D. (1988). *BMDP5V: Unbalanced measures model with structured covariance matrices* (Tech. Rep. 86). Los Angeles, CA: BMDP Statistical Software, Inc.

Stebbins, L. B., St. Pierre, R. G., Proper, E. C., Anderson, R. B., & Cerva, T. P. (1977). *Education as experimentation: A planned variation model* (Vol. IV-A, An evaluation of project follow through). Boston, MA: Abt Associates.

Travers, K. J., & Westbury, I. (Eds.). (1989). *The IEA study of mathematics I: Anaysis of mathematics curricula.* Oxford: Pergamon Press.

Wiley, D. W. (1976). Another hour, another day. In R. A. Hauser, W. H. Sewell, & D. Alwin (Eds.), *Schooling and achievement in American society.* New York: Academic Press.

Wisler, C. E. (1974). Partitioning the explained variance in a regression analysis. In G. W. Mayeske, A. E. Beaton, C. E. Wisler, J. Okado, & W. M. Cohen (Eds.), *Technical supplement to a study of the achievement of our nation's students.* Washington, DC: U.S. Department of Health, Education, and Welfare.

10

Schooling and Achievement: Additive Versus Interactive Models*

Adam Gamoran

University of Wisconsin
Department of Sociology
Madison, Wisconsin

Why do some students learn more than others? One answer is that students differ in the experiences they have in schools. This proposition has received increasing attention, in part because an alter-

* This chapter was published previously in *Schools, Classrooms, and Pupils: International Studies of Schooling from a Multi-level Perspective*, edited by S. W. Raudenbush and J. D. Willms (1991). San Diego: Academic Press, and is reprinted here with the permission of Academic Press. The author appreciates the collaboration of Martin Nystrand, and the research assistance of Mark Berends, Jock Evanson, Dae-dong Hahn, Jim Ladwig, and John Knapp. Maureen Hallinan, Bill Pendelton, Andrew Porter, and Doug Willms provided helpful comments on an earlier draft. This chapter was prepared at the National Center on Effective Secondary Schools, Wisconsin Center for Education Research, School of Education, University of Wisconsin-Madison, which is supported by a grant from the Office of Educational Research and Improvement (Grant No. G-008690007-89). Any opinions, findings, and conclusions are those of the author and do not necessarily reflect the views of this agency or the U.S. Department of Education.

native answer—that some students attend schools with better resources—turned out to have surprisingly little explanatory power
(e.g., Coleman, Campbell, Hobson, McPartland, Mood, Weinfield, &
York, 1966). The notion of examining differences inside schools
draws on the reasoning that because student achievement mainly
varies within schools, it makes sense to seek the sources of that
variation within schools (e.g., Bidwell & Kasarda, 1980). Classroom
instruction, in particular, is likely both to vary within schools and to
contribute to achievement. In recent years, differences in opportunities for learning have become a central focus in the sociology of
schooling.

This chapter extends that line of research in two main ways.
First, it applies a statistically appropriate hierarchical model to a
problem that has been conceptualized in a multilevel framework but
analyzed with single-level models. Second, it contrasts two distinct
specifications of how within-school effects on achievement occur.
One is an *additive model*, in which achievement rises as a linear
function of increasing opportunities to learn. The other is an *interactive model*, in which learning opportunities do not influence
learning directly; instead, as they increase they provide growing
benefits to additional ability and effort. The goal of this chapter,
then, is to test these competing models in a multilevel framework.

THE ADDITIVE MODEL OF SCHOOLING EFFECTS

In the additive model, classroom instruction is viewed as a crucial
force in the production of achievement. Stimulated by the discour-
aging results of between-school analyses of school effects, this perspective has opened the "black box" of schools in order to see what
happens to students inside them. Among the key proponents are
Barr and Dreeben (1977, 1983), who view schools as "nested layers"
in which the outcomes of one hierarchical level constitute the inputs
at the next. In their formulation, district and school administrators
allocate resources to classrooms. Key resources include time, curricular materials, and the competencies of teachers and students;
learning occurs when teachers make use of these resources in their
classrooms. Thus, the process is viewed as a technological one:
achievement is produced as a result of instructional activities that
make use of available resources.

Students' individual characteristics—background and prior
achievement, for example—play a relatively minor role in this perspective. Conceptually, they are important mainly as aggregates,

because the composition of the class or instructional group constitutes an important part of the context in which instruction occurs. For example, Barr and Drecben (1983) showed that much of the association of reading aptitude with first-grade reading achievement could be attributed to the influence of the aptitude composition of reading groups on the groups' rate of progress through the curriculum. Individual characteristics also exert direct effects on achievement; such effects are well known, but deemed less interesting because they are not open to manipulation through educational policy (see further, Gamoran, 1988). In general, this model pays less attention to effects on achievement attributable to individuals, and places more emphasis on within-school effects deriving from classes and instructional groups (see especially, Barr & Dreeben, 1983; Dreeben & Barr, 1988b).

By drawing attention to instructional processes, the additive model offers an important advance over earlier studies of the production of school achievement. Whereas earlier work had examined the inputs and outputs related to schooling (e.g., Coleman et al., 1966; for reviews see Averch, Carroll, Donaldson, Kiesling, & Pincus, 1972; and Hanushek, 1986), the additive model examines the production process itself (Barr & Dreeben, 1977, 1983; Gamoran, 1986, 1987a; Rowan & Miracle, 1983). A prominent difficulty in this approach is the complexity of measuring instruction. Most studies use indicators of the quantity of instruction, such as the amount of instructional time or the extent of content covered during the year. Using these measures, researchers have established support for the model. For example, the more words taught during first grade reading (that is, the more "content coverage"), the more students learn by the end of the year (Barr & Dreeben, 1983; Dreeben & Gamoran, 1986; Gamoran, 1986). Similarly, Rowan and Miracle (1983) found that covering more levels in the reading series increased reading achievement for fourth graders. Instructional time—measured variously as the length of the school year (Wiley & Harnischfeger, 1974), the number of months spent in high school (Shavit & Featherman, 1988), daily time teachers devote to instruction (Dreeben & Barr, 1988b; Gamoran & Dreeben, 1986), and the time students spend engaged in academic work (Denham & Lieberman, 1980)—also contributes to achievement. Other studies have shown that high school achievement depends on the number of academic courses students take, particularly in mathematics and science (Alexander & Cook, 1982; Alexander & Pallas, 1984; Gamoran, 1987a).

Some advocates of this perspective have called for measures of the quality of instruction as well. As Karweit (1983) argued, additional time will contribute little to instruction unless it is used effectively.

Similarly, the effects of content coverage must depend in part on how well the content is covered (Gamoran, 1989). One would expect higher achievement in areas covered with greater depth. Until now, however, little progress has been made on measuring instructional quality because of the conceptual and operational difficulties involved.

THE INTERACTIVE MODEL
OF SCHOOLING EFFECTS

Students' academic experiences are also critical in the interactive model of schooling effects, but the process is viewed quite differently. Learning is seen not as a function of instruction per se but as a result of student ability and effort. The impact of these individual characteristics, however, depends on the availability of opportunities for learning. The more opportunities for learning—for example, the more content coverage or the more instructional time—the greater the payoff to having more ability or exerting greater effort. "Thus, school effects due to opportunities for learning are interactive effects that determine the effect of ability and effort on learning" (Sørensen & Hallinan, 1977, p.288). The interactive model views learning as a consequence of interaction between individual characteristics on the one hand, and features of the class or instructional group on the other.

Ability and effort are present in the additive model, but they operate primarily as precursors to learning opportunities. Content coverage in particular is seen as sensitive to the qualities of students in the group or class. Thus, in the additive model, instruction mediates the impact of ability and effort on achievement: more ability and effort results in more complex and faster instruction, which in turn produces higher achievement. By contrast, instruction largely determines the impact of ability and effort in the interactive model. If there were no opportunities for learning, ability and effort would have little value for achievement; conversely, even when opportunities were great they would hardly matter if ability and effort were too low to take advantage of them (Sørensen & Hallinan, 1977, 1986).

Another difference between the models concerns the relation between learning opportunities and educational inequality. In the additive model, an equal distribution of opportunities would result in no change in inequality: students who began with higher achievement would remain ahead, but the gap would not increase. Moreover, inequality could actually decline if instruction were distributed in a compensatory fashion; for example, if more instructional time were devoted to low-ability groups (see Dreeben & Barr, 1988b). However, in the interactive model an equal distribution of opportunities leads to an increase in inequality. This occurs because students who are more able at the start benefit more from the same opportunities. Compensating for inequality is thus more difficult if this model is correct; one way to do so would be to convince low-ability students to exert more effort.

Although the interactive approach has parallels in a long tradition of research on "aptitude-treatment interactions" (Cronbach & Snow, 1977), it is Sørensen and Hallinan (1977, 1986) who formulated it explicitly as a model of the production of school achievement. Unlike the additive model, it has received few empirical tests. Sørensen and Hallinan (1986) provided only limited support because their data contained no measures of effort or of opportunities for learning. Using ability group placement as a proxy for opportunities, they found significant effects of the interaction of prior achievement and group level.

MODEL SPECIFICATION

An innovative feature of both models is their conceptualization as multilevel processes. Earlier studies of school effects considered effects at a single level—generally that of the individual (e.g., Coleman et al., 1966; Jencks, Smith, Acland, Bane, Cohen, Gintis, Heyns, & Michaelson, 1972). But authors such as Barr and Dreeben and Sørensen and Hallinan recognized that school production occurs on many levels simultaneously. As Barr and Dreeben (1983, p. 41) argued, "the preoccupation with one level or another obscures the possibility that productive events occur over several levels."

Barr and Dreeben have emphasized the collective nature of schooling. Students receive instruction in groups (such as classes or within-class groups), so it is the characteristics of the group that must be most closely tied to the instruction that occurs in a given context (see especially, Dreeben & Barr, 1988a). Still, learning is a cognitive process that occurs in the minds of individual students. Thus, instruction is a group-level outcome with consequences for the individual-level process of learning. Studies of school production, according to Barr and Dreeben, must consider at least these two levels. Their formulation looks back from the classroom to the school and district as well, although their analyses mainly focus on the class, instructional group, and student (but see Gamoran & Dreeben, 1986).

Although the specifics of their model are different, Sørensen and Hallinan (1977, 1986) also have emphasized the hierarchical nature of educational effects. They recognized that opportunities for learning apply to classes, not individual students in isolation. In their formulation, class-level variables (opportunities for learning) affect the relation between individual-level inputs (ability and effort) and outputs (achievement).

Despite these multilevel conceptualizations, the methodological approaches of both models have remained at a single level. Typically, analyses have been conducted at the level of the dependent variable: group-level dependent variables were examined with group-level data, even when some of the predictors varied within groups (Barr & Dreeben, 1983, Chapter 5; Dreeben & Barr, 1988a, 1988b); and individual-level dependent variables were analyzed with data at that level even though some of the variables actually pertained to collectivities, not individuals (e.g., Barr & Dreeben, 1983, Chapter 6; Gamoran, 1986; Rowan & Miracle, 1983; Sørensen & Hallinan, 1986).

Recent advances in statistical estimation have shown that single-level methods are not optimal for estimating multilevel models. Problems of aggregation bias and misestimation of standard errors have distorted single-level estimates of multilevel processes (see Bryk & Raudenbush, 1988, for further discussion of these difficulties). As Bryk and Raudenbush (1988, p. 68) indicated, "the 'choice of unit' is the wrong question." Statistical methods are now available that permit one to examine data at more than one level simultaneously, so that each variable can be measured at its own level.

Multilevel versions of the additive and interactive models of schooling effects can be specified as follows. The additive model states that instruction applied to a class of students affects the average of learning in the class, after the average is adjusted for between-class differences in individual characteristics such as background and prior achievement. This formulation requires two equations. The first is an individual-level equation estimated for each class:

$$\text{(Achievement)}_{ij} = \beta_{0j} + \beta_{1j}\,\text{(Ability)}_{ij} + \beta_{2j}\,\text{(Effort)}_{ij} + \beta_{3j}\,\text{(Background)}_{ij} + \epsilon_{ij} \tag{1}$$

The second is a class-level equation in which instruction predicts between-class differences in the within-class intercepts, that is, the β_{0j}'s:

$$\beta_{0j} = + \theta_{00} + \theta_{01} \text{ (learning opportunities)}_j + v_{0j}. \tag{2}$$

The interactive model differs in that instruction predicts between-class differences not in the intercept, but in the slopes for ability and effort, that is, β_1 and β_2. Thus, in addition to the within-class Equation (1), the interactive model requires two between-class equations:

$$\beta_{1j} = \theta_{10} + \theta_{11} \text{ (learning opportunities)}_j + v_{1j} \tag{3}$$

$$\beta_{2j} = \theta_{20} + \theta_{21} \text{ (learning opportunities)}_j + v_{2j}. \tag{4}$$

DATA SETS

I will use two data sets on teaching and learning in eighth-grade classes to compare the success of the additive and interactive models. One is the United States sample from SIMS. This is a nationwide sample, although probably not nationally representative due to sampling difficulties (Gamoran, 1987b). I used data from the 218 classes, including about 5,700 students, which provided data on instruction and on fall and spring mathematics achievement. The second data set was derived from a study of eighth-grade literature achievement carried out at the National Center for Effective Secondary Schools (NCESS) in Madison, Wisconsin during 1987–88 (Nystrand & Gamoran, 1991). These data were drawn from 58 eighth-grade English classes located in 16 midwestern schools. The sample comprised both public and Catholic schools, which varied in community contexts, including urban, suburban, and rural areas.

SIMS EIGHTH-GRADE MATHEMATICS DATA

Learning and Teaching

In the fall and spring, students in the SIMS study completed a test of mathematics achievement. The test included 40 core items covering five areas: fractions, algebra, geometry, measurement, and ratio and proportion. Researchers attempted to ensure that the test items constituted a fair representation of the universe of content that might be covered in eighth-grade mathematics (Travers, 1985). Instruction was then gauged by asking teachers how many of the test items were covered during the year. Classes that covered more items are viewed as having more content coverage. Thus, the instructional variable in this data set is a measure of the quantity of instruction. Table 10.1 presents means and standard deviations for all variables.

Ability and Effort

The fall achievement test serves as a proxy for ability, a tactic following that of Hallinan and Sørensen (1986). An indicator of effort was obtained from students' reports of their willingness to work in school. It consisted of the spring questionnaire response, on a five-point scale from "strongly disagree" to "strongly agree," to the statement "I will work a long time in order to understand a new idea in mathematics."

Other Background Variables

I included data on three additional background variables: gender was measured with a dummy variable (1 = female, 0 = male), as

TABLE 10.1
Means and Standard Deviations of Variables

	Mean	Standard Deviation
SIMS 8th-Grade Mathematics Data		
Student-level Variables (N = 3915)		
Spring achievement	20.357	9.084
Fall achievement	16.056	7.864
Sex (1 = female)	.529	.499
Ethnicity (1 = minority)	.140	.347
Parents' education	3.413	.577
Willingness to work	3.254	1.016
Class-level Variables (N = 186)		
Class mean fall achievement	15.202	5.916
Class mean willingness to work	3.246	.258
Content coverage	27.301	7.546
NCESS 8th-Grade English Data		
Student-level Variables (N = 919)		
Literature achievement	14.665	6.787
Fall reading score	21.619	5.340
Sex (1 = female)	.509	.500
Ethnicity (1 = minority)	.192	.394
Socioeconomic status	− .009	.827
Willingness to work	3.038	.605
Class-level Variables (N = 5)		
Class mean fall reading score	21.196	3.280
Class mean willingness to work	3.025	.210
Discourse quality	.196	.620

Note. Uncentered data. See text for information on centering of student-level variables.

was ethnicity (1 = Black or Hispanic, 0 = others); socioeconomic status was indicated by the average of mother's and father's education on a four-point scale.

NCESS EIGHTH GRADE LITERATURE DATA

Learning and Teaching

As in the SIMS study, the NCESS researchers desired to test students on material covered in class. They designed a test to assess students' mastery of the literature assigned in class during the year, with questions ranging from simple recall to ones requiring in-depth understanding and synthesis. Although the questions on each test were the same (for example, "What was the theme of [title of story]?"), the selections they concerned differed, depending on what students had been assigned to read during the year. A representative sample of five readings was chosen for the test for each class. Tests were scored holistically on dimensions such as extent of recall and depth of understanding. Each was scored by two raters whose scores were averaged. Interrater agreement on total scores was computed as a correlation of .90.

Rather than measuring the *quantity* of instructional content as in the SIMS data, the NCESS study obtained information on instructional *quality*. It utilized the perspective of Nystrand and Gamoran (1988, 1991; see further Nystrand 1986, 1987), which suggests that achievement will be higher when students participate more fully in creating the processes of instruction. According to this view, the quality of instruction is reflected in the quality of discourse between teachers and students. Discourse that is fragmented, and that fails to acknowledge students as sources of information in their own right, is seen as less engaging and is expected to produce less learning. In this formulation, discourse refers not only to classroom talk, but also to teacher–student exchanges occurring through reading and writing assignments.

Preliminary analysis of item-level data (see Nystrand & Gamoran, 1991) suggested that two aspects of instructional discourse are particularly important: its "authenticity," the extent to which teacher questions and assignments are open-ended or otherwise call for genuine input on the part of students, rather than requiring students to simply list what teachers already know; and its "contiguity," the strength of overlap and connections between writing, reading, and oral discourse in the classroom. Several components of each variable were measured using classroom observations (each class was observed four times) and teacher questionnaires. The components were then standardized and averaged to compute a single indicator of "discourse quality." A list of the observational and questionnaire items may be found in the Appendix.

Recall that in both data sets achievement was measured at the individual level but instruction at the class level. Instruction is assumed to vary between classes, but not within them. Although that is an oversimplification, it is a closer approximation of reality than using school-level indicators of instructional resources (for examples, per-pupil expenditures).

Ability and Effort

The measure of ability in the NCESS data is a National Assessment of Educational Progress (NAEP) test of reading power, administered in the fall, which asked multiple-choice comprehension questions about a set of short passages. It also required a brief writing sample. Because this test is not curriculum specific, it is closer to the kind of ability measure that the interactive approach calls for than the fall achievement test available in the SIMS data. At the same time, it provides a reasonable control for performance on the spring literature test because it indicates students' reading and writing skills at the beginning of the year.

Effort was again measured as student-reported willingness to work in school. In the NCESS data, three spring questionnaire items were combined to form an unweighted composite on a four-point scale: "I have put a great deal of effort into most things at school because they are important to me"; "Skipping school is OK as long as you don't flunk any classes"; and "The best way to get through most days at school is to goof off with my friends." (All three items were scored so that higher values indicated greater effort.) This scale has an alpha reliability of .71.

Other Background Variables

Gender and ethnicity were again measured with dummy variables. In the NCESS data, socioeconomic status was computed as an unweighted composite of mother's and father's education, the higher of mother's or father's occupation on an updated Duncan SEI scale (Stevens & Cho, 1985), and possession of a set of home resources.

RESULTS

The data were analyzed using HLM, a program for estimating hierarchical linear models (Bryk, Raudenbush, Seltzer, & Congdon, 1988). Analyses consisted of within- and between-class models as described earlier. To facilitate computation and interpretation, within-class variables were centered around their grand means (for variables fixed to have constant slopes across classes) or their class means (for variables whose slopes were free to vary between classes). Missing data were deleted listwise at both the class and individual levels, and only classes containing ten or more students were included. This resulted in samples of 186 classes and 3,915 students (SIMS; 85% of the classes and 68% of students) and 51 classes and 919 students (NCESS; 89% of the classes and 78% of students).

I estimated four models for each data set: (a) a baseline model, with no instructional predictors; (b) the additive model, in which instruction affects class achievement (adjusted for the within-class variables); (c) the interactive model, in which instruction predicts differences in the effects of prior achievement and effort; and (d) a combined model containing estimates of instructional effects on variation in both the intercepts and the slopes. The results appear in Tables 10.2 and 10.3.

The baseline model of the SIMS mathematics data shows that fall achievement, ethnicity, parents' education, and willingness to work all exert significant effects on student achievement. Class means for fall achievement and willingness to work are included as predictors of the intercept in this and subsequent models in order to adjust the intercept for these variables, which are centered around the class means in the within-class equations. Fall achievement has significant between- and within-class components, whereas willingness to work matters only as an individual-level variable.

Content coverage is added as a predictor of net class achievement in the second column. Its small but statistically significant effect is evidence of additive schooling effects.

The third column of Table 10.2 provides partial support for the interactive model. Although the effect of willingness to work is not significantly influenced by between-class variation in content coverage, the fall achievement slopes are sensitive to coverage differences. The positive coefficient indicates that initially higher achieving students benefit more from additional content coverage than their lower achieving counterparts. This finding is consistent with the expectations of the interactive model.

Moreover, the interactive approach provides a better account of the overall pattern of effects observed for prior achievement than does the additive approach. Besides the significant interaction, in comparing the first and third columns one notes a decline in the coefficient for base fall achievement from .737 to .594. This drop, which is about 20 percent, indicates that the apparent advantage of high initial achievement partly reflects the interaction between cov-

TABLE 10.2
Effects of Schooling on 8th Grade Mathematics Achievement (SIMS Data)

	Baseline Model		Additive Model		Interactive Model		Combined Model	
	Effect	(SE)	Effect	(SE)	Effect	(SE)	Effect	(SE)
Effects of Student-Level Variables:								
Intercept	.970	(2.625)	-1.655	(2.732)	1.034	(2.630)	-1.783	(2.733)
Fall Ach.	.737**	(.019)	.738**	(.019)	.594**	(.069)	.582**	(.070)
Will. to Work	.182*	(.081)	.181*	(.081)	.102	(.304)	.236	(.307)
Sex	.225	(.155)	.224	(.155)	.225	(.155)	.223	(.155)
Ethnicity	-.600*	(.283)	-.612*	(.283)	-.591*	(.283)	-.602*	(.283)
Parents' Educ.	.314*	(.148)	.310*	(.148)	.316*	(.148)	.310*	(.148)
Effects of Class-Level Variables on:								
Intercept								
Mean Fall Ach.	1.051**	(.036)	1.064**	(.035)	1.049**	(.036)	1.064**	(.035)
Will. to Work	.838	(.804)	.919	(.790)	.827	(.806)	.916	(.789)
Content Coverage			.080**	(.027)			.085**	(.027)
Fall Achievement								
Content Coverage					.005*	(.002)	.006*	(.002)
Willingness to Work								
Content Coverage					.003	(.011)	-.002	(.011)
Proportion of net class-level variance explained								
Intercept			.049				.049	
Fall Achievement					.068		.068	
Willingness to work					.000		.000	

Note. Standard errors in parentheses. $N = 186$ classes, 3,915 students.
*$p < .05$ **$p < .01$

TABLE 10.3
Effects of Schooling on 8th Grade Literature Achievement (NCESS Data)

	Baseline Model		Additive Model		Interactive Model		Combined Model	
	Effect	(SE)	Effect	(SE)	Effect	(SE)	Effect	(SE)
Effects of Student-Level Variables:								
Intercept	−11.892	(6.946)	−8.484	(5.863)	−12.487	(6.995)	−8.468	(5.859)
Fall Ach.	.264**	(.038)	.265**	(.037)	.263**	(.039)	.258**	(.039)
Will. to Work	.690*	(.303)	.711*	(.296)	.772	(.309)	.799*	(.309)
Sex	1.264**	(.329)	1.257**	(.328)	1.260**	(.329)	1.249**	(.329)
Ethnicity	−1.251*	(.463)	−1.283*	(.461)	−1.253*	(.463)	−1.287*	(.461)
SES	.796**	(.231)	.810**	(.229)	.799**	(.231)	.819**	(.229)
Effects of Class-Level Variables on:								
Intercept								
Mean Fall Ach.	.947**	(.145)	.795**	(.126)	.949**	(.146)	.792**	(.126)
Will. to Work	2.058	(2.269)	1.819	(1.903)	2.236	(2.284)	1.822	(1.902)
Discourse Quality			3.001*	(.635)			3.096**	(.640)
Fall Achievement								
Discourse Quality					.004	(.053)	.038	(.053)
Willingness to Work								
Discourse Quality					−.511	(.519)	−.658	(.521)
Proportion of net class-level variance explained								
Intercept			.373				.374	
Fall Achievement					.000		.000	
Willingness to work					.056		.060	

Note. Standard errors in parentheses. $N = 51$ classes, 916 students.
*$p < .05$ **$p < .01$

erage and prior skills, as predicted by the interactive approach. The additive view would have expected a drop in the coefficient for class mean achievement from the first to the second columns, because it maintains that class composition affects outcomes by influencing the quantity of instruction. This, however, does not appear in the results.

The combined equation in the final column provides support for both the additive and the interactive models—content coverage raises achievement for all students, but especially for those who begin at a higher level. Although the effects are statistically significant, substantively they appear modest. A 15-point increase in coverage (two standard deviations) would raise average achievement by just over one and one-quarter points on the test (about 14% of a standard deviation). A two-standard-deviation advantage in fall achievement (also about 15 points) would increase the benefits of additional coverage by less than a tenth of a point per additional point of coverage. All in all, providing 15 points more coverage to a student with 15 points higher fall achievement would add 2.63 points to the spring test score [(15 × .085) + (15 × 15 × .006) = 2.625], a bonus of 29 percent of a standard deviation.

Table 10.3 presents the results for the NCESS literature data. Despite the measurement differences, the baseline results are similar: prior skills, ethnicity, family background, and willingness to work all exhibit significant effects, with significant class-level effects of the fall test but not of class mean willingness to work. Unlike the mathematics analysis, though, girls score significantly higher than boys in literature achievement, a result consistent with previous studies reporting a female advantage in verbal achievement (e.g., Gamoran, 1987a).

The second column again provides support for the additive model of schooling effects. Classes exhibiting higher quality instructional discourse produce higher achievement. However, in contrast to the mathematics analysis, the literature data do not support the interactive model. As the third column shows, the class-level instructional variable fails to interact significantly with either the fall reading score or the indicator of effort. Further, in this case the pattern of effects for the fall test conforms to the predictions of the additive model: the class-level fall reading effect of .947 in the baseline model drops to .795 in the additive model, suggesting that the advantage of classes with high levels of initial skills results in part from the higher quality of discourse that occurs within them.

These findings are sustained in the combined model. Instruction affects average achievement to an important extent—an increase of two standard deviations in discourse quality would raise achieve-ment by almost a full standard deviation—but the effects of fall reading score and of willingness to work do not depend on instruc-tional conditions.

DISCUSSION AND CONCLUSIONS

Although this chapter focuses on differences between the additive and interactive models, it is important not to lose sight of their overall similarities. Both emphasize the value of opportunities for learning, and in this respect both are supported by the analyses. In comparison to earlier views, the perspectives are more alike than different, and their mutual interest in classroom instruction is most strongly supported in the analyses presented here.

Nevertheless, the two specifications differed in the levels of sup-port engendered by the analyses. Results from both data sets were consistent with the additive approach. More content coverage in mathematics, and a higher quality of instructional discourse in English, lead to greater achievement in their respective subjects. Substantively, the effects of instructional discourse on literature achievement appear particularly strong. This finding underscores the importance of examining not only instructional quantity, but quality as well.

The interactive model found support only in the mathematics data, and only for the prior achievement slopes. There, the more able the students, the more they benefited from greater content coverage. Why would this interaction not have occurred in the literature data as well? The answer may lie in the different approaches to measur-ing instruction. Fast-paced instruction may be especially valuable to a high-achieving student, who is able to catch on quickly and needs less repetition and review. Increasing coverage by the same amount would thus be less helpful to the student who is already behind. In contrast, improving the quality of instruction, as measured in the NCESS data, benefits the low achiever as much as it does the high.

Although this interpretation seems plausible, one cannot dismiss the alternative that differences in the nature of the subject matter account for the varying results. Is mathematics learning more de-pendent than literature mastery on cognitive skills? In this study, it is impossible to disentangle subject matter from instructional indi-cator effects, because quantity was measured in mathematics and quality in English.

Several improvements in the data might help sort out these ambiguities. First, it would be useful to obtain indicators of instructional quantity *and* quality in the same data set. Second, a measure of ability independent of prior achievement might reveal stronger interactive effects. According to the interactive formulation, more learning opportunities provide greater benefit to more talented students; those who have accumulated more knowledge, but are not more skilled cognitively, would not necessarily have a special advantage in turning opportunities into achievement. One assumes that those with more knowledge have greater cognitive skills; that is why achievement serves as a reasonable proxy. But the interactive model calls for a direct measure of ability (Sørensen & Hallinan, 1977, 1986). It is worth noting, however, that in this study the English data contained a closer approximation of an ability measure (the fall reading power test), and yet the interactive effect appeared only in the mathematics data, where an achievement pretest stood for ability.

A third improvement would be to measure within-class instructional variation. Despite this chapter's assumption to the contrary, teachers do not treat all their students alike, and more able students may receive greater learning opportunities. Information on differential treatment within classes would allow a better test of both the additive and the interactive models: the additive effects of instruction would be measured more precisely; and one could examine individual-level as well as cross-level interactions among ability, effort, and instruction.

To the extent my interpretation is valid—that varying support for the interactive model reflects differences in the measurement of instruction—the results have implications for educational inequality. They suggest that improving instruction by increasing content coverage would have a differentiating effect, allowing high-achieving students to increase their advantage. Even if low-achieving students covered as much ground—which is unlikely under current curricular arrangements, and which some practitioners argue is inappropriate anyway—they would still fall further and further behind. The quality of instructional discourse, however, does not have this differentiating effect, for its benefits are similar across the range of student skill levels. Furthermore, whereas educators may advocate fast-paced instruction for high-achieving students, they would presumably wish to maintain a high quality of classroom discourse for all students. Thus, a policy that emphasized improving the quality of instructional discourse for low-achieving students would serve to equalize results, or at least prevent them from spreading out further.

APPENDIX
COMPONENTS OF DISCOURSE QUALITY VARIABLE IN NCESS LITERATURE DATA SET

Aspect of Discourse	Description of Item	Source
I. Authenticity		
A. Writing	"About how often are your writing assignments open-ended, requiring students to express opinions or to write about questions to which you cannot predict their answers?"	Teacher Questionnaire
	"About how often do your students write about things you don't know much about (including information about themselves and subjects about which they may have some expertise)?"	Teacher Questionnaire
B. Reading	"When you ask students about their reading assignments in class, how frequently do you attempt to do each of the following? Ask them for their opinions. Ask them to relate what they have read to their own experiences."	Teacher Questionnaire
C. Classroom	Authenticity rate, computed as number of teacher questions avoiding prespecified answers, plus one-half the number of questions partially prespecifying answers, divided by total teacher questions.	Classroom Observation
	"Sometimes teachers ask questions to probe their students' knowledge or thinking or to discover their opinions. Often these questions have no fixed or prespecified answers. About how often do you ask such questions?"	Teacher Questionnaire
	"When you ask your students questions, which of the following are you trying to do? See if students have done homework [negative item] Make sure students are learning [negative item] Elicit ideas and opinions Get students to express themselves Brainstorm informally"	Teacher Questionnaire
	"During class discussion, how often do students do the following? Give their opinion"	Teacher Questionnaire
II. Contiguity		
A. Writing	"About how often do students in your class write about (or in response to) things they have read?"	Teacher Questionnaire
	"About how often do you discuss writing topics with students before asking them to write?	Teacher Questionnaire

Appendix (cont.)

Aspect of Discourse	Description of Item	Source
B. Reading	"About how often do you and your class discuss the readings you assign?"	Teacher Questionnaire
	"When you ask students about their reading assignments in class, how frequently do you attempt to do each of the following? Ask them to relate what they have read to their other readings."	Teacher Questionnaire
C. Classroom	Percent of teacher questions incorporating student responses to previous questions (uptake).	Classroom Observation
	"About how often does your class relate its discussion to previous discussions you have had?"	Teacher Questionnaire
	"About how often do you and your class discuss things students have written about?"	Teacher Questionnaire

REFERENCES

Alexander, K. L., & Cook, M. A. (1982). Curricula and coursework: A surprise ending to a familiar story. *American Sociological Review, 47,* 626–640.

Alexander, K. L., & Pallas, A. M. (1984). Curriculum reform and school performance: An evaluation of the 'New Basics.' *American Journal of Education, 92,* 391–420.

Averch, H., Carroll, S. J., Donaldson, T. S., Kiesling, H. J., & Pincus, J. (1972). *How effective is schooling?* Santa Monica, CA: Rand Corporation.

Barr, R., & Dreeben, R. (1977). Instruction in classrooms. In L. S. Shulman (Ed.), *Review of research in education:* (Vol. 5). Itasca, IL: Peacock.

Barr, R., & Dreeben, R. (1980). *How schools work.* Chicago: University of Chicago Press.

Bidwell, C. E., & Kasarda, J. D. (1980). Conceptualizing and measuring the effects of school and schooling. *American Journal of Education, 88,* 401–430.

Bryk, A. S., & Raudenbush, S. W. (1988). Towards a more appropriate conceptualization of research on school effects: A three-level linear model. *American Journal of Education, 97,* 65–108.

Bryk, A. S., & Raudenbush, S. W., Seltzer, M., & Congdon, R. T. (1988). *An introduction to HLM: Computer program and users guide.* (Version 2.0.) Chicago: Department of Education, University of Chicago.

Coleman, J., Campbell, E., Hobson, C., McPartland, J., Mood, A., Weinfield, J., & York, R. (1966). *Equality of educational opportunity.* Washington, DC: U.S. Government Printing Office.

Cronbach, L. J. & Snow, R. E. (1977). *Aptitudes and instructional methods.* New York: Irvington.

Denham, C., & Lieberman, A. (Eds.). (1980). *Time to learn*. Washington, DC: National Institute of Education.

Dreeben, R., & Barr, R. (1988a). Classroom composition and the design of instruction. *Sociology of Education, 61*, 129–142.

Dreeben, R., & Barr, R. (1988b). The formation and instruction of ability groups. *American Journal of Education, 97*, 34–64.

Dreeben, R., & Gamoran, A. (1986). Rate, instruction, and learning. *American Sociological Review, 51*, 660–669.

Gamoran, A. (1986). Instructional and institutional effects of ability grouping. *Sociology of Education, 59*, 185–198.

Gamoran, A. (1987a). The stratification of high school learning opportunities. *Sociology of Education, 60*, 135–155.

Gamoran, A. (1987b). *Instruction and the effects of schooling*. Paper presented at the annual meetings of the American Sociological Association, Chicago.

Gamoran, A. (1988). Resource allocation and the effects of schooling: A sociological perspective. In D. H. Monk & J. Underwood (Eds.), *Micro-level school finance: Issues and implications for policy* (pp. 207–232). Cambridge, MA: Ballinger.

Gamoran, A. (1989). Measuring curriculum differentiation. *American Journal of Education, 97*, 129–143.

Gamoran, A., & Dreeben, R. (1986). Coupling and control in educational organizations. *Administrative Science Quarterly, 31*, 612–632.

Hanushek, E. (1986). The economics of schooling: Production and efficiency in the public schools. *Journal of Economic Literature, 24*, 1141–1177.

Jencks, C., Smith, M., Acland, H., Bane, M. J., Cohen, D., Gintis, H., Heyns, B., & Michaelson, S. (1972). *Inequality: A reassessment of the effects of family and schooling in America*. New York: Basic Books.

Karweit, N. (1983). *Time on task: A research review* (Tech. Rep. No. 332). Baltimore MD: Center for the Social Organization of Schools.

Nystrand, M. (1986). *The structure of written communication: Studies in reciprocity between writers and readers*. New York: Academic Press.

Nystrand, M. (1987). *A scheme for measuring the quality of instructional discourse in English and social studies*. Paper presented at the Annual Meeting of the American Educational Research Association, Washington, DC.

Nystrand, M., & Gamoran, A. (1988). *A study of instruction as discourse*. Paper presented at the Annual Meeting of the American Educational Research Association New Orleans.

Nystrand, M., & Gamoran, A. (1991). Instructional discourse, student engagement, and literature achievement. *Research in the Teaching of English, 25*, 261–290.

Rowan, B., & Miracle, A. W., Jr. (1983). Systems of ability grouping and the stratification of achievement in elementary schools. *Sociology of Education, 56*, 133–144.

Shavit, Y., & Featherman, D. L. (1988). Schooling, tracking, and teenage intelligence. *Sociology of Education, 61*, 42–51.

Sørensen, A. B., & Hallinan, M. T. (1977) A reconceptualization of school effects. *Sociology of Education, 50,* 273–289.

Sørensen, A. B., & Hallinan, M. T. (1986). Effects of ability grouping on growth in academic achievement. *American Educational Research Journal, 23,* 519–542.

Stevens, G., & Cho, J. H. (1985). Socioeconomic indexes and the new 1980 census occupational classification scheme. *Social Science Research, 14,* 142–168.

Travers, K. J. (1985). *Second International Mathematics Study: Summary report for the United States.* Urbana, IL: Stipes.

Wiley, D. E., & Harnischfeger, A. (1974). Explosion of a myth: Quantity of schooling and exposure to instruction, major educational vehicle. *Educational Researcher, 3,* 7–12.

11

Instructionally Sensitive Psychometrics: Applications to The Second International Mathematics Study

Bengt O. Muthén

CRESST and Graduate School of Education
University of California, Los Angeles
Los Angeles, CA

This chapter discusses new psychometric analyses that improve capabilities for relating performance on achievement test items to instruction received by the examinees. The modeling discussion will be closely tied to the SIMS data for U.S. eighth-grade students.

Item Response Theory (IRT) is a standard psychometric approach for analyzing a set of dichotomously scored test items. Standard IRT modeling assumes that the items measure a unidimensional latent trait, a hypothetical or unobserved characteristic (for example, mathematical ability). Latent trait models describe the relationship between the observable test performance and the unobservable traits or characteristics that are assumed to influence performance on the test. This particular kind of latent trait model is used to assess the measurement qualities of each item and to give each examinee a latent trait score (the examinee's standing on the latent trait). However, as will be shown, IRT modeling is limited in ways that are a hindrance to properly relating achievement responses to instructional experiences. Taking IRT as a starting point, this chapter summarizes some work on a set of new analytic techniques that give a richer description of achievement-instruction relations.

Six topics that expand standard IRT and specifically deal with effects of varying instructional opportunities will be discussed:

1. *Variation in latent trait measurement characteristics.* This relates to the classic IRT concern of "item bias," here translated as the advantage or disadvantage to OTL in getting an item right.
2. *Multidimensional modeling.* Inclusion of narrowly defined, specific factors closely related to instructional units in the presence of a general, dominant trait.
3. *Modeling with heterogeneity in levels.* Analyses that take into account that achievement data often are not sampled from a single student population but one with heterogeneity of performance levels.
4. *Estimation of trait scores.* Deriving scores based on both performance and background information for both general and specific traits.
5. *Predicting achievement.* Latent trait modeling that relates the trait to student background variables.
6. *Analyzing change.* Relating change in general and specific traits to opportunity to learn.

The SIMS data will be used throughout to illustrate the new methods. All analyses will be carried out within the modeling framework of the LISCOMP computer program (Muthén, 1984, 1987).

The first part of this chapter describes the data to be analyzed. The second part describes general features of the psychometric problem. The third part presents a descriptive analysis of the achievement–instruction relation for the SIMS data and sets the stage for later modeling. The final sections of the chapter discuss methods appropriate for Topics 1–6 listed above.

THE SIMS DATA

We will concentrate our analysis on the U.S. eighth-graders (for whom there are about 4,000 observations from both fall and spring) sampled from about 200 randomly sampled classrooms varying in size from about 5 to 35 students. For the part of the sample that we will be concerned with, the core test was administered both during the fall and the spring to all students in the study while the rotated forms varied in their use pattern. We will be particularly concerned with analyses of the 40 core items but will also report on analyses of the four rotated forms. The rotated form analyses will be presented as a cross-validation of findings for the core items. The SIMS data provide a uniquely rich set of data with which to study instructionally sensitive psychometrics.

It is well known that eighth-grade mathematics curricula vary widely for students in the United States. Part of this information *opportunity to learn* (OTL) for the topics covered by each test item. As noted in previous chapters, for each item on the cognitive test, teachers were asked two questions:

Question 1. During this school year did you teach or review the mathematics needed to answer the item correctly?

1. No
2. Yes
3. No response

Question 2. If in the school year you did not teach or review the mathematics needed to answer this item correctly, was it mainly because?

1. It had been taught prior to this school year
2. It will be taught later (this year or later)
3. It is not in the school curriculum at all
4. For other reasons
5. No response

Using these responses, OTL level is defined as:

No OTL: Question 1 = 1; Question 2 = 2,3,4, or 5
Prior OTL: Question 1 = 1 or 3; Question 2 = 1
This Year OTL: Question 1 = 2; Question 2 = 5 (other response combinations had zero frequencies)

In most analyses to follow, *Prior OTL* and *This Year OTL* will be combined into a single OTL category.

For the U.S. eighth-grade mathematics students, information was also collected in order to make a distinction between "tracks" or class types, yielding a categorization into *remedial*, *typical*, *enriched* (or *pre-algebra*), and *algebra* classes. This classification was based on the SIMS teacher questionnaire data. Other teacher-related information was also collected, as well as student background information on family, career interests, and attitudes. Some of this additional information will also be used in some of the analyses to follow.

THE GENERAL PROBLEM

In general, psychometric modeling assumes independent and identically distributed observations (*i.i.d.*) from some relevant population. This assumption is also made in IRT. Because of the varying curricula and instructional histories of the students in a study like SIMS, the assumption of identically distributed observations is not realistic to describe either relationships between what is measured (achievement responses) and what the measurements are attempting to capture (the traits) or how traits vary with relevant covariates such as instructional exposure and student background.

The distribution of responses for various values of the latent trait cannot be expected to be identical for a student who has had no specific instruction on the item topic and a student who has had instruction. The trait distribution cannot be expected to be the same for students in *enriched* classes as for students in *typical* classes. The students are naturally sampled from heterogeneous populations. Increased homogeneity can be obtained by dividing the students into groups based on instructional experiences; however, such groupings may have to be very detailed to achieve their purpose and any simple grouping may be quite arbitrary.

A more satisfactory approach is to use modeling that allows for heterogeneity, using parameters that vary for varying instructional experiences. Such modeling also accomplishes the goal of instructionally sensitive psychometrics by explicitly describing achievement response-instructional experiences relations.

DESCRIPTIVE ANALYSES

It is informative to consider descriptively how achievement responses within SIMS vary with instructional exposure. This forms a basis for our subsequent modeling efforts. We will first study this in terms of univariate achievement distributions using the posttest core items. We will also study the change in univariate responses from pretest to posttest.

Univariate Response

Consider first the univariate responses for the posttest. The proportion correct for these items is presented in Table 11.1, broken down by the class-type categories *remedial, typical, enriched,* and *algebra* and by the OTL categories *No OTL, This Year OTL,* and *Prior OTL*. From the totals it is seen that both class type and OTL have a strong effect on proportion correct.

For most items the proportion correct is higher for enriched and algebra classes than for remedial and typical classes. For almost all items the proportion correct increases when moving from No OTL to This Year OTL to Prior OTL. The reason why Prior OTL gives higher proportion correct than This Year OTL is partly because Prior OTL is more common for enriched and algebra classes to which we presume students of higher achievement levels have been selected.

OTL appears to also have an overall positive effect on proportion correct when controlling for class type, at least for typical classes. Also, when controlling for OTL, class type seems to still have a strong effect. These univariate relationships are informative but confound effects of instructional exposure with effects of student achievement level. For example, the higher proportion correct for a certain item for students with Prior OTL may be solely due to such students having a higher achievement level on the whole test. It would be of interest to know if students with the same achievement level perform differently on a certain item for different instructional exposure.

To explore this possibility, we may consider the total score on the posttest as the general mathematics achievement level of each student. Then, for each general achievement level, we could study the variation of proportion correct for each item as a function of instructional exposure. We have carried this out using the dichotomous version of OTL, combining Prior OTL with This Year OTL into a single OTL category.

For each value of the achievement variable we then have a proportion correct for a No OTL and an OTL group and can study whether OTL makes a difference. Conversely, for each of the two OTL categories we will present the distribution of the achievement variable in order to study whether having OTL for an item implies that these students have a higher general achievement level. These plots are given in Figures 11.1-11.4

TABLE 11.1
Percentage of Students and Percentage Correct for Selected Core Items
by OTL and Class Type

	Total*		No OTL			This Year OTL			Prior OTL		
Item	PR	PO	ST	PR	PO	ST	PR	PO	ST	PR	PO
ME01											
TOT	35	43	21	22	26	59	36	47	20	44	48
REM	11	18	33	7	8	60	12	23	7	21	21
TYP	30	38	24	21	27	64	34	43	12	28	43
ENR	42	52	17	25	24	71	48	63	12	29	29
ALG	61	64	6	64	64	5	39	50	89	62	65
AR02											
TOT	47	60	3	34	53	89	45	59	8	74	78
REM	12	21	9	17	33	91	11	20	0	0	0
TYP	42	57	3	34	40	97	42	57	0	0	0
ENR	58	74	4	46	86	90	57	73	6	74	81
ALG	74	75	0	0	0	43	73	71	57	74	78
AL03											
TOT	9	21	38	8	9	61	10	28	1	3	19
REM	15	9	78	15	8	22	13	13	0	0	0
TYP	8	14	49	7	9	50	8	18	2	3	19
ENR	8	21	16	12	11	84	7	23	0	0	0
ALG	16	64	7	0	19	94	17	68	0	0	0
ME06											
TOT	49	55	28	48	54	59	48	55	13	52	59
REM	20	31	41	23	35	45	21	31	14	11	22
TYP	47	52	27	48	53	65	48	52	8	42	47
ENR	52	61	32	51	60	65	52	62	2	82	68
ALG	66	73	10	83	80	28	68	75	62	63	72
ME08											
TOT	89	89	17	89	88	58	88	88	25	93	92
REM	67	61	34	62	55	58	69	64	8	76	67
TYP	89	89	17	94	93	66	88	89	18	89	88
ENR	93	93	16	90	91	59	93	93	26	96	94
ALG	98	97	14	96	100	12	96	98	74	99	97
ME09											
TOT	42	52	14	41	48	56	38	50	30	50	59
REM	16	18	27	18	19	58	15	18	15	21	15
TYP	37	48	14	41	49	62	36	47	23	38	49
ENR	48	64	11	42	53	63	46	65	27	56	65
ALG	67	73	12	76	78	2	56	33	85	66	73
AL16											
TOT	23	58	6	9	16	92	24	60	2	37	88
REM	9	14	52	10	9	48	7	20	0	0	0
TYP	18	50	3	6	11	97	18	52	0	0	0
ENR	28	74	2	17	89	94	28	73	4	34	94
ALG	53	89	0	0	0	94	53	89	6	41	77
GE17											
TOT	47	59	13	39	38	72	46	62	15	59	63
REM	24	24	41	22	15	48	25	26	10	29	46

TABLE 11.1 (cont.)
Percentage of Students and Percentage Correct for Selected Core Items by OTL and Class Type

Item	Total*		No OTL			This Year OTL			Prior OTL		
	PR	PO	ST	PR	PO	ST	PR	PO	ST	PR	PO
TYP	42	56	11	42	37	82	43	60	8	35	40
ENR	53	68	12	44	44	80	55	72	8	53	68
ALG	76	80	10	61	85	18	78	93	72	78	77
GE19											
TOT	23	33	76	23	32	23	22	38	1	52	57
REM	10	19	0	10	19	0	0	0	0	0	0
TYP	22	30	72	22	29	28	21	33	0	0	0
ENR	25	39	71	25	35	29	25	49	0	0	0
ALG	39	49	89	38	48	0	0	0	11	52	57
GE21											
TOT	20	34	60	20	30	37	21	39	3	23	39
REM	16	16	97	16	17	3	25	13	0	0	0
TYP	18	30	60	17	29	39	20	33	1	22	11
ENR	20	39	46	20	34	52	20	44	2	6	33
ALG	34	50	65	33	45	18	44	71	17	28	49
GE22											
TOT	37	59	13	26	26	80	37	64	7	62	67
REM	21	18	79	23	19	17	9	11	4	30	40
TYP	33	55	8	28	26	90	33	58	2	29	37
ENR	40	71	6	20	15	92	40	75	2	59	59
ALG	70	81	9	47	82	44	70	85	47	73	78
AL25											
TOT	42	46	7	28	34	92	42	47	2	70	59
REM	12	15	28	8	13	72	13	16	0	0	0
TYP	38	42	7	36	40	92	37	43	2	68	44
ENR	48	55	3	40	60	97	49	55	0	0	0
ALG	69	67	0	0	0	94	69	66	6	73	86
AR34											
TOT	24	39	4	16	19	90	22	39	7	45	53
REM	10	15	19	14	16	81	9	14	0	0	0
TYP	19	34	4	17	22	96	19	34	0	0	0
ENR	29	54	0	0	0	97	29	54	3	39	35
ALG	44	53	0	0	0	43	43	50	57	45	55

*Percentages of students by class type are:
  REM = Remedial: 7.1 (N = 268), TYP = Typical: 57.6 (N = 2148)
  ENR = Enriched: 24.4 (N = 909), ALG = Algebra: 10.7 (N = 399)
ST = Percentage students   ME = Measurement
PR = Percentage correct for pretest   AR = Arithmetic
PO = Percentage correct for posttest   AL = Algebra
                                        GE = Geometry

Figure 11.1 describes Items 1, 2, and 3. The left-most panel shows the total score distribution given No OTL and OTL, respectively. We note that the score distributions have different means with the OTL distribution having a somewhat higher mean, supporting the notion that students who receive OTL perform better as measured by

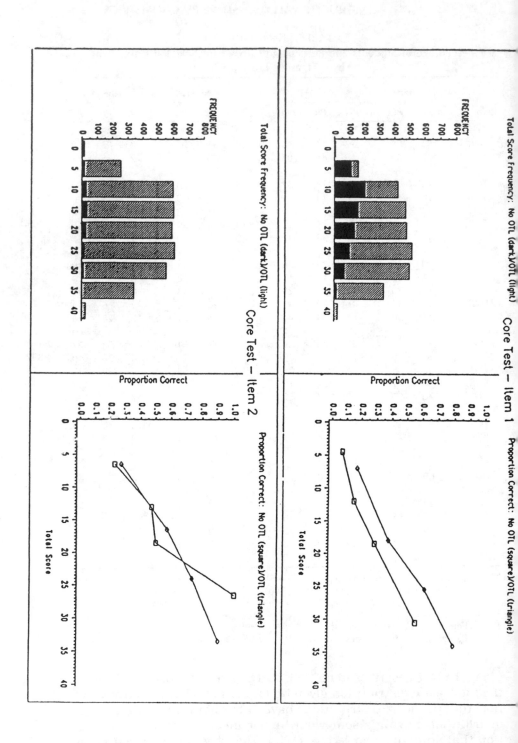

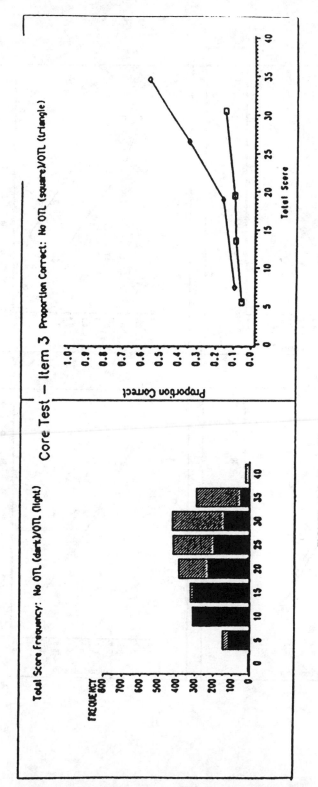

FIGURE 11.1 Score Distributions for Core Items 1, 2, and 3

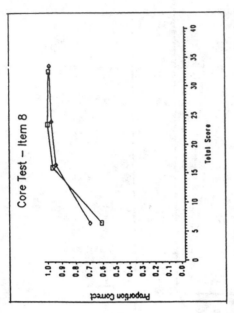

Core Test — Item 6

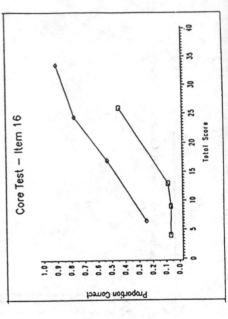

Core Test — Item 8

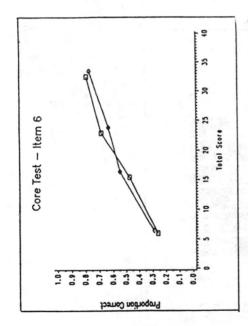

Core Test — Item 9

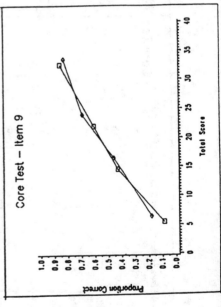

Core Test — Item 16

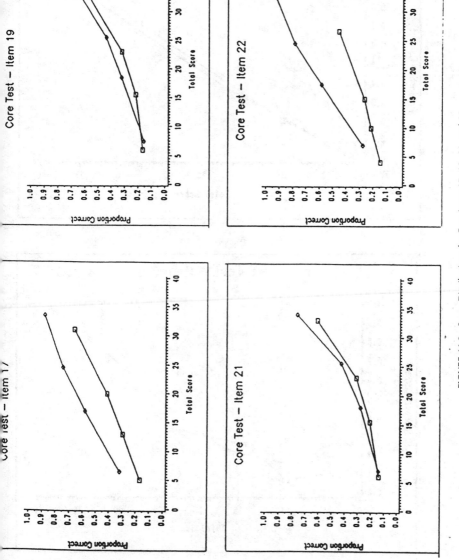

FIGURE 11.3 Score Distributions for Core Items 17, 19, 21, and 22

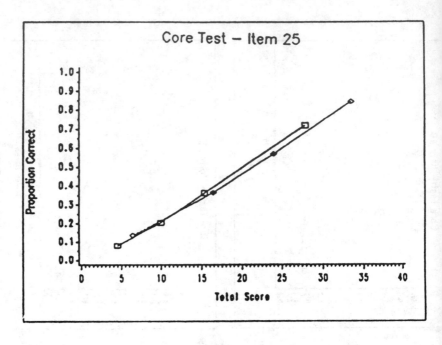

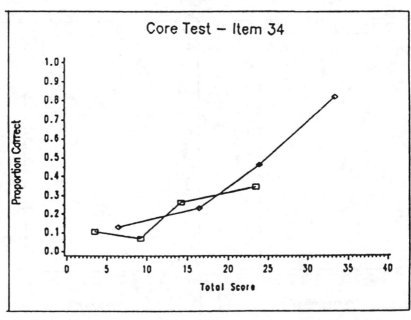

FIGURE 11.4 Score Distributions for Core Items 25 and 34

this test. We also note that the variances of the two distributions are about the same. The score distributions shown are representative of all core items.

The right-most part of Figure 11.1 and Figures 11.2-11.4 contain curves showing the proportion correct for a given total score for the two OTL categories. For each item and both OTL categories, proportion correct increases with total score indicating that for both OTL categories the item is a good indicator of the general achievement variable that the total score represents. It is particularly noteworthy that this is true also for the No OTL category and that the No OTL and OTL curves most often are very close. The students who, according to their teachers, have not been taught the mathematics needed to answer the item correctly still appear to have a high probability of answering the item correctly and this probability increases with increasing total score. This may indicate that students can, to a large degree, draw on related knowledge to solve the item. It may also indicate unreliability in the teachers' OTL responses. However, the differences in score distributions for the core items show that the OTL measures have consistent and strong relations to the total score. Instead of unreliability there may be a component of invalidity involved in the teachers' responses, where OTL may to some extent be confounded with average achievement level in the class and/or the item's difficulty.

The score distributions show that OTL is correlated with performance. Our hypothesis is that OTL helps to induce an increased level of general achievement and that, in general, it is this increased level that increases the probability of a correct answer, not OTL directly. In this way, moving from the No OTL status to the OTL status implies a move upwards to the right along the common curve for No OTL and OTL.

There are some exceptions to the general finding of common curves for the No OTL and OTL categories. For example, Items 3 and 17 show a large positive effect of having OTL. Several other items with sizeable numbers of students in the two OTL categories also show positive effects. This means that for these items, the added advantage of having OTL is not fully explained by a corresponding increase in total score. OTL directly affects success in answering the item correctly. From Table 11.1 we find that for the three items listed, the proportion correct increases strongly when moving from the No OTL category to the OTL categories.

However, Table 11.1 cannot be counted on for finding items with direct OTL effects of this kind since several other items also show strong increases in proportion correct due to OTL. For example, in Table 11.1, Item 25 shows substantial increases in proportion correct moving from the No OTL to the OTL categories, but the curves shown in Figure 11.4 are essentially the same. We will return to the interpretation of this type of effect in Section 4. Note also that with the exception of Item 3 any OTL effect appears to be such that the two curves are approximately parallel, implying that the OTL effect is constant across achievement levels. For Item 3 the OTL advantage increases with increasing achievement level, perhaps because it is a difficult item.

Change of Univariate Responses

The SIMS core items also provide the opportunity to study changes in proportion correct for each item from the fall to the spring testing. This change can be related to OTL. For each item we may distinguish between three groups of students: those who did not have OTL before the pretest or before the posttest (the No OTL group); those who had OTL before the pretest (Prior OTL); and those who did not have OTL before the pretest but did have OTL before the posttest (This Year OTL).

The change for the No OTL group gives an indication of change due to learning on related topics. The change for the Prior OTL group gives an indication of effects related to practice, review, and, perhaps, forgetting. The change for the group having This Year OTL reflects the direct exposure to the topic represented by the item. These changes can also be studied in Table 11.1. Table 11.1 shows that where changes occur, they are largely positive for each OTL category, with the largest changes occurring for students in the category of This Year OTL as expected. They may be taken to support the dependability of the teacher-reported OTL measure.

VARIATIONS IN LATENT TRAIT MEASUREMENT CHARACTERISTICS

The study of the univariate achievement responses above showed that the set of core test items served as good indicators of the total test score. We may hypothesize that this test score is a proxy for a general mathematics achievement variable as measured by the combined content of the set of core items. However, the total test score is a fallible measure and what we are interested in are the relationships between the items and the true score and estimates of the true scores. This is a situation for which Item Response Theory (IRT) has been proposed as being appropriate (see, for example, Lord, 1980).

The curves of Figures 11.1 to 11.4 are, in IRT language, empirical item characteristic curves, which as theoretical counterparts have conditional probability curves describing the probability correct on an item given a latent trait score. We will now describe the IRT model and how it can be extended to take into account instructional heterogeneity in its measurement characteristic.[1]

In this part of the chapter we investigate descriptively whether the proportion correct for a given total test score varied across OTL groups. In IRT language this is referred to as investigating *item bias* or, using a more neutral term, *differential item functioning*. Standard IRT assumes that the item functions in the same way for different groups of individuals. Concerns about item bias due to instructional heterogeneity have recently been raised in the educational measurement literature. (See Chapter 8.) A variety of bias detection schemes related to IRT have been discussed in the literature. Conflicting results have been found in empirical studies. For example, Mehrens and Phillips (1986, 1987) found little differences in the measurement characteristics of standardized tests due to varying curricula in schools; however, Miller and Linn (1988), using the SIMS data, found large differences related to opportunity to learn, although these differences were not always interpretable.

---

[1] In formulas the IRT model may be briefly described as follows: Let y^* be a p vector of continuous latent response variables that correspond to specific skills needed to solve each item correctly. For item j,

$$y_j = 0, \text{ if } y^*_j \leq \tau_j \tag{1}$$

$$1, \text{ otherwise}$$

where 0 denotes the incorrect answer, 1 denotes the correct answer, and τ_j is a threshold parameter for item j corresponding to its difficulty. Assume also that the latent response variable y^*_j is a function of a single continuous latent trait η and a residual ϵ_j,

$$y^*_j = \lambda_j \eta + \epsilon_j \tag{2}$$

where λ_j is a slope parameter for Item j, interpretable as a factor loading. With proper assumptions on the right-hand-side variables, this gives rise to the two-parameter normal ogive IRT model. For each item there are two parameters, τ_j and λ_j. The conditional probability of a correct response on Item j is

$$P(y_j = 1|\eta) = \Phi \left[(-\tau_j + \lambda_j \eta) \phi^{-1/2} \right] \tag{3}$$

where ϕ is the variance of ϵ_j. This means that the threshold τ_j determines the item's difficulty, that is the horizontal location of the probability curve, and the loading λ_j determines the slope of the probability curve.

Muthén (1989b) pointed out methodological problems in assessing differential item functioning when many items may be biased. He suggested a new approach based on a model which extends the standard IRT. The analysis is carried out by the LISCOMP program (Muthén 1987). This approach is particularly suitable to the SIMS data situation with its item specific OTL information.[2]

The model disentangles the effects of OTL in an interesting way. It states that OTL has a direct effect on the general achievement trait. Here we are interested in finding positive effects of instruction. Through the expected increase in the general achievement trait, such effects also have an indirect positive effect on the probability of a correct item response.

In addition to the indirect effect of OTL for an item, there is also the possibility of a direct OTL effect on an item. Any direct effect indicates that the specific skill needed to solve the item draws not only on the general achievement trait but also on OTL. The size of the OTL effect on the general achievement trait indicates the extent to which the trait is sensitive to instruction. The size of the OTL

---

[2]Let x be a vector of p OTL variables, one for each achievement item. The x variables may be continuous, but assume for simplicity that x_j is dichotomous with $x_j = 0$ for *No OTL* and $x_j = 1$ for *OTL*. Consider the modification of Equation (2)

$$y^* = \lambda\eta + B x + \epsilon \tag{4}$$

where in general we restrict B to be a diagonal $p \times p$ matrix. The diagonal element for Item j is denoted β_j. The OTL variables are also seen as influencing the trait η,

$$\eta = \gamma x + \zeta \tag{5}$$

where γ is a p-vector of regression parameter slopes and ζ is a residual. It follows that

$$P(y_j = 1|\eta, x_j) = \Phi [(-\tau_j + \beta_j x_j + \lambda_j\eta)V(y^*_j|\eta)^{-1/2} \tag{6}$$

In effect, then, the β_j coefficient indicates the added or reduced difficulty in the item due to OTL. Equivalently, using equation (4), we may see this effect as increasing y^*_j, the specific skill needed to solve Item j.

We note that this model allows for differential item functioning in terms of difficulty but not in terms of the slope related parameter λ_j. This is in line with the data analysis findings of Section 3.1 where little difference in slopes of the conditional proportion correct curves was found across OTL groups (Item 3 was an exception; we assume that this item will be reasonably well fitted by a varying difficulty model). More general modeling is in principle possible, but the data features do not seem to warrant such an extra effort.

effect on the probability of a correct response indicates the amount of exposure sensitivity, or instructional oversensitivity, in the item.

While positive effects on the general achievement trait correspond to a positive educational outcome, possible direct effects on items are of less educational interest in that they demonstrate effects of teaching that influence very narrow content domains. From a test construction point of view, items that show such exposure sensitivity are less suitable for inclusion in standardized tests since they are prone to "item bias" in groups of examinees with varying instructional history. If such item bias goes undetected, IRT analysis is distorted. However, in the modeling presented here exposure sensitivity is allowed for and the analysis does not suffer from the presence of such effects.

Muthén, Kao, and Burstein (1991) present examples of analysis of exposure sensitivity using the dichotomous OTL groupings. However, we will first consider an example where the OTL categories *No OTL*, *This Year OTL*, and *Prior OTL* were used. Figure 11.5 shows the estimated item characteristic curves for Item 17, which has to do with acute angles. Since there are three OTL categories, there are three curves corresponding to three difficulty values. Since the curves for both This Year OTL and Prior OTL are above the No OTL curve, the direct effects of OTL on the probability of a correct response are positive for these two OTL groups. Exposure to the concept of acute angles produces a specific skill, which has the same effect as a reduced item difficulty, and this skill is not included in the general achievement trait.

It is interesting to relate this finding to the percentage correct on Item 17 broken down by OTL group as given in Table 11.1. Percentage correct increases dramatically from the No OTL category to the OTL categories, but the percentage correct is slightly higher for Prior OTL than for This Year OTL. For Item 17 the Prior OTL students may do better than This Year OTL students, but Figure 11.5 shows that the recency of OTL gives an advantage for students at the same achievement trait level. Comparing the estimated item characteristic curves of Figure 11.5 with the empirical curves of Figure 11.3 we find a large degree of similarity but also differences. The estimated curves represent more correct and precise estimates of these curves.

Muthén et al. (1991) found substantial exposure sensitivity in Items 3 (solving for x), 16 (product of negative integers), and 17 (acute angles), 38 (percentages), and 39 (coordinate system). While Items 3, 17, and 39 provided rather poor measurements of the achievement trait as indicated by their estimated factor loadings,

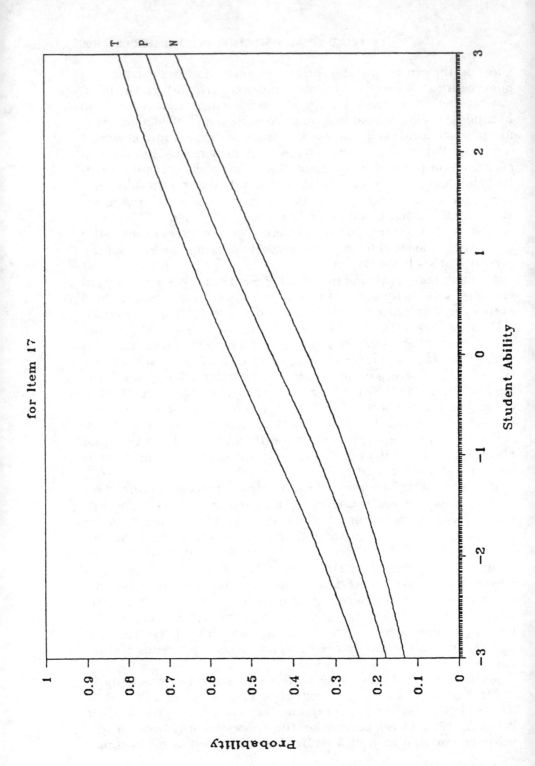

for Item 17

that was not the case for the other two. We hypothesized that the exposure sensitivity corresponded to early learning of a definitional nature.

Further analyses of the rotated form items, carried out by Kao (1990), supported this hypothesis. For example, the rotated forms showed exposure sensitivity for items covering square root problems. Overall, about 15 to 30 percent of the items exhibit mild exposure sensitivity, while only about 10 to 15 percent exhibit strong exposure sensitivity. We may note that these percentages are considerably lower than Miller and Linn's (1988) findings using related parts of the SIMS data and standard IRT methodology. The effects of OTL on the achievement trait will be discussed in later sections.

MULTIDIMENSIONAL MODELING

Standard IRT modeling assumes a unidimensional trait. For a carefully selected set of test items, this is often a good approximation. However, in many achievement applications, it is reasonable to assume that sets of items draw on more than one achievement trait.

Although of great substantive interest, models with many minor factors are very hard to identify by the means of analysis that are commonly used. For instance, assume, as we will for the SIMS data, that a general achievement factor is the dominant factor in that it influences the responses to all items. Assume further that, in addition to this general factor, there are several specific factors, uncorrelated with the general factor, that influence small sets of items with a common, narrow content. It is well known that such models with continuous data cannot be easily recovered by ordinary exploratory factor analysis techniques involving rotations.[3] This problem carries over directly to dimensionality analysis of dichotomous items using tetrachoric correlations.

---

[3]Muthén (1978) presented a method for the factor analysis of dichotomous items, where the model is

$$y^* = \Lambda\eta + \epsilon \qquad (7)$$

$$V(y^*) = \Lambda\Psi\Lambda' + \Theta \qquad (8)$$

where Λ is a $p \times m$ factor loading matrix, Ψ is a factor covariance matrix, and Θ is a diagonal matrix of residual variances. In line with item analysis tradition (see Lord and Novick, 1968), Muthén fitted the model to a matrix of sample tetrachorics. For an overview of factor analysis with dichotomous items, see Mislevy (1986).

Consider as an illustration of the problem an artificial model for 40 dichotomous items. Assume that one general factor influences all items and eight specific factors each influence a set of five items. Let the general factor loadings be 0.5 and 0.6 while the specific factor loadings are 0.3 and 0.4. Let the factors be standardized to unit variances and let the factors be uncorrelated. The eigenvalues of the corresponding artificial correlation matrix are shown in Figure 11.6.

Such a "scree plot" is used for determining the number of factors in an item set. The number of factors is taken to correspond to the first break point in the plot where the eigenvalues level off. If the first eigenvalue is considerably larger than the others and the others are approximately equal, this is usually taken as a strong indication of unidimensionality. Figure 11.6 clearly indicates unidimensionality despite the existence of the eight specific factors. There would be no reason to consider solutions of higher dimensionality. As a comparison, Figure 11.7 shows the eigenvalues for the tetrachoric correlation matrix for the 39 core items of the SIMS data. The two eigenvalue plots are rather similar.

Models similar to the artificial one considered above have been studied by Schmid and Leiman (1957). They pointed out that the situation with one general factor and k specific factors uncorrelated with the general factor could also be represented as a k-factor model with correlated factors. Hence, they used the term *hierarchical factor analysis.*

The usefulness of hierarchical factor analysis has recently been pointed out by Gustafsson (1988a, 1988b). He sought to circumvent the difficulties of exploratory factor analysis by formulating confirmatory factor analysis models. Hypothesizing a certain specific factor structure in addition to a general factor, the confirmatory model enables the estimation of factors with very narrow content. (Applications of this type of modeling to the SIMS data are being considered by the author in collaboration with Burstein, Gustafsson, Webb, Kim, Novak, and Short.)

In line with our previous modeling, we may consider a simplified version of the confirmatory model.[4] In this simplified version of the

---

[4]We may write a simple version of this model as

$$y^*_j = \lambda_{G_j} \eta_G + \lambda_{S_j} \eta_{S_k} + \epsilon_j \tag{9}$$

where y^* is the latent response variable for Item j (cf. the Section 3 model), η_G is the general achievement factor, η_{S_k} is the specific factor for Item j, and ϵ_j is a residual. The three right-hand side variables are taken to be uncorrelated. This means that the items belonging to a certain specific factor correlate not only due to the general factor but also due to this specific factor.

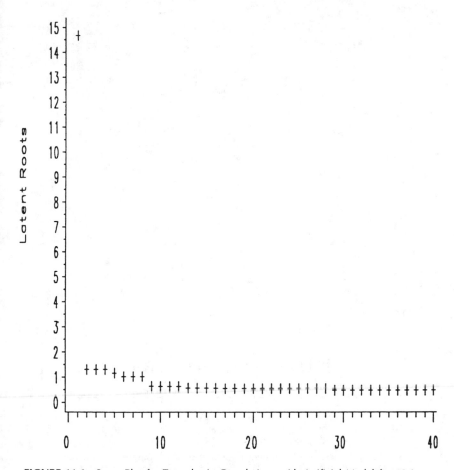

FIGURE 11.6   Scree Plot for Tetrachoric Correlations with Artificial Model for 40 Items

model, it is assumed that each item measures only one specific factor. For identification purposes we assume that each specific factor is measured by at least two items. The general factor is assumed to influence each item to a different degree, while the specific factor has the same influence on all items in the corresponding set.

The multidimensional confirmatory factor analysis model allows an interesting variance component model interpretation. The model implies a decomposition of the latent response variable variances into a general factor component, a specific factor component, and

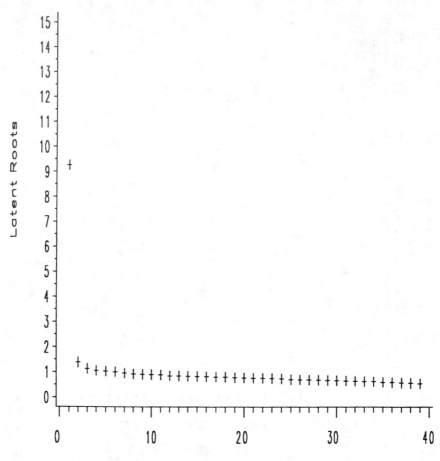

FIGURE 11.7   Scree Plot of Latent Roots for 39 Items Based on Tetrachorics

an error component.[5] The relative sizes of the general and the specific components are of particular interest. The specific component can also be interpreted as the average correlation remaining between items belonging to specific factor k when holding the general factor constant. The model can be estimated by confirmatory factor

---

[5]The variance component model is estimated by standardizing the general factor variance to unity, while letting the specific factor variances be free parameters. The decomposition is:

$$V(y^*_j) = \lambda_{G_j}^2 + \psi_{S_k} + \theta_j \tag{10}$$

where ψ_{Sk} is the variance of the specific factor k. Since the items are dichotomous, the variances of the y^*'s are standardized to one by restrictions on the θ_j's.

analysis techniques for dichotomous items using the LISCOMP computer program (see Muthén, 1978, 1987).

The SIMS items of the core and the rotated forms were classified into subsets corresponding to specific factors defined both by content and procedure. Examples of the narrow item domains that were considered are: arithmetic with signed numbers (Core Items 3, 16, 25), percent calculations (Core Items 2, 34, 36, 38), estimation skills (size, distance; Core Items 6, 8, 9), and angular measurements (Core Items 17, 19, 21, 22).

The analysis steps are as follows: For a given hypothesized set of specific factors, a confirmatory factor analysis can be performed. The initial model may then be refined in several steps. An inappropriate combination of items for a specific factor gives rise to a low or negative variance component estimate for this specific factor. Modifications may be assisted by inspection of model misfit indices.

For this model a useful index is related to the loadings of the specific factors that are fixed to unity in the baseline model. The sign and size of the derivatives of these loadings are of interest. A positive value for a certain item indicates that if the loading is free to be estimated, the estimated value will be smaller than one. In effect, this allows the estimate of the variance component for the specific factor at hand to increase. This is because the specific variance component is related to the average correlation of the specific factor items, conditional on the general factor, where the decrease in the factor loading for a certain item means that the contribution from this item is weighted down. Thus, modifying the initial analysis, items that obtain very low or negative specific factor loadings are candidates for exclusion from the set assigned to this specific factor. This modification process may be performed in several iterations. In the analyses performed for the SIMS data, this procedure appeared to produce substantively meaningful results in that the items that were signaled out clearly had features that distinguished them from the others in the set.

Table 11.2 gives the estimated variance components for core items corresponding to three of the specific factors. It is seen that the variance contribution from the specific factors can be as large as 50 percent of that of the general factor and are therefore of great practical significance. This is particularly so since the sets of items for a specific factor correspond closely to instructional units. Analyses of the rotated forms replicated most of the specific factors found for the core.

The confirmatory factor analysis procedure described is a cumbersome one, involving many iterations and many subjective decisions. An attempt was therefore made to find an approach that would involve fewer steps and a more objective analysis. It was

TABLE 11.2
Variance Components for Selected Items from the SIMS Population A
Test Core*

Item	General Factor	Specific Factors		Angular Measurement
		Percent	Estimate	
AR02	33 (24)	9 (9)		
AR24	39 (32)	9 (9)		
AR36	32 (27)	9 (9)		
AR38	35 (26)	9 (9)		
ME06	20 (14)		9 (10)	
ME08	38 (27)		9 (10)	
ME09	38 (29)		9 (10)	
GE17	28 (17)			11 (12)
GE19	17 (12)			11 (12)
GE21	24 (17)			11 (12)
GE22	43 (30)			11 (12)

*The estimate when controlling for mean level heterogeneity is given in parentheses (See Section 5).

reasoned that if the influence of the general factor could be removed from the item correlations, the remaining correlations would be due to the specific factors alone. Such residual correlations could then be factor analyzed by regular exploratory techniques, at least if nesting of specific factors within each other was ignored. Given a proxy for the general factor, the residual correlations could be obtained by bivariate probit regressions of all pairs of items on the proxy using the LISCOMP program.

An attempt was first made to approximate the general factor for the posttest core items with the posttest total score. However, this produced almost zero residual correlations. Instead, the pretest total score was used for the posttest items. An exploratory factor analysis of these residual correlations, using an orthogonal rotation by Varimax, resulted in 11 factors with eigenvalues greater than one.

The interpretation of these factors showed an extraordinary high degree of agreement with the specific factors previously obtained. The best agreement was obtained for factors that had obtained the largest variance component estimates. The exploratory analysis also suggested a few items to be added to the specific factors as defined earlier. The agreement of these two very different approaches is remarkable and it is interesting that the pretest score appears to be a better proxy for the general factor at the posttest occasion than the posttest score. This may indicate that the general factor is a relatively stable trait related to the achievement level before eighth grade instruction (we note from Table 11.1 that This Year OTL is the most prevalent category). In contrast, controlling for posttest score may control for a combination of the general factor and specific factors.

It is interesting to note that analyses of the core items administered at the pretest gave very similar results in terms of specific factors identified by the confirmatory approach. This indicates stability of the specific factors over the eighth grade. Attempting to compute residual correlations for exploratory factor analysis again gave near zero values when controlling for the total score, the pretest in this case, and this approach had to be abandoned.

MODELING WITH HETEROGENEITY IN LEVELS

The factor analysis described in the previous section was performed under the regular assumption of identically distributed observations. That is, all students are assumed to be sampled from the same population with one set of parameters. However, we have already noted that the students have widely varying instructional histories and that the homogeneity of student populations is not a realistic assumption. This is a common problem in analysis of educational data and has been given little attention. We may ask how this heterogeneity affects our analysis and if it can be taken into account in our modeling.

Muthén (1989a) considers covariance structure modeling in populations with heterogeneous mean levels. He considers the effect of incorrectly ignoring the heterogeneity, and proposes a method to build the heterogeneity into the model. The method is directly applicable to the multidimensional factor analysis model considered in the previous section and can also be carried out within the LISCOMP framework.[6] This modeling has two important outcomes. The

---

[6]Consider the model of Equation (7)

$$y^* = \Lambda\eta + \epsilon \tag{11}$$

In the previous section we made the usual standardization of $E(\eta_i) = 0$ for all observations i and assumed $V(\eta_i) = \Psi$. However, we know that it is unrealistic to assume that, for example, students from different class types have the same factor means levels. We may instead want to assume that the means vary with class type such that for Student i in Class c we have $E(\eta_{i_c}) = \alpha_c$. As pointed out in Muthén (1989a) this may be accomplished by considering in addition to (11) the equation

dimensionality analysis can be carried out without distortion due to the differences in factor mean levels across class types, and the factor mean levels can be estimated.

A mean-adjusted analysis was carried out on the SIMS core items using the multidimensional factor model from Table 11.2. Factor mean differences were allowed for class type using three dummy variables and also gender. We will concentrate our discussion of the results on the factor structure.

Despite large mean differences across class type for the general achievement factor, a factor structure very similar to the previous one emerged. The same specific factors showed large and small variances, respectively. Hence, the potential for a distorted structure is not realized in these data. The results are presented in parentheses in Table 11.2. It is seen that the variance contributions to the general factor are considerably reduced as compared to the first approach.

$$\eta_{i_c} = \Gamma x_c + \zeta_{i_c} \tag{12}$$

where x_c represents a vector of class type dummy variable values for Class c, Γ is a parameter matrix, and ζ_{ic} is a residual vector for Student i in Class c. We assume that conditional on class-type membership the factor means vary while the factor covariance matrix remains constant,

$$E(\eta_{i_c}|x_c) = \Gamma x_c \tag{13}$$

$$V(\eta_{i_c}|x_c) = \Psi \tag{14}$$

The modeling also assumes that the matrices Λ and Θ are constant across class types, so that

$$E(y^*|x_c) = \Lambda\Gamma x_c \tag{15}$$

$$V(y^*|x_c) = \Lambda\Psi\Lambda' + \Theta \tag{16}$$

It is interesting to note that the assumption of constancy of the conditional covariance matrix $V(y^*/x_c)$ is in line with the findings of constancy of the homogeneity of correlations.

The structure imposed on the parameter matrices of (15) and (16) may correspond to an exploratory or a confirmatory factor analysis model. Muthén (1989a) points out that the conditional covariance matrix of (16) is not in general the same as the marginal covariance matrix $V(y^*)$. In our context this means that even when we have the same factor analysis structure in the different class types this covariance structure does not hold in the total group of students. The approach outlined here essentially provides a mean-adjusted analysis of pooled covariance matrices assumed to be equal in the population. In our situation the analysis effectively is carried out on pooled tetrachoric correlation matrices.

The reduction in variance contribution from the general factor is natural, since holding class type constant reduces the individual difference in the general achievement trait due to selection of students. If the inference is to the mix of students encountered in the SIMS data, the unreduced variation in the trait is the correct one; but this variation is not representative for a student from any given class type. It is also interesting to note that the specific factor variances are not similarly reduced by holding class type constant, presumably indicating that these specific skills are largely unrelated to the student differences represented by class type.

ESTIMATION OF TRAIT SCORES

So far in this chapter, we have considered various factor analysis models for the achievement responses. Assuming known or well-estimated parameter values for these models, it is of interest to estimate each student's score on the factors of these models. For the standard, unidimensional IRT model, estimation of the trait values is a standard task which may be carried out by maximum likelihood, Bayes' model (maximum a posteriori), or expected a posteriori estimators (see for example, Bock & Mislevy, 1986).

However, the instructionally sensitive models we have considered for the SIMS data have brought us outside this standard situation in the following three respects:

1. In line with Section 4, we want to consider factor score estimation that takes into account that certain items have different difficulty levels depending on the students' OTL level.

2. In line with Section 5, we want to consider factor scores for both the general achievement factor and the specific factors in the multidimensional model.

3. In line with Section 6, we want to consider factor scores estimation that takes into account differences in student achievement level.

We note that (1) and (3) are quite controversial since these points raise the issue of estimating achievement scores based not only on the student's test responses but also on his or her instructional background. Bock (1972) has argued that prior information on groups should not be used in comparisons of individuals across groups. Nevertheless, it would seem that students who have had very limited OTL on a set of test items will be unfairly disadvantaged in comparison with students with substantial exposure. The aim may instead be to obtain achievement scores for given instructional experiences.

Point (2) is of considerable interest. While a rough proxy for the general achievement score is easily obtainable as the total test score, adding of items corresponding to specific factors would involve only a few items resulting in a very unreliable score. As a contrast, estimating the specific factor scores draws on the correlated responses from all other items.

Muthén and Short (1988)[7] considered an example of the situation of (1) and (3). They generated a random sample of 1,000 observations from a model with 40 items measuring a unidimensional trait. Observations were also generated from 40 OTL variables and five other background variables. All background variables were assumed to influence the trait while the first 20 OTL variables had direct effects on their corresponding items, giving rise to exposure sensitivity in these items.

Among other results, Muthén and Short considered differences in factor score estimates using the above method and the traditional IRT method. In Table 11.3 comparisons of the two corresponding score distributions are presented by quartiles, broken down in two parts—students with a high total sum of OTL and students with a low sum. The table demonstrates that for students of the low OTL group, estimated scores are on the whole higher with the new method, corresponding to an adjustment for having had less exposure, while for the high OTL group the estimated scores are on the whole lower for the new method.

Other work by Muthén and Short has investigated Situation (2) and the precision with which scores for specific factors can be estimated. Once the estimated factor scores have been calculated

---

[7]The following estimation procedure was discussed in Muthén and Short (1988) and handles all three cases above. For various density and probability functions g, consider the posteriori distribution of the factors of η,

$$g(\eta|y,x) = \phi(\eta|x)g(y|\eta,x)|g(y|x) \tag{17}$$

Here, the first term on the right-hand side represents a normal prior distribution for η conditional on x, where as before x represents instructional background variables such as OTL and class type. In line with Section 5, the factor covariance matrix may be taken as constant given x, while the factor means may vary with x. The second term on the right-hand side represents the product of the item characteristic curves, which may vary in difficulty across OTL levels as discussed in Section 3.

TABLE 11.3
Trait Estimates by Traditional and New Approaches*

Low OTL Group

NEW	Traditional 25%	Traditional 50%	Traditional 75%	Traditional 100%	Total
	136	6	0	0	142
25%	−1.323	−0.610			−1.293
	−1.255	−0.724			−1.233
	10	125	5	0	140
50%	−0.783	−0.361	0.037		−0.375
	−0.624	−0.338	−0.119		−0.351
	0	13	111	7	131
75%		−0.094	0.309	0.827	0.297
	0.058	0.316	0.691		0.311
	0	0	6	124	130
100%			0.691	1.282	1.255
			0.834	1.308	1.286
Total	146	144	122	131	543
	−1.286	−0.347	0.317	1.257	
	−1.212	−0.318	0.324	1.275	

High OTL Group

NEW	Traditional 25%	Traditional 50%	Traditional 75%	Traditional 100%	Total
	99	9	0	0	108
25%	−1.306	−0.578			−1.245
	−1.349	−0.743			−1.298
	5	94	12	0	111
50%	−0.726	−0.340	0.049		−0.315
	−0.581	−0.366	−0.119		−0.349
	0	3	110	5	118
75%		−0.167	0.345	0.870	0.355
	0.022	0.322	0.640		0.327
	0	0	6	114	120
100%			0.653	1.386	1.349
			0.782	1.334	1.306
Total	104	106	128	119	457
	−1.278	−0.355	0.332	1.364	
	−1.312	−0.389	0.302	1.305	

*Entries are: Frequency
  Mean value by the traditional approach
  Mean value by the new approach

they may conveniently be related to various instructional variables and may also be studied for change from pretest to posttest.

PREDICTING ACHIEVEMENT

Given the explorations outlined in the previous sections, we may attempt to formulate a more comprehensive model for the data. Muthén (1988) proposed the use of structural equation modeling for this task. He discussed a model that extends ordinary structural modeling to dichotomous response variables, while at the same time extending ordinary IRT to include predictors of the trait. He studied part of the SIMS data using a model that attempted to predict a unidimensional algebra trait at the posttest using a set of instructional and student background variables from the pretest.

The set of predictors used and their standardized effects are given in Table 11.4. While pretest scores have strong expected effects,

TABLE 11.4
Structural Parameters with the Latent Construct
as Dependent Variable

Regressor	Estimate	Estimate/S.E.
PREALG	0.68	11
PREMEAS	0.45	7
PREGEOM	0.33	5
PREARITH	2.09	16
FAED	0.07	1
MOED	0.02	0
MORED	0.18	3
USEFUL	0.45	7
ATTRACT	0.04	1
NONWHITE	−0.02	0
REMEDIAL	0.07	1
ENRICHED	0.22	3
ALGEBRA	0.56	4
FEMALE	0.14	6
LOWOCC	0.02	1
HIGHOCC	0.12	3
MISSOCC	0.05	2
NONW × REM	0.10	1
NONW × ENR	0.19	3
NONW × ALG	−0.18	−1
PREARITH × REM	−1.45	−3
PREARITH × ENR	−0.10	−1
PREARITH × ALG	−0.54	−2
NONW × PREARITH	−0.19	−1

class type, being female, father being in a high occupational category, and finding mathematics useful to future needs also had strong effects. The OTL variables had very small effects overall, perhaps due to the fact that each item's OTL variable has rather little power in predicting this general trait. Given the results of the previous sections, this modeling approach can be extended to include a multi-dimensional model for the set of both pretest and posttest items, predicting posttest factors from pretest factors, using instructional and student background variables as covariates, and allowing for differential item functioning in terms of exposure sensitivity.

ANALYZING CHANGE

The structural modeling discussed in the previous section is also suitable for modeling of change from pretest to posttest. Earlier in the chapter we pointed out that in terms of change, the SIMS data again exemplified complex population heterogeneity. For each item, a student may belong to one of three OTL groups, corresponding to the two types of no new learning and learning during the year. To again reach the goal of instructionally sensitive psychometrics for this new situation, we should explicitly model this heterogeneity. However, to properly model such complex heterogeneity is a very challenging task.

A basic assumption is that change is different for groups of students of different class types and OTL patterns. In a structural model where posttest factors are regressed on pretest factors, the slopes may be viewed as varying across such student groups, where student groups for whom a large degree of learning during the year (as measured by the set of OTL variables) has taken place, are assumed to have steeper slopes than the other students. Such an approach is rare in the field of psychometrics.

REFERENCES

Bock, R. D. (1972). Review of The dependability of behavioral measurements. *Science*, *178*, 1275–1275A.

Bock, R. D., & Mislevy R. J. (1986). Adaptive EAP estimation of ability in a microcomputer environment. *Applied Psychological Measurement*, *6*, 431–444.

Crosswhite, F. J., Dossey, J. A., Swafford, J. O., McKnight, C. C. & Cooney, T. J. (1985). *Second International Mathematics Study: Summary report for the United States*. Champaign, IL: Stipes.

Gustafsson, J. E. (1988a). Hierarchical models of individual differences in cognitive abilities. In R. J. Sternberg, (Ed.), *Advances in the psychology of human intelligence*, (Vol. 4). Hillsdale, NJ: Lawrence Erlbaum.

Gustafsson, J. E. (1988b). Broad and narrow abilities in research on learning and instruction. *Learning and individual differences: Abilities, motivation, methodology*. Symposium conducted at the Minnesota Symposium, Minneapolis.

Kao, C. F. (1990). *An investigation of instructional sensitivity in mathematics achievement test items for U.S. 8th grade students*. Doctoral dissertation, University of California at Los Angeles, Los Angeles, CA.

Lord, F. M. (1980). *Application of item response theory to practical testing problems*. Hillsdale, NJ: Lawrence Erlbaum.

Lord, F. M., & Novick, M. R. (1968). *Statistical theories of mental test scores*. Reading, MA: Addison-Wesley.

Mehrens, W. A., & Phillips, S. E. (1986). Detecting impacts of curricular differences in achievement test data. *Journal of Educational Measurement*, *23*, 185-196.

Mehrens, W. A., & Phillips, S. E. (1987). Sensitivity of item difficulties to curricular validity. *Journal of Educational Measurement*, *24*, 357–370.

Miller, M. D., & Linn, R. L. (1988). Invariance of item characteristic functions with variations in instructional coverage. *Journal of Educational Measurement*, *25*, 205–219.

Mislevy, R. J. (1986). Recent developments in the factor analysis of categorical variables. *Journal of Educational Statistics*, *11*, 3–31.

Muthén, B. (1978). Contributions to factor analysis of dichotomous variables. *Psychometrika*, *43*, 551–560.

Muthén, B. (1984). A general structural equation model with dichotomous, ordered categorical, and continuous latent variable indicators. *Psychometrika*, *49*, 115–132.

Muthén, B. (1987). *LISCOMP: Analysis of linear structural equations with a comprehensive measurement model: User's Guide*. Mooresville, IN: Scientific Software, Inc.

Muthén, B. (1988). Some uses of structural equation modeling in validity studies: Extending IRT to external variables. In H. Wainer & H. I. Braun (Eds.), *Test Validity*. Hillsdale, NJ: Lawrence Erlbaum.

Muthén, B. (1989a). Latent variable modeling in heterogeneous populations. *Psychometrika*, *54*, 557–585.

Muthén, B. (1989b). Using item-specific instructional information in achieving modeling. *Psychometrika*, *54*, 385–396.

Muthén, B., Kao, C. F., & Burnstein, L. (1991). Instructional sensitivity in mathematics achievement test items: Application of a new IRT-based detection technique. *Journal of Educational Measurement*, *28*, 1–22.

Muthén, B., & Short, L. M. (1988). *Estimation of ability by IRT models allowing for heterogeneous instructional background*. Paper presented at 1988 American Educational Research Association meeting. New Orleans.

Schmid, J., & Leiman, J. M. (1957). The development of hierarchical factor solutions. *Psychometrika*, *22*, 53–61.

Author Index

Subject Index